Hegel and Capitalism

Hegel and Capitalism

Edited by

Andrew Buchwalter

Cover: *Berliner Hinterhäuser im Schnee*, by Adolf Friedrich Erdmann von Menzel, 1847

Published by State University of New York Press, Albany

For information, contact State University of New York Press, Albany, NY
www.sunypress.edu

Production, Dana Foote
Marketing, Fran Keneston

Library of Congress Cataloging-in-Publication Data

Hegel and capitalism / edited by Andrew Buchwalter.
    pages cm
  Includes bibliographical references.
  ISBN 978-1-4384-5875-5 (hc : alk. paper)—978-1-4384-5876-2 (pb : alk. paper)
  ISBN 978-1-4384-5877-9 (e-book)
1. Hegel, Georg Wilhelm Friedrich, 1770–1831.   2. Capitalism.   I. Buchwalter,
Andrew, editor.
  B2948.H31738 2015
  330.12'2—dc23   2015001350

10 9 8 7 6 5 4 3 2 1

Contents

Acknowledgments

The original versions of the chapters contained in this book were presented at the twenty-second biennial meeting of the Hegel Society of America (HSA), held at DePaul University in October 2012. I thank DePaul's Department of Philosophy for its support of the event and Professor Kevin Thompson for coordinating local arrangements. Thanks are also owed the HSA members who evaluated conference paper submissions.

In addition, I thank the contributors to this volume for their commitment and cooperation; State University of New York Press acquisitions editor Andrew Kenyon for his interest in the project; production editor Dana Foote for her conscientious oversight of the production process; Lauren Hambidge, Donatella SchianoMoriello, and other members of the Center for Instructional Research and Technology at the University of North Florida (UNF) for assistance in preparing the manuscript; Gayle Stillson of the UNF Department of Philosophy for help in preparing permission and release forms; and Katharine Rowe for her counsel throughout. Finally, I wish to express my appreciation to UNF for the funding provided through the John A. Delaney Presidential Professorship, which helped support my work on this project.

Richard Dien Winfield's chapter, "Economy and Ethical Community," was first published in his book *Hegel and the Future of Systematic Philosophy* (Basingstoke, UK: Palgrave Macmillan, 2014).

Introduction

Hegel and Capitalism

ANDREW BUCHWALTER

Hegel and the Contemporary Discourse on Capitalism

Capitalism, whose historical triumph was for many confirmed with the collapse of the Soviet Union, has in recent years become a topic of significant public consideration. The 2008 financial crisis, declining growth rates, economic stagnation, prolonged unemployment, mounting income inequality, decreasing social mobility, growing personal and public indebtedness, an ongoing housing crisis, the commercialization of more spheres of life, the increasing monetarization of social relations, environmental degradation stemming from industrial production, and a globalization process fueled by multinational corporations operating relatively free from public accountability, have all contributed to growing concerns about the nature, stability, and even legitimacy of Western market economies. In addition, economic globalization has triggered in advanced industrial societies a predilection for austerity measures that, coupled with persistent neoliberal challenges to welfare state policies, have called into question common assumptions about the shape and trajectory of capitalism in postwar societies.

Accompanying these developments has been the proliferation of academic studies devoted to capitalist economies. In recent years such writers as Luc Boltanski and Ève Chiapello, James Galbraith, David Harvey, Thomas Piketty, Debra Satz, Wolfgang Streeck, and Joseph Stiglitz, to name just a few, have authored works that in differing ways address the state of contemporary market economies. In addition, historians in growing numbers have made capitalism a central category of disciplinary inquiry. And there has been a renewed interest in theorists historically associated with the analysis of market economies, including writers so diverse as Adam Smith, Karl Marx, and Friedrich Hayek.

So far, however, only a small effort has been made to mine the work of G.W.F. Hegel for understanding the current state of capitalism. This is perhaps not surprising, given that for many Hegel remains first and foremost a champion of the Prussian state and state power generally. Whatever one might say of this assessment, it is nonetheless a mistake to disregard his possible contribution to reflections on the nature and status of capitalist market societies. Even if Hegel rarely used the term *capitalism* itself, his thought—not only his social theory but his political philosophy and his practical philosophy generally—does represent a sustained and distinctive engagement with the prospects and problems of modern market societies. Indeed, given his contention that philosophy itself represents a response to the tensions and "bifurcations" (*Entzweiungen*) he associated with modern economic life, his general conceptual framework, expressed above all in its notion of dialectics, can itself be construed as a response to the phenomenon of modern capitalism.

The *locus classicus* for Hegel's understanding of capitalism is the sphere of civil society (*bürgerliche Gesellschaft*), the middle zone in the theory of ethical life or ethicality (*Sittlichkeit*) he elaborates in his 1821 *Philosophy of Right*. Here Hegel advances a nuanced and multifaceted analysis of modern market economies. On the one hand, he clearly highlights what he perceives as the strengths and achievements of market societies. He attributes to such societies realization of a defining feature of the modern age: the right of subjective freedom. He locates in modern economies conditions for realizing a principle whose first articulation he attributes to Protestantism: the right to subjective satisfaction. He discerns in the increasing mechanization of labor possibilities for greater human emancipation. He claims that modern market economies, committed in principle to the meritocratic evaluation of individual performance, condition realization of the idea of universal human rights. He calls attention to the cosmopolitan dimension of modern commerce, noting how trade fostered through civil society surpasses national borders in ways that contribute to worldwide adoption of uniform norms of person, property, and contract, while cultivating more developed forms of international cooperation. He also assigns normative status to the capitalist division of labor, which, in forging wide-ranging relations of interdependence between individual and community, underwrites modern accounts of constitutional law, republican politics, and forms of sociality based on mutuality and social cooperation.

On the other hand, Hegel was also an acute and highly prescient observer of the problems and pathologies of modern market economies. The account of "the system of needs" (*das System der Bedürfnisse*) he presents in the section on civil society describes the deadening effect mechanized labor has on the mental and physical well-being of human beings. There Hegel also details how this new social order promotes forms of gratuitous and conspicuous consumption that foster and perpetuate vast wealth disparities between rich and poor. He demonstrates how modern market economies, systemically gripped by boom-bust cycles, generate an impoverished underclass characterized not only by material but above all by psychological deprivations. He describes how such deprivations cultivate in the underclass, termed by him a "rabble" (*Pöbel*), a sense of indignation directed not only at the performance and achievement expectations of modern society but at the modern social order itself. He explains how civil society also promotes the emergence of a "wealthy rabble" typified not only by its material avarice but by an insouciant and disdainful attitude toward less fortunate members of society. He details as well how problems in the functioning of individual market economies trigger a colonizing search for new markets that not only replicates original pathologies but promotes worldwide conflict and bellicosity. In all these ways, Hegel maintains, modern market societies, their considerable resources notwithstanding, afford, as he famously notes in introducing his analysis of civil society, "a spectacle of extravagance and misery as well as of the physical and ethical corruption common to both."

Hegel was not sanguine about the prospects for solving the maladies he associated with modern market societies. Indeed, he asserts that some presumed solutions—public assistance projects and public works programs—may only replicate the problems in question. One partial solution, however, lies with "corporations"—voluntary work-related cooperatives that hark back to the mediaeval and early modern guild systems and find attenuated reaffirmation today in labor unions, trade organizations, and professional associations. There are various respects in which such corporate bodies can counter the ill effects of market societies. They provide various forms of assistance to those adversely affected by market forces. They recognize members simply in virtue of their membership alone, thus counteracting both the dehumanizing humiliation experienced by the poor in market societies and the expectation on the part of the affluent that status is conferred through conspicuous consumption and ostentatious displays of wealth. Inasmuch, further, as corporate members themselves help to counteract the deleterious effects of market forces, their actions circumvent the externally imposed institutional solutions that often reinforce pathologies in question. And because corporate members participate

in efforts that foster cooperation, mutuality, and commitment to shared
ends, their actions both contribute to and instantiate the ethicality that
for Hegel is crucial to offsetting the atomistic, self-seeking individualism
basic to the aporias of modern market societies.

Hegel is aware of the limitations of the corporatist solution to these
aporias. Although the theory of corporations provides elements of a
uniquely polyarchic form of civic republicanism, it also lends support to
an interest group particularism that can contribute to the societal atomism
in question. A more comprehensive solution is available only in a differentiated polity comprised of diverse individuals and groups committed to
the ends of political community as such. Yet if in his scheme this mandates
transition from civil society to the state and the domain of politics proper,
Hegel does not thereby invoke external norms and criteria in confronting
the problems of market economies. Against such "abstract" negation, he
proffers a "determinate" negation, predicated on further developing and
realizing resources implicit in market societies themselves. The principle
of ethicality that Hegel contraposes to the pathologies of market economies itself derives from the wide-ranging interdependence of individual
and community present, however inadequately, in the modern system of
political economy. As with his dialectic generally, Hegel's dialectic of civil
society is informed by the view that the source of problems also contains
tools for their correction.

One can question the plausibility and adequacy of such "immanent
transcendence" of the challenges posed by capitalist economies. Yet such
questions should not mute appreciation of the broader nature of Hegel's
reception of modern market societies. Basic to that reception is a philosophical holism that, on the model of a differentiated and reflexively constituted totality, delineates the possibilities and problems of modern market
societies while considering how those societies can themselves address the
challenges confronting them. At a time when those challenges seem especially daunting, an approach like Hegel's, comprehensive in scope and
eschewing conventional disciplinary divisions, still merits consideration.

Themes and Arguments

This volume examines the value of Hegel's thought for understanding
and assessing capitalism, both as encountered by Hegel himself and in the
forms it takes today. It comprises contributions from an array of prominent and internationally diverse Hegel scholars who approach the theme
"Hegel and Capitalism" from a wide range of perspectives and orientations.
Their contributions also address a myriad of themes and topics. Some

authors explore specific issues, like Hegel's treatment of poverty, conspicuous consumption, mechanized labor, the bearing of market imperatives of the conditions for human subjectivity, and the relationship of religion and capitalism. Others examine Hegel's understanding of capitalism with regard to his general account of the project of modernity, while still others ask whether Hegel's critique of capitalism mandates the latter's reform and further realization or its rejection altogether. Those in the former camp examine Hegel's proposals for "taming" capitalism, differentiating between institutional and cultural, economic and sociological, or "top-down" and "bottom-up" approaches. Some contributors consider the compatibility of market mechanisms with broader accounts of ethical community, the role of recognitive relations in the assessment of capitalist social structures, the place of republican politics in response to the vicissitudes of market economies, and the moral obligations individual do and do not owe to capitalist institutions. Various authors examine Hegel's conception and evolving understanding of capitalism in specific texts, including the 1802/03 *System of Ethical Life*, the 1805/06 Jena *Realphilosophie*, 1806 *Phenomenology of Spirit*, 1812 *Science of Logic*, as well as the 1821 *Philosophy of Right*. Several authors compare Hegel's reflections on capitalism to those of other important thinkers, including Adam Smith, Immanuel Kant, Johann Gottlieb Fichte, Karl Marx, Max Weber, Theodor Adorno, Václav Havel, Wilfred Cantwell Smith, as well as contemporary social theorists and theorists of economic ethics. Yet others relate Hegel to issues pertaining to capitalism today, such as economic globalization, the adequacy of models of utility maximization for comprehending contemporary market societies, the subordination of ever more spheres of human life to the logic of economic imperatives, and the responsibilities individuals must accept in light of the power of such imperatives.

As a whole, the chapters in this book reflect the breadth and depth of Hegel's analysis of capitalism as well as the holistic character of his thought generally. They also articulate anew what in the Preface to the *Philosophy of Right* Hegel proffers as the defining feature of philosophy itself: "its own time apprehended in thought." In what remains I provide a brief summary of the main argument of each chapter, noting as well connections among the various discussions and the contribution those discussions make to the discourse on capitalism.

In the opening chapter, Michalis Skomvoulis details Hegel's very "discovery" of capitalism. According to Skomvoulis, this discovery occurred in the early 1800s when Hegel first encountered the theories of modern political economy associated with thinkers like Adam Smith, Adam Ferguson, and James Steuart. This encounter had important consequences as much for Hegel's logical and metaphysical theory as for his social and political thought. In both cases, appreciation of the modalities of modern economic life—for example, self-seeking individualism, market competition, the division of labor, and the centrality of labor itself—led Hegel to integrate principles of "negativity" and "finitude" into his account of absolute philosophy. In the logico-metaphysical writings, this entailed acknowledging "bifurcation" as the motivating force for philosophy itself. It also entailed formulating a conception of dialectics, where—through such principles as "determinate negation" and "the labor of the negative"—one position's negation could be deemed a preservation resulting in a higher and more encompassing conceptual form. Similar features are evident, according to Skomvoulis, in Hegel's social and political writings. If prior to 1800 Hegel championed a notion of political life based on an organic, unmediated, and even religiously based union of individual and community, now he asserts that a proper account of political community must integrate elements associated with negativity and finitude. On this view, Hegel advances a differentiated and highly mediated account of community, one in which a political order predicated on a system of interdependencies goes hand in hand with the economic individualism central to a view of social relations oriented to principles of labor and material well-being.

Hegel thus advances, for Skomvoulis, a nuanced view of the role of political economy in modern social life. On the one hand, the realities of modern economic life lead to a new account of sociality, one in which social relations are elevated beyond the domain of nature and fashioned as the conscious product of human will. Via the dialectical "cunning" underwriting modern market life, competitive struggles reflective of an economic state of nature lead to a system of social-juridical relations based on law and the mutual recognition of individual rights. On the other hand, the modes of mediation fueling modern economic exchange also serve to mechanize labor and monetarize social relations in ways that undermine the forms of human autonomy that the structures of modern economic life empower. Modern economic structures thereby serve to renaturalize society, subjecting it to reified, impersonal laws operating independently of autonomous subjects and in reference to ends removed from human control. Hegel thus presents as structural features of capitalism phenomena he considers more fully in his later writings: the alienating character of the division of labor, the growing polarization of rich and poor, and the regularity of economic crises. This analysis also leads Hegel to posit the need for an intervening state that stabilizes market relations while affirming conscious attention to the ends of the social whole.

In "Beyond Recognition in Capitalism: From Violence and Caprice to Recognition and Solidarity," Kohei Saito also considers Hegel's early treatment of capitalism, comparing it to the position advanced by Johann Fichte in the latter's 1800 *Closed Commercial State*. The comparison is instructive as both thinkers sought to rearticulate the conditions for human freedom and equality in the face of challenges posed by emergent capitalism and the new system of political economy. In the *Closed Commercial State* Fichte presents an especially damning indictment of capitalism, asserting not only that it distorts human needs and desires but occasions European subjugation of the rest of the world. In response, Fichte proposes a system of state control directed to the coercive regulation of European individuals and states. Hegel shares Fichte's concerns regarding the pathological dimensions of modern capitalism, even if he does not connect them so emphatically to European imperialism. He, too, sees modern capitalism as gripped by arbitrary cycles of overproduction and unemployment, with vast disparities in wealth and corresponding forms of domination. Yet, as is clear from his 1802/3 *System of Ethical Life*, Hegel differs in his response. Against Fichte's advocacy of an external system of market regulation administered by an interventionist state, Hegel, attentive to the freedoms also part of modern economic life, champions instead an "internal regulative practice" rooted in the system of economic life itself. Focusing on relations of commodity exchange central to the "system of needs," modern market societies generate modes of mutual dependence able to counteract the forms of inequality and subordination occasioned by the market. As Hegel also argues in his later writings, such modes are manifest in work-related corporations and other occupational cooperatives. These corporate bodies are important, however, not just because they address the ills experienced by those directly affected by the caprice of the market. Hegel contends as well that they empower worker-based forms of collective agency able to challenge market pathologies, and in ways that supplant a system of social antagonism with one committed to greater societal cohesion.

On the basis of this analysis, Saito presents a distinctive account of Hegel's famous struggle for recognition. This struggle is not to be understood in the way already articulated by Fichte, as an effort to secure recognition for the rights and liberties formally held by autonomous individuals or "persons." Instead, it takes the form of individuals contesting the modes of dependence and inequality associated with market societies, those that a purely formal account of recognition can actually promote. In addition, this approach does not gainsay the antagonisms associated with modern market societies, but construes them in a manner contributive to their resolution, that is, as elements in a social practice of contestation meant to adjust social norms and structures so as to foster relations of mutuality and cooperation in the economy and society generally. Both reflect Hegel's broader effort to respond to market tensions, not through the exogenously imposed solutions proposed by Fichte, but by cultivating resources present in market relations themselves. Saito leaves open the question of which solution may be more compelling in light of growing economic inequalities today.

In "Anonymity, Responsibility, and the Many Faces of Capitalism: Hegel and the Crisis of the Modern Self," Ardis Collins explores how the 1806 *Phenomenology of Spirit* sheds light on Hegel's understanding of capitalism. Collins' central concern is the opposition between the imperatives of impersonal economic systems—she includes here not only versions of capitalism but forms of socialism as well—and the conditions for the autonomous subjectivity of persons. Following Václav Havel and Wilfred Cantwell Smith, she claims that the autonomization of the economic domain results in the latter's loss of orientating relation to the human self, a state of affairs that deprives the economic order of unifying purpose while fostering in individuals an economic narcissism devoid of attention to higher ends and obligations. In appealing to the *Phenomenology*, Collins focuses on its general account of the developmental formation of consciousness. This process details how seeming opposites are gradually surmounted in a reciprocally transformative dynamic whereby each side acknowledges its limitations while integrating the partial truth of the other. After analyzing various stages in this self-formative process, Collins attends to the reconciliation represented by revealed religion, whose notion of "self-sharing spirit" both binds objective economic exigencies to the requirements of subjective autonomy and inculcates in individuals a sense of objective responsibility transcending their private concerns.

For Collins, self-sharing spirit can be construed in terms of a transcendent God or as the highest aspiration of the human spirit. In either case, it has a threefold significance with regard to the goal of addressing the conflict, central to capitalism, between objective economic imperatives and autonomous subjectivity. First, the objective science of economics would be affirmed, yet in a way acknowledging that its proper use depends on norms forged in appreciation of humankind's higher purposes. Second, participants in economic relations would have the right to recognize themselves in the way each is represented in the words and actions of other participants. Third, different interests, subject to norms of mutuality, would learn to forgive the way each becomes subordinated to others, as such shift in dominance belongs to the necessary conditions for genuine action.

In "The Purest Inequality: Hegel's Critique of the Labor Contract and Capitalism," Nicholas Mowad also considers the account of capitalism advanced in the *Phenomenology*, focusing on its relation to the more explicit treatment detailed in the 1821 *Philosophy of Right*. In both works, Hegel, according to Mowad, shows how in capitalist societies, understood as complex and wide-ranging systems of mutual interdependency, individual value and merit are linked to societal norms and expectations regarding performance and achievement. Both works also make clear that, uniquely under capitalism, value and merit are understood in monetary terms, a point Hegel makes in identifying the word "valuation" (*gelten*) with "money" (*Geld*) and by suggesting that people have worth to the degree that they "count" (*gilt*). Both works also reveal how this monetarization of human value entails a host of social pathologies that devalue individuals, and not just the underemployed poor but also the wealthy, who increasingly must demonstrate worth through conspicuous consumption. This phenomenon is captured by what Hegel in the *Phenomenology* terms the "purest inequality," whereby the worth and identity of individuals are construed wholly in terms of their opposite—objectively calculable cash value. The works differ, however, in two respects. The first concerns the nature of Hegel's depiction of the monetarization of human value. In the *Philosophy of Right* Hegel focuses directly on modern industrial society and in particular the labor contract, the practice specific to capitalism in which money is exchanged not for a commodity of a fixed value but for the power to create value. In the *Phenomenology*, by contrast, the issue is addressed through changes in culture, especially with regard to nobility and the "noble-minded consciousness," where public service comes to be valued monetarily rather than, as had traditionally been the case, in terms of honor. The second difference concerns Hegel's assessment of the phenomenon of monetarization. In the *Philosophy of Right* Hegel advanced only a partial critique of capitalism, asserting that the labor contract is problematic not per se, but only inasmuch as the alienation it entails becomes a general phenomenon rather than one restricted to a limited period of time. By contrast, human devalorization as presented in the *Phenomenology* results in a more global indictment, including one of capitalism itself. For Mowad, the differing assessments raise questions about Hegel's real view of the nature of capitalism. They also raise questions about the internal consistency of the *Philosophy of Right*, as even a qualified acceptance of the devalorization Hegel associates with the labor contract would seem to conflict with a central principle of civil society: that individuals are to receive "satisfaction" via general societal mediation.

In "Hegel's Notion of Abstract Labor in the *Elements of the Philosophy of Right*," Giorgio Cesarale continues the exploration of Hegel's account of labor under capitalism pursued by Mowad and others. His specific concern is the division of labor, and how it entails a process of abstraction—understood as the reduction of quality to quantity—that leads both to the increasing mechanization of labor and an increased reliance on machines. For Cesarale, this development reflects ambivalence in Hegel's thinking regarding abstract labor. On the one hand, Hegel espoused the view, both in his Heidelberg and Berlin periods, that machines can have an emancipatory function, liberating human beings from the drudgery of labor, thereby furnishing conditions for a freer and more dignified life. Yet he also maintains that the capitalist mode of production, as evident especially in England, engendered a physically and mentally debilitating form of mechanization that undermined its emancipatory potential. Indeed, the increasing reliance of humans on machines led, for Hegel, to the emergence of a new and potentially fatal form of human subjectivity—a mechanistic sort, where subjectivity is little more than the composite of diverse and unrelated elements. Lost thereby is the more genuine sort based on the organic-teleological model of a self-conscious unity expressed and sustained in its objective differentiations. The process of abstract labor under capitalism thus proceeds isomorphically with the reification of subjectivity and the increasing transformation of the self into a thing.

Cesarale's analysis entails a revision of some conventional readings of Hegel's thought, including those involving the relationship of spirit and nature. According to the standard view—represented here by Theodor Adorno, Hegel is said to nullify nature as he charts the evolving formation of spirit. By contrast, Cesarale shows that the forms of reification accompanying capitalist-based mechanization entail an increasing naturalization of spirit. In social labor spirit may overcome nature but only by becoming more like nature itself. This also explains why abstract labor is so problematic for Hegel: the structures of spirit that might free human beings from the yoke of reification themselves contribute to that very reification.

In "Hegel's Torment: Poverty and the Rationality of the Modern State," C. J. Pereira Di Salvo considers another problem Hegel identifies with modern market societies: poverty. He does so by comparing the position Hegel elaborates in the *Philosophy of Right* with the distinctive view on the same topic advanced by Kant in his 1797 *Metaphysical First Principles of the Doctrine of Right*. For Kant, poverty, unlike mere physical deprivation, denotes a relationship of individuals. An impoverished person is one who lacks the means to meet basic needs in a social order where those means are owned by other people. Poverty on this account is a problem specifically for a political community that affirms a right of private property and allows for the rightful ownership of all things. In such a community, consistent with Kant's view of a legitimate polity, an impoverished person can survive only by depending on the generosity of others. Yet because such dependence is inconsistent with a right of freedom (independence of all constraint by others in conjunction with the right of all) that supposedly is secured in a society that guarantees the right of private property, poverty for Kant is a wrong, understood as the illicit dependence of one person on another. It is, moreover, a wrong that can be rectified only by securing the freedom and independence of the impoverished individual, achievable through redistribution measures based on direct transfers rather than through more conditional measures (e.g., poor houses and work requirements) that can undermine independence.

For Pereira Di Salvo, Hegel also posits a connection among personhood, property, and poverty in modern societies. Yet for Hegel that connection is more fundamental than in Kant. At stake here is how poverty undermines autonomous personality itself. Proceeding from the view that individuals are persons not as such but only as they attain concrete embodiment for their will, Hegel claims that personhood minimally depends on owning property, that is, entities enabling the external expression of will. Yet what characterizes the poor is precisely that they do not own property. Indeed, Hegel contends that the nature of modern society—reflected in structural unemployment and the growing replacement of workers by machines—is such that the poor increasingly lack even the opportunity to acquire property through their labor. Poverty is thus problematic, for Hegel, for reasons more profound than for Kant. Whereas for Kant poverty is problematic because it places persons in a wrongful relation of dependence on others, poverty is problematic for Hegel because it prevents human beings from realizing the capacity for personhood itself. Pereira Di Salvo notes that Hegel is not fully clear on the policy measures needed to address modern poverty. Yet his analysis does make clear that for Hegel poverty, conducive to the condition of the "socially frustrated personality," undermines the conditions for autonomous personality. Since fostering such conditions is, for Hegel, a central function of the modern state, addressing the problem of poverty must be deemed a central task not just of the *Philosophy of Right* but of modernity itself.

For Michael Thompson, the pathologies associated by Hegel with capitalist economies lead to a view of his political philosophy as essentially "anti-capitalist." In "Capitalism as Deficient Modernity: Hegel against the Modern Economy," Thompson elaborates this view by proceeding from a conception of capitalism that expands upon and updates Hegel's own understanding. Whereas Hegel understood capitalism more narrowly as an autonomous system of market exchange coordinated by economic self-interest, Thompson, consonant with theories of late capitalism, construes it as the dominant logic of social institutions and social relations generally, one in which exchange relations infuse all spheres of life. Contemporary state interventionist capitalism, fueled by forces of globalization, has reshaped market relations so that not only work but culture and indeed all aspects of everyday life—schooling and family life included—are organized around the economic imperatives of efficiency, productivity, and consumption.

On this basis, Thompson asserts that Hegel construes capitalism as a "deficient modernity." For Hegel, modernity is predicated on commitment to the freedom and rationality of the individual. Proper to this view is a republican account of societal life, where relations of communality and mutuality are conditions for individual freedom, agency, and self-determination. Yet capitalism, with its systematic and wide-ranging promotion of, *inter alia,* atomistic individualism, hedonic self-interest, particularist class interest, commodification, and hierarchical power structures, distorts republican sociality, rendering impossible the individual freedom it could facilitate. Such distortion is reflected, for Thompson, in a range of societal pathologies illustrative of the general loss of ethical life Hegel discerns in modern civil society. These are the pathologies of: *socialization,* caused by deficient forms of social structure and social integration; *recognition,* where individuals become unable to perceive in others the commonality needed for greater social interdependence; and *rationality,* where individuals become unable to grasp the principle of freedom that should inform their will and the social institutions constituting their lives.

According to Thompson, Hegel does not dispute the legitimacy of modernity itself. The basic institutions of the modern world—family, civil society, and the state—are, for Hegel, intrinsically rational and worthy of assent. This is so, however, only as they promote the free individuality and rationality of agents. Inasmuch as capitalism does not do so, it cannot, Thompson argues, command the assent of modern individuals, who in turn have no obligation to support its institutions.

An alternate account of Hegel's assessment of capitalism is offered by Richard Winfield in "Economy and Ethical Community." No less than Thompson and others in this volume, Winfield is mindful of the pathologies that Hegel associated with modern market economies. Yet for him their appreciation does not entail a wholesale indictment of such economies or, for that matter, capitalism itself. Such indictment might be warranted if Hegel's civil society were understood, as it often is, simply in terms of the self-seeking individualism common to the liberal-contractarian tradition. Yet for Winfield this understanding fails to capture Hegel's general account of civil society. Distinctively reflected in the logic of commodity exchange central to "the systems of needs," this account denotes a wide-ranging system of interdependence in which the freedom of one is inextricably tied to the freedom of others. On this view, civil society represents an ethical community predicated on norms of reciprocity, mutual respect, and communal well-being—norms that can be invoked to challenge pathologies associated with unbridled market mechanisms. This normative commitment is facilitated, according to Winfield, through a system of justice supportive of rights meant to ensure that everyone can participate in the economic life of the community. Included here are not only property and contract rights, but also employment rights (supported, as needed, by public works projects) and rights to participate in the political regulation of the economy.

Winfield does challenge features of Hegel's position. He is critical, for instance, of Hegel's appeal to particular social interest groups (corporations) to counteract market pathologies. On his view, an account of economic community predicated on a system of interdependence requires a more comprehensively political mode of economic regulation. Yet acknowledging such limitations should not hinder appreciation of Hegel's account of civil society as an ethical community or its capacity to promote what Winfield calls "capitalism with a human face."

In "Two Ways of 'Taming' the Market: Why Hegel Needs the Police *and* the Corporations," Lisa Herzog also considers Hegel's proposals to "tame" the effects of untrammeled market mechanisms. In her view, Hegel presents two distinct options for achieving this end: an "economic" and a "sociological." The economic, identified with the institution of the public authority or the police (*Polizei*), presumes that individuals, on the *homo oeconomicus* model of rational choice theory, are utility maximizers whose preferences and even identities are fixed. On this view, market maladies are to be addressed in the manner also proposed by Adam Smith: with institutional measures that, through the availability of more or less costly options, incentivize profit-oriented individuals to make some choices rather than others. By contrast, the sociological model is identified with the corporations discussed by Winfield and others in this volume. On Herzog's reading, corporations represent the site where preferences and identities are not simply fixed or given but shaped in processes of social interaction. As such, corporate existence serves to cultivate a "republican" ethos of shared interest and citizenship, and not only at the occupational level but at the political level as well.

Herzog concludes by considering the continuing relevance of the market-taming proposals proffered by Hegel, focusing especially on recent discussions in business and economic ethics. On the one hand, she invokes the work of Karl Homann who, influenced by James Buchanan, champions the "economic" approach, one that through institutional incentives aims to redirect fixed preferences and given strivings for wealth maximization. On the other hand, she references the sociological approach promoted by Peter Ulrich, who, influenced by Jürgen Habermas, seeks to transform preferences in a way contributive to an ethos of responsible citizenship. Herzog allows that any current taming of the market must draw on both approaches. But she also asserts, especially given the academic predominance of approaches oriented to utility maximization, that greater attention must be accorded the sociological approach, and those that seek to transform preferences in ways that might foster more republican responses to market maladies. This is particularly the case, she contends, given that forces of economic globalization have undermined the state-centric institutional structures that traditionally have sustained incentive based approaches.

In "Hegel's Logical Critique of Capitalism: The Paradox of Dependence and the Model of Reciprocal Mediation," Nathan Ross explores a topic also addressed by Michalis Skomvoulis: the connection between Hegel's logico-metaphysical and social-political writings. In particular, Ross draws on the *Science of Logic* to shed light on Hegel's "determinate negation" of capitalism, one that advances a trenchant critique of the latter even while engaging the resources of capitalism itself. Ross begins by appealing to the logic of mechanism to elucidate Hegel's view of the contradictory nature of capitalist economic life. For Hegel, the logic of mechanism details the dependence of self-sufficiently isolated objects on external forces and aggregated coordinating relations that are not a feature of their own nature. In like manner, capitalist market societies, reflected above all in Hegel's account of the system of needs, depict a social order in which the seemingly autonomous pursuit of individual self-interest entails dependence on broader coordinating structures that not only escape the control of individuals but result in pathologies—for example, increasingly dehumanized labor and an impoverished underclass—that undermine autonomy itself.

Against the "ethical untenability" of the form of capitalism thus illuminated, Hegel seeks to fashion, according to Ross, a more ethical mode of social being. Yet he does so neither by jettisoning capitalism itself nor by appealing to outside political institutions meant to regulate its excesses. Instead, his determinate negation of capitalism consists in a highly mediated account of political and economic structures, one that Ross details by appealing to the logic of reciprocal mediation contained in the *Logic*'s treatment of absolute mechanism. Drawing on the concept of the "syllogism of syllogisms" there elaborated, Ross presents Hegel as advancing a view of modern social life understood as a concrete and differentiated totality, whose component parts reciprocally entail and presuppose one another. Thus, although the contradictions of modern economic life do require the political intervention of a regulatory state, the latter in turn depends for its legitimacy on modes of representation best expressed through work-related interest groups (corporations, again), which in turn depend on individuals who appreciate how their needs and labor are intertwined with the needs and labor of others.

For Ross, this reading of Hegel's assessment of capitalism demonstrates how modern economic life, however much it may contribute to

alienation and forms of social antagonism, contains resources for modes
of civic engagement that can also challenge modern social pathologies. It
eschews the abstract separation of political and economic concerns found
as much in liberal as in Marxist understandings of modern society. It also
sheds light on how the economic forms of social organization associated
with capitalism can be seen, consonant with the goals of Hegel's political
philosophy, as part of a broader account of ethical life, where the social
whole, in line with an animating notion of freedom understood as *bei-sich-
Selbst-sein*, is created and sustained in the complex interpenetration of its
component parts.

In "Hegel and Capitalism: Marxian Perspectives," Tony Smith also
considers how the categories of Hegel's logic might be used to comprehend modern capitalist economies. Yet his focus is on how this application was performed, not by Hegel himself, but by Marx, well-known for
his assertion that Hegel's logic was "of great use" in the formulation of a
critique of political economy. Smith begins by noting the distinctive features of Hegel's analysis of modern political economy, calling attention to
its account of generalized commodity production and exchange. According to Smith, Marx accepts much of Hegel's analysis. He differs most
decisively, however, in his comprehension of the nature of generalized
commodity exchange, and in particular the role occupied by money. As
with other political economists, Hegel claims that money here is simply a
means enabling human beings to further chosen ends. By contrast, Marx
discerns the distinctiveness of modern political economy to lie in a state
of affairs where money, in the form of capital, becomes an end in itself,
while human ends now become mere tools for its accumulation. In clarifying this point, Marx appeals to Hegel's logico-metaphysical writings and in
particular the concept of Absolute Spirit. However much it may mystify the
real relation of thought and being, Absolute Spirit does represent an accurate depiction of the perverted logic of a social order where human ends
are subordinated to the exigencies of capital accumulation. Like Absolute
Spirit, capital assumes the form of a self-moving substance for which all
forms of human agency are simply expressions and manifestations.

While allowing that the tools of Hegel's logic were of unquestioned
value in Marx's own analysis of capitalism, Smith disputes their particular
deployment by Marx. A central issue is the "homology thesis" itself, the
claim that the concept of Absolute Spirit is directly identifiable with the
logic of capital. For Smith, this thesis fails to recognize—here he invokes
the system of syllogisms discussed as well by Ross—how Hegel's logic also
contains tools to mount a normative challenge to a social order that subordinates human freedom to the dominion of reified forces. Thus, instead
of invoking the homology thesis to explain the value of Hegel's logic for

Marx's account of capitalism, Smith appeals to the logic of essence, for which things depend for their reality on reflection in entities other than themselves. On this reading, Marx can be said to appeal to *two* distinct forms of a logic of essence in explicating the nature of modern societies. On the one hand, he indicates how the process of commodity production and exchange is to be understood in the context of a generalized system of social reproduction, one that, based strictly on mechanisms of monetary valuation, liberates individuals from the forms of personal domination characteristic of premodern societies. On the other hand, this system under capitalism is to be understood via a notion of *dissociated* sociality, where all activity and value is subordinated to the dominion of capital. In this way, Hegel's logic is employed both to demonstrate how capitalism can in fact be deemed a system that subordinates individuals to alien ends *and* to assert that that system represents a historically particular manifestation that can be challenged from the perspective of an account of social reproduction free from such subordination.

In "Hegel's Ethic of *Beruf* and the Spirit of Capitalism," Louis Carré compares Hegel's account of capitalism to that of another important successor, Max Weber. In particular, he details affinities between Hegel's practical philosophy and Max Weber's thesis on the Protestant origins of capitalism in order to grasp the distinctive "spirit" that informs modern capitalism as an economic system. Carré is especially interested in the concept of the human subject that both thinkers assert is demanded by modern capitalism, something decisively shaped by their respective receptions of Protestantism. In the case of Weber, Protestant notions of asceticism and divinely ordained "calling" (*Beruf*) cultivated in individuals dispositions uniquely supportive of modern capitalism, those that construe work and the legitimate pursuit of economic gain, not just as means to satisfy materials needs, but as components in a methodically directed mundane life-practice understood as an end in itself. In Hegel's case, Protestantism's understanding of the relationship of the human and the divine not only fortified human subjectivity, but did so in a way that saw work and other worldly activities, in contradistinction to the conventional Catholic separation of spiritual and worldly concerns, as realizations of spirit itself. In addition, Hegel also characterized the cultivation of human subjectivity as a "calling," but one understood in wholly secular terms—not as fulfillment of a divine task, but through successful integration into the vocational requirements of modern civil society.

Carré further considers the distinctive response each thinker provides to confront the "fate" of capitalism. These responses reflect divergent assessments of the project of modernity. For Weber, modernity is a process of disenchantment that, in gradually depriving occupational existence of religious foundation, renders work in capitalist societies increasingly devoid of meaning. This is a state of affairs that for Weber could be countered only through the emergence of an aesthetic elite that, on the model of fellow *fin de siècle* thinker Friedrich Nietzsche, confronts an alienating capitalism with the values of authentic individualism. Hegel, by contrast, understands modernity as the progressive realization of spirit in the world and, in particular, the further actualization of human autonomy. Thus, though no less mindful of the alienating features of modern capitalism, Hegel advances a solution that consists, not in a new existential aesthetic, but in forms of intersubjective sociality that better realize the conditions for autonomous subjectivity.

1

Hegel Discovers Capitalism

Critique of Individualism, Social Labor,
and Reification during the Jena Period (1801–1807)

Michalis Skomvoulis

Introduction: Jena or Philosophy
as the Need for Unification

What seems astonishing for someone studying the evolution of Hegel's sociopolitical thought is the degree to which his writings from before 1800 differ from the mature work of his *Philosophy of Right*. The early works present an image of political virtue that Hyppolite calls "heroic" and Lukács "republican."[1] This is an image of an unmediated political life[2] attached to the hope for the resurrection of the organic ideal of the ancient city as a civil religion; it is an image as well of a certain political radicalism aroused by the French Revolution and expressed in the demand to surpass the state, which treats human beings as cogs in a machine. In the mature work, we find a completely different image of the political sphere, strongly mediated and to a certain extent conditioned by bourgeois civil society. Moreover, politics is presented in the form not of religion but a state understood as a rationally structured organization.

If we ask what intervenes between these two very different images we find ourselves confronted with the Jena years, an extremely dense period, which was to prove decisive in the formation of Hegel's political and epistemological thought. One of its main characteristics is Hegel's understanding of the particularity of the modern epoch as one in which, as the French Revolution had shown, "history becomes philosophy and philosophy history."[3] This constitutes, for Hegel, the first great discovery of the specificity of capitalist modernity: philosophy in the modern world must accept the necessary mediation of historical reality in its negativity and finitude. Taking into account finitude as a necessary moment in the construction of philosophical identity would become the second discovery of modernity in Hegel's thought during this period. Infinity could no longer simply subsume finitude, it had itself to be subsumed under finitude in order to become genuine infinity; henceforth, infinity would really be *in-fini*.[4] As we will see, the discovery of the *real dynamics* of the capitalist economy in the modern world will be, for Hegel, a decisive element in this reevaluation of the importance of finitude.

For Hegel, the appreciation of finitude initially takes the form of a fragmentation. It begins as an observation regarding "bifurcation," the "tearing apart" brought about by the onset of modernity, meaning above all else the fragmentation of every traditional bond attendant on the emergence of modern bourgeois-civil society. It is this bifurcation, this real negativity, that triggers the *need of philosophy*.

The comprehension of the negativity of the real thus has as its point of departure a practical need to rethink unity under conditions of fragmentation. We can already find signs of such a comprehension in the text of the *German Constitution*, in which recognition of a social playroom (*Spielraum*) for the free interaction of individuals (*W1/GC* 484/22), as well as references to Machiavelli, mark the end of Hegel's constant efforts during the Frankfurt period to found the power of social unification upon the affective relations of "life" and "love."

It was Georg Lukács' *The Young Hegel*, which, despite weaknesses stemming from its dependence on a Soviet type of Marxism, had demonstrated that Hegel is actually one of the radical philosophers (with Machiavelli, Hobbes, and Mandeville) who affirm that progress in history is propelled through human passions and occurs through violent revolutionary action.[5] True, this dialectic, according to Lukács, found its systematic articulation in Hegel's search for a *reconciliation* of the opposing forces of modernity. Still, Lukács' book, written as a polemic against all those who considered Hegel a metaphysician unconcerned with material reality, broke new ground in affirming that one of the decisive factors in Hegel's comprehension of the dynamics of the modern epoch—which also means its negativity—was his encounter with political economy.

Political economy as a mode of thought emerged in its various categories with the development of the capitalist economy, which went hand in hand with the monetarization of commercial exchange and a process of mass production based on both the division of labor and the subsumption of workers under capital. The central category of political economy is *labor*, both as the source of useful products for satisfying individual needs (use value) and as the uniform measure permitting the exchange of different products (exchange value).[6] It was Adam Smith who in his *Wealth of Nations* had already underscored the significance of the division of labor, along with the dominating importance of money as a universal means of exchange.

However, Hegel did not restrict himself to the famous analyses of Adam Smith. Instead, he seems to have been the only philosopher in early nineteenth-century Germany who—from the moment he read Steuart's *Inquiry into the Principles of Political Economy*[7] (preparing notes that have unfortunately been lost)—never ceased observing the evolution of concepts of political economy or displaying an interest in socioeconomic life. The question we have initially to consider concerns the influence this interest had on the central feature of his philosophical approach and theoretical framework: the dialectical method. To answer this question, it is useful to begin at the end of the period in question with the enigmatic formulation of the "labor of the negative" we find in the *Phenomenology of Spirit*.

The Negative Labor of the Concept

The Preface to *Phenomenology* further develops the methodological motifs central to Hegel's "dialecticization" of philosophy. During deployment of knowledge of objectivity as a dynamic process, certain elements that we consider as given are annulled, which means that they are sacrificed in order to be refashioned in a higher form. However, these elements are simultaneously preserved as traces (*PhG/PhS* 24/16), being somehow imprinted each time on what is "present." This simultaneous process of annulment and preservation (known as *Aufhebung* or sublation) is rooted in Hegel's thematization of a procedure, termed *determinate negation*, focused on the immanent transition from an initial to a more developed form, something emanating from the negation of what is, each time conceived as a positive "reality." It is this procedure that Hegel calls the "the labor of the negative" (*PhG/PhS* 18/10). The negative labor of the concept would henceforth distinguish Hegel's philosophy as a mode of thought opposed on the one hand to an attitude that should be called

> material thinking, a contingent consciousness absorbed only in material stuff, and thus is challenged to extricate the [thinking] self from such matter so that it can be with itself alone. Equally opposed, however, is a form of argumentation expressed as freedom

from all content and a sense of vanity toward it. What is sought instead is an effort that renounces this vain freedom, and, rather than arbitrarily defining content from without, locates this freedom in the content itself, allowing the latter to determine itself spontaneously according to its own nature—a process that thought then simply contemplates. (*PhG/PhS* 42/35–36)

With his conceptualization of the labor of the negative Hegel thus turns against two epistemological attitudes. He turns first against the empiricist approach, which remains trapped in the contingency of the empirical "given"; Hegelian epistemology is strongly opposed to any evidentiary logic presuming that external things are static and given immediately. Refuting this reliance on the empirical given is the point of departure for the dialectic of (natural) consciousness in the *Phenomenology of Spirit*, which is realized through the relativization of the existence of an individual spatio-temporal given. The "now" and the "here" of the individual thing cannot resist spatio-temporal alteration (*PhG/PhS* 64–65/60–61); in order to speak of a here and a now, we must construct a universal here and now through the labor of conceptual mediation. Cognitive universality emerges as the condition of any "sense certainty."[8]

The other attitude that Hegel contests is the formalist rationalism of Kant and, especially, Fichte—the abstract freedom that regards content from the top down, arbitrarily imposing its laws.[9] It should be emphasized that Hegel fashioned here a polemic on the basis of a political argument: in the *Difference Between Fichte's and Schelling's System of Philosophy* he already expressed his concerns about the domination of the bifurcating power of the understanding (*Verstand*). This domination is especially prevalent in the writings of Fichte, proponent of a system in which the unity of subject and object can be achieved only as a subjective unity, given that the absolute identity as the principle of the system is posited in a dogmatic way and has not been constructed from *inside* the system itself (*W2/Diff.* 60–61/126). The antinomical character of this system of understanding is completely confirmed in Fichte's doctrine of natural law, a theory of right in which enforcement of law becomes an end in itself, presenting the curious spectacle of freedom being imposed through its restriction and thus its "limitless limitation." This system finds its application in the *Closed Commercial State*, the Fichtean system of political economy, which—based on the idea of an "autarkic" economy—is incompatible with the dynamics of the modern (capitalist) world[10] and, as Hegel clearly implies, could lead directly to an authoritarian regime.[11]

Faced with these effects of the mechanical domination of reflective understanding, Hegel searched for a different solution to the unification of the subject with the external world. He appeals, in the initial phase of the Jena period, to Spinoza's monist tradition, and tends to consider the unified formation of the subject with a productive nature—depicted in Schelling's identity philosophy—as the real solution. But after 1803 he quickly distances himself from an approach based, as this one was, on an intuitive totality. Finally, in the *Phenomenology of Spirit*, he comes to defend both empirical differentiations and the requisite scientific formalism against a notion of the absolute as an intuitive identity[12]—thus breaking with Schelling and Schellingians, confirmed in a highly polemical way in the Preface to the *Phenomenology of Spirit*. At the same time, he strongly opposed views such as Schlegel's—what might be termed *romantic aesthticism*—which attempted to replace conceptual processes with the expression of natural sentiments. In combining philosophy and poetry, this popular "philosophizing by the light of nature which regards itself as too good for the Notion, and as being an intuitive and poetic thinking in virtue of this deficiency, brings to market the arbitrary combinations of an imagination that has only been disorganized by its thoughts, an imagery that is neither fish nor foul, neither poetry nor philosophy" (*PhG/PhS* 50/42).

This brings us to a first conclusion. The critical confrontation of the labor of the negative with the theoretical aspects of individualism led Hegel to three philosophical oppositional stances: against empiricism, against formalism, and against romanticism.

Critique of Individualism and Sociohistorical Holism: A Structured Historical Totality

This conclusion helps us ask under what conditions Hegel employed the formulation of the "labor of the negative" to go beyond romantic irrationalism and, more importantly, beyond the dualism of subjective transcendental philosophy.[13] It is this very labor of the concept that leads, in the *Phenomenology of Spirit*, to the cultural dynamic of the "labor of spirit," thereby justifying the social aspects of modern (abstract) labor. What is the significance of the fact that such a theoretical use occurs after the dense political and social texts of the Jena period?[14] An analysis of these texts seems to be indispensable. We pursue such an analysis by focusing on the two *Philosophies of Spirit* (*Realphilosophie* I and II) in tandem with the *Phenomenology of Spirit*, given that both are integral to Hegel's thought during the Jena period.

It is clear that Hegel's intention is to extend the concept of labor beyond its strictly economic signification so as to reveal its cognitive function.[15] In objectifying itself, the subject annihilates the object; at the same

time, because of this objectification, it can conceptualize fully, it can sub-
late the object precisely because this object acquires the *self-same structure
of the subject* (*JS3/PoS* 200/99). Through its activity, the ego renders itself
intuitive, but it requires the mediation of an *instrument* during the process
of objectification to elevate itself beyond the simple passivity of thingness
(*Dinglichkeit*). This integration of the instrument into Hegel's conceptual
apparatus is crucial, because it entails a new form of rationality, one characterized by a certain *separation* from nature through the latter's "exploitation." Spirit becomes a relatively autonomous sphere, one that reproduces
itself *in its own element*, thus prescribing to itself a high degree of autonomy
in relation to its natural referents. In this way, Hegel fashions a new concept of rationality, one expressed in a coupling of *mechanical-material and
cognitive-spiritual* elements.[16] This implies a rupture with natural dependence, one much stronger than the rationality of the subjective spontaneity
we find in Kant and Fichte. We argue that this new conceptualization of
rationality implies a concept of *speculative materiality* that Hegel takes up
again with the great innovation he introduces in his *Realphilosophie* II: the
concept of *cunning*.

   The concept of cunning is established by means of reference to the
feminine element associated with it. The use of this metaphor parallels
the phenomenon associated with a certain historical rupture, namely the
abandonment of the ideal of "courage" in modern complex societies (an
argument we also find in the British social thinkers of capitalist modernity,
principally Smith and Ferguson). This autonomy of the artificial-spiritual
element introduces a new *sociality based on juridical recognition*. Henceforth,
the movement of recognition denotes an exit from the natural condition
of a struggle and signifies a transition to juridical relations, which results
in acknowledging the rights of individuals in civil society. Hegel characterizes the object produced by these relations as a *creation of right* (*Erzeugen
des Rechts–JS3/PoS* 215/111), which consists precisely in a sublation (*Aufhebung*) of the state of nature. Thus, the transformation of the struggle for
recognition into a sociojuridical state of affairs results from the general
revalorization of the *autonomy of the artificial element*.

   If the right of the state of nature meant the exclusion of the other,
legitimate right is to be found in its mediation by that which is already
recognized. The specificity of this right is that it is recognized by others,
a state of affairs that accentuates transition from the act of recognition
to the phenomenon of *being recognized*.[17] "But what is it, exactly, that the
others recognize? It is that which I have, which I possess. The content
[of 'property'] therefore emanates from my possession. Can I therefore
have whatever and as much as I want? I cannot take it from a third party
and expect recognition [as owner], because what he has is already recog-

nized" (*JS3/PoS* 216/112). The motive behind the struggle for recognition is evidently preserved, but this struggle now centers on the product of a sociojuridically mediated form of labor that emerges as the third term (*JS3/PoS* 219/115). The product of labor is transformed into the common context of any struggle for recognition.

This may be an appropriate point to respond to a reading of Hegel that absolutizes the existence of the concept of recognition in his pre-*Phenomenology* texts. This reading, which has become very popular following its formulation by A. Honneth, is problematic, as it seeks to locate the source of normativity in a presocial natural struggle for recognition, and thus proposes the existence of an originary *intersubjective community*.[18] This approach sees the concept of recognition progressively concretized, initially in juridical norms and then in social relations, characterizing them as a primordial normative claim. In fact, however, Hegel did not follow a method of progressively concretizing certain originary claims. Instead, he seems to have adopted the *progressive-regressive* method[19] evident in the texts of the Jena period onward, according to which a holistic framework is revealed to be the presupposition of earlier, more abstract moments. It is a quasi-objective (*gegenständlich*) sociohistorical framework—rather than a "monological" philosophy of consciousness—that emerges as the condition of possibility for recognition between subjects, integrating them into an artificial (namely sociohistorical) and *already structured totality*. This is a movement that for Hegel explicitly marks the historical transition into the modern world,[20] a transition that the *Phenomenology of Spirit* presupposes but does not present in its historical linearity, as it seeks only to reconstructs its constitutive/structural elements.

The integration of the isolated consciousness into an already structured sociohistorical totality, which finds its complete formulation in the *Phenomenology of Spirit*, constitutes a decisive break on Hegel's part with both the abstract subject of Kant and Fichte and the methodological individualism of political economy. Hegel posits the requirements for a *gradual sublation* of the point of view of the simple individual consciousness into the framework of spirit: the exposition of the representational schemes of consciousness in the *Phenomenology of Spirit* comprehends the deployment of the social, aesthetic and religious *representational structure* of modernity— a structure that operates "behind the backs" of the particular consciousnesses, while also creating the condition of their existence. Already in the chapter on "Reason" in the *Phenomenology of Spirit*, Hegel focuses on the effective realization of self-consciousness through a historical people's ethical-objective framework (*Sittlichkeit*), which is characterized as the "truth" of individual self-consciousness (*PhG/PhS* 193/212). Self-conscious reason finds its effective reality in the life of people, a framework that in the modern world is simultaneously only realized through a multiplicity of individuals. Their labor acquires its importance in the context of the reproduction of a complex-differentiated system; the individual reproduces the whole without knowing it (*PhG/PhS* 194–195/213).

Within this context, Hegel proceeds to a particularly penetrating treatment of what we can without exaggeration call the spirit of capitalism, referring to the "spiritual animal kingdom." This is a formulation that thematizes in a very strong way representations that are close to an antagonistically shaped market economy. In this "kingdom," bourgeois individuality presents itself as if it were "originally natural" (*PhG/PhS* 216/237), and attempts to manifest its natural domination, acting by positing ends for its own realization. Each individual struggles to promote its own specific activity as universal; the task of self-consciousness, appearing here as something to be exposed to others, thus creates an *action-mediated* universal space for mutual comparison and valorization (*PhG/PhS* 220–221/242–243). Within this generalized antagonism, individual consciousnesses, each in their own way, distinguish between aspects they retain for themselves and those they externally present to others. This play of individualities finally leads to a state of mutual deception (*PhG/PhS* 226/249–250). Nonetheless, in trying to promote their own distinct work, individuals find themselves forcibly entwined with the universal work; even if they wish to present the thing as *their* own, the thing becomes *everyone's*; the thing itself has become the universal *Subjekt* (*PhG* 226–228/250–252).

Abstract Social Labor, Reification, and the Dynamics of Market Economy

In order to understand the real bases of the representational scheme detailed in the "spiritual animal kingdom," we must turn to an elaboration of the concept of social labor in the texts of *Realphilosophie* I and II. In the first *Philosophy of Spirit*, labor is already distinguished from the universalization of its results, as artificial *instruments* are the principal expression of this universality. In its social function, the instrument transforms natural reality while preserving the materiality of the human activity. Yet in the mechanical dimension of labor, even the activity of the subject is finally eliminated as such. The cunning that the human subject uses against nature "takes its revenge upon him" (*JS1/PoS I* 320/247). Taking this as his starting point, Hegel inaugurates a particularly original appropriation of the issue of the *division of labor*: the mechanization of labor, promoted by its division, is accompanied by the augmentation of the *total value* produced by society, one that becomes possible only because the value of the individual's particular labor tasks is diminished. Yet the value of that labor is not only diminished, it deteriorates: human labor becomes an abstract and formal unit that corresponds to a universal need.[21] In this way, the satisfaction of needs is no longer accomplished through a correspondence between particular labor and concrete need, but through the totality of social labor.

The general interdependence thus emerging is not founded on relations of reciprocity, as in traditional societies, but on a generalization of *relations of contingency*.[22] (This is a notion that chronologically parallels the formulation of Say's law [1803], by which the contingent character of exchange plays a crucial role in the constitution of the space of the market.) Hegel organizes his appropriation of the reality of the division of labor into four nodal points (*JS1/PoS I* 323–324/248–249): (1) The observed augmentation of the product results from the fact that the value of individual labor diminishes in accordance with the extension of the division of labor; (2) with the mechanization of production, the workers' consciousness is identified with this deteriorated labor and is *reified* in the process; (3) the interconnection between the specialized labors creates a system of *blind interdependence* that subordinates the labor of a whole social class (Hegel uses the word *Klasse*); (4) the accomplishment of this transition results in the formation of a complete *second nature* that renders binding definition of individuals by the abstract market forms and the "new" luxury needs incorporated into the dynamics of bourgeois civil society. (We are thus presented here with a conceptual reconstruction of James Steuart's argument on the consolidation of the representations of "surplus" as a stimulus that triggers the dynamics of the accumulation of wealth.) This shift in social representations, which co-exists with a multiplication of needs, necessarily implies a space of general mediation between these needs and the labor that produces them, a state of affairs that introduces into Hegel's treatment the problem of the exchange forms of the *market*.

The aforementioned autonomization of the artificial element in the modern world now takes on the systematic character of an entire *second nature*, which is to be found in the market's reificatory forms and in their internal correlation with the capitalist division of labor. The particularity of Hegel's treatment lies precisely in the fact that, from the very beginning, he connects this problem with *money as a material form of mediation*.[23] In money we find the necessary dynamic means that correspond to the development of a "great" (modern) people. This is a people who no longer correspond to the "beautiful" ancient Greek immediacy, but express themselves in the mediated form of a "monstrous system" (*JS1/PoS I* 324/249). The introduction of these elements thus underscores the consolidation of the concepts of political economy in Hegel's thought, while also highlighting an important change of perspective within the text of the first *Philosophy of Spirit*: references to "courage" as a superior value disappear to make room for references to specialized individual relations.

The consequences of differentiation through the division of labor are treated in much greater depth in *Realphilosophie II*. Initially, we have a repetition of a common motif: pursuing the satisfaction of his needs, man works on inorganic nature, positing himself in it.[24] But here these needs rapidly exceed the satisfaction of immediate natural needs: they become the needs of society in general. The satisfaction of abstract needs necessitates a *common essence*, which, shared by the products of the different labor activities, transforms them as *exchange values*. The way to this transformation of what is individually diverse to the universal is established by *abstract labor*.[25] Henceforth, "human" labor is only meaningful as socially abstract labor.

> In the element of universality, it is such that it becomes abstract labor. The needs are many. The incorporation of their multiplicity in the I, that is, labor, is an abstraction of universal models (*Bilder*), yet [it is] a self-propelling process of formation (*Bilden*). The I, which is for-itself, is abstract I; but it does labor, hence its labor is abstract as well. The need in general is analyzed into its many aspects—what is abstract in its movement is the being-for-itself, activity, labor. Since work is performed only [to satisfy] the need as abstract being-for-itself, working becomes abstract as well (*so wird auch nur abstrakt gearbeitet*). (*JS3/PoS II* 224/121)

At the same time, the text indicates Hegel's profound understanding of the logic of a capitalist society that compels this type of labor—an understanding highlighted by the importance he attributes to the structures of mediation. It is these structures that form the movement of abstraction, whose most important result is the monetarization of social relations: money becomes the "universal equivalent" or the "transcendental framework" of capitalist society, as Alfred Sohn-Rethel would later put it.[26] Anticipating later theorists, Hegel emphasizes that the common element to be found in the products of abstract labor should be condensed into a universal notion—value—and that this universality should *manifest* itself in a *real* object: namely, money[27] (*JS3/PoS II* 226/121–122). It is clear that Hegel owes to Steuart the profound nature of his understanding of the formative power of money as the condition of the abstract exchange, a power that drives the entire process implied in the relationship between abstract labor and exchange. Steuart is perhaps the most important economist who, rejecting the orthodoxy of monetary thought (the quantitative theory of money of Hume, Smith, and Ricardo), conceived of money as an *endogenous* element in production relations.[28] Nevertheless, Hegel's appropriation of the Steuartian perspective on the monetary constitution of production is also a transformation whose character we can define as speculative constructivism, a viewpoint based on the *productive mediation* of spiritual forms. Money, this great "invention" according to Hegel, is the artificial material thing that transforms needs into something "merely represented (*vorgestellten*)" (*JS3/PoS II*, 269/166). It thus seems that for Hegel money plays the mediating role in the reconcretization of the product of abstract labor as a "useful" product, positing the conditions of exchange *in general*, while being an eminent case of what we called speculative materiality. In such a framework, the productive artificiality of money is thus a condition of possibility, forming the context of existence for both exchange value *and* use value.

The generalized dynamic of mediation through money becomes civil society's *element of equilibrium*. This means that, contrary to the harmonizing conception we encounter in certain aspects of the thought of Adam Smith and, more explicitly, Ricardo and Say, Hegel understands modern society to be stabilized not in spite of its dynamic, but *through* and *because of* this dynamic. For this reason, the contingency and conflictual antagonism provoked by this dynamic function not as an element of destruction but as one of equilibrium: "This necessity, which is the complete contingency of individual existence, is at the same time its sustaining substance" (*JS3/ PoS II* 244/140).

It is evident that Hegel does not confront the dynamic processes of capitalist society from the romantic point of view of a loss of an idyllic origin. Instead, he evaluates positively the importance of the creation of a social sphere for the free interaction of individuals, a sphere supported by a respect for individual rights systematized as the juridical code of modern civil society. Still, it is no surprise that Hegel also demonstrates a profound dialectical understanding of the fact that these emancipatory aspects are accompanied by the inherent instability of modern capitalist society, which brings about an explosion in the *fractures* and *inequalities* in its structure, along with an extreme increase in wealth. Hegel understands that from the moment needs become increasingly abstract and multiple, the labor that serves them becomes equally mechanical and dominated by the impersonal, reified forces of the market. In *Realphilosophie* II, he describes the progressive but simultaneously alienating character of the capitalist division of labor in far from rosy hues, focusing on the precarious conditions it produces for a large mass of the population, structured as it is on the polarization between rich and poor and on periodic economic crises as its *structural elements*.[29] The image of the market that emerges from this description is not that of a harmonious order, but of a complex mechanism that is inherently unstable and *not necessarily self-regulated*. The reified forms of commercial society that ensue from the division of labor do not, in the main, entail the subordination of a class of people by means of explicit and physical violence, as was the case in the slave regimes of antiquity. Hegel seems to understand that inequality and the concentration of wealth at certain stages in capital accumulation bring about an intense but *abstract form* of violence founded on a continuous movement, exercising a generalized *competitive pressure* coupled with the inherent periodic crises of the dynamic modern market economy:

> Thus a vast number of people are condemned to a labour that is totally stupefying, unhealthy and unsafe—in workshops, factories, mines, etc.—shrinking their skills. And entire branches of industry, which supported a large class of people, go dry all at once because of [changes in] fashion or a fall in prices due to inventions in other countries, etc.—and this huge population is thrown into helpless poverty.
>
> The contrast [between] great wealth and great poverty appears: the poverty for which it becomes impossible to do anything; [the] wealth [which], like any mass, makes itself into a force. (*JS3/PhS*, 244/139–140)

Conclusion

We leave aside here some enormously important questions: whether, for example, Hegel considers political institutions to be primarily produced within the aforementioned socioeconomic processes, or to have an autonomous logic and existence. Or whether Hegel, frightened at the spectacle of his own discovery of the conflictual nature and dynamic of modern capitalist society, really did retreat into contemplation, as Lukács reproached him, repressing history and positing the state as the "mythological" form of authority. What we have seen, however, is that Hegel has clearly understood and demonstrated that capitalist modernity is characterized by an autonomization and expansion of a sphere of obligatory interdependence that transforms natural needs into abstract needs and natural labor into abstract social labor. He has simultaneously shown that this sphere functions through reified forms that constitute an artificial second nature governed by laws as mechanical as those of inorganic nature. For Hegel, the economy is *the inorganic moment of the ethical organization* of society;[30] it is a process that works without autonomous subjects and without autonomous ends.

It is particularly significant that, when the crisis conditions provoked by the dynamic expansion of this sphere become apparent, Hegel introduced, already during the Jena period, the stabilizing exigencies of the universal class, integrating the state into civil society. Even at this early stage in Hegel's thought, it is the political state, as the *singularization of the universal*, which assumes the burden of elevating modern society to absolute spirit: art, religion, and philosophy. But this is a matter for another essay.

Notes

1. Hyppolite 1983, 93, and Lukács 1975, chapter 1.

2. On Hegel's pure "politicism" prior to the text of the *German Constitution* and the emergence of an autonomous social space, see Kervégan 1991, 191–193.

3. Bourgeois 1969, 33.

4. Koyré 1971, 162 and 166.

5. Lukács 1975, 355.

6. Smith 1976, 32–34.

7. Chamley 1963, 57–58.

8. On the necessary intervention of mediation in every form of sense perception, given that empirical observation is already concept laden, see Adorno 1993, 57–58. That is why the deeper we progress into conceptual mediation, the more we conceive the object in its totality; "the later is always richer," Adorno 1993, 64.

9. On Hegel's rupture with the arrogant (Cartesian) attitude toward representation, see Lebrun 1972, 109–110.

10. On the differences between Fichte and Hegel on this issue, see Nakano 2004.

11. In the text of the *Difference* we find a clear allusion to Fichte's *Natural Law* as an authoritarian practical philosophy that fully accepts the Hobbesian motif that Hegel calls the system of "atomistic" (*W2/Diff.*, 146 and 149).

12. On the necessary formalism *PhG/PhS* 16–17/9. See also Lukács 1975, 434–438.

13. See the study by A. Arndt (Arndt 1985, 110–111), which examines how Hegel reappropriates (through Hölderlin) the notion of labor as *poiesis* in order to overcome the oppositions of the "philosophy of understanding." Habermas had also emphasized the importance of labor for a synthesis that goes beyond the abstract "I," before the development of his dualism between the strategic and communicative action (Habermas 1973).

14. See Arndt 1985, 101. Adorno also clearly links Hegel's analyses on the abstract social labor with his discovery of the "labor of the concept" (Adorno 1993, 25–26).

15. See also Chamley 1965, 256.

16. A comparison with Marx's account of the instrument is here instructive: "An instrument of labour is a thing, or a complex of things, which the worker interposes between himself and the object of his labour and which serves as a conductor, directing his activity onto that object. He makes use of the mechanical, physical and chemical properties of some substances in order to set them to work on other substances as instruments of his power, and in accordance with his purposes" (Marx 1976, 285). See also the observations of Bienenstock 1992, 187, 201.

17. Contrary to the prevailing view that overemphasizes the normative exigency of a primordial recognition, what already seems to be crucial for Hegel in this text is the condition of *being recognized* (see also Taminiaux 1984, 54–56). Bienenstock also pertinently underscores that the act of recognition is only an initial stage in the development of Hegel's argument (Bienenstock 1992, 18).

18. In a characteristic passage, Honneth criticizes Hegel because his "turn to the philosophy of consciousness allows Hegel to completely lose sight of the idea of an original intersubjectivity of humankind and blocks the way to the completely different solution that would have consisted in making the necessary distinctions between various degrees of personal autonomy within the framework of a theory of intersubjectivity" (Honneth 1995, 30).

19. On the function of this method in the *Philosophy of Right*, see Kervégan (2004) and K. Hartmann (1982). It seems that this methodological tendency is already present in the Jena writings.

20. It seems that Hegel recognizes this, explicitly emphasizing the transition to a "new world" at the end of "Absolute Knowledge," as he puts it: "Thus absorbed in itself, it is sunk in the night of its self-consciousness; but in that night its vanished outer existence is preserved, and this transformed existence—the former one, but now reborn of the Spirit's knowledge—is the new existence, a new world and a new shape of Spirit. In the immediacy of this new existence, the Spirit has to start afresh to bring itself to maturity as if, for it, all that preceded were lost and it had learned nothing from the experience of the earlier Spirits. But recollection, the *inwardizing*, of that experience, has preserved it and is the inner being, and in fact the higher form of the substance" (*PhG/PhS* 433/492).

21. "The satisfaction of needs is a universal dependence of everyone upon one another; for everyone all security and certainty that his labour as a single agent is directly adequate to his needs disappears; as a singular complex of needs he becomes a universal. Through the division of labour the skill of anyone for the labour to be done is immediately greater; all the relations of nature to the singular circumstances of man come more fully under his command, *comfort* increases. [. . .] The consciousness [of this universality] is not an absoluteness in which these connections are nullified; it is directed toward the cancelling of this privacy, the freeing of the labouring [agent] from his dependence on nature; need and labour are elevated into the form of consciousness; they are simplified, but their simplicity is formally universal, abstract simplicity" (*JS1/PoS I*, 322–323/247–248).

22. Hegel's treatment of this issue here tacitly implies a reference to the crucial issue of the transition from a subsistence economy to a market economy. On the importance of this question for the modern social system, see Luhmann 1988, 202 and 246.

23. See also Ahrweiler 1976, 59.

24. On the immanence of the self in the thing realized by the activity of labor, see Schmidt am Busch 2001, 33. Schmidt am Busch nevertheless attempts to detach labor from reification, which we would consider impossible in the conditions of modern society.

25. Hegel is here explicitly referencing Adam Smith's famous example of the pin factory. On Hegel's contact with the text of *Wealth of Nations*, but also for the

different uses to which he would later put this example in his lectures on the *Philosophy of Right*, see N. Waszek 1988, 128–131.

26. Sohn-Rethel 1972, 21.

27. On the necessity of value's objectification as money in Hegel, see Arthur 2002, 182.

28. See Steuart 1966, 36, 44, 155–157, 314–316, 325. For a parallel analysis between Steuart and Hegel on this issue, see Caboret 1998.

29. On the important observation that Hegel does not consider unemployment and precarious labor conditions as "market failures" external to the rationality of the market, but rather as endogenous elements of its dynamic, see Priddat 1990, 55.

30. On the place of economy as the inorganic part of the social organism, Dickey 1987, 213–214, 240–241, 264.

Works Cited

Abbreviations for Works by G.W.F. Hegel

JS1/PoS I   *Jenaer Systementwürfe* I, Bd 6 GW. Hamburg: Felix Meiner, 1975. "Hegel's First Philosophy of Spirit." In *System of Ethical Life and First Philosophy of Spirit.* Translated by H. S. Harris and T. M. Knox. Albany: State University of New York Press, 1979.

JS3/PoS II   *Jenaer Systementwürfe* III, Bd 8 GW. Hamburg: Felix Meiner, 1976. *Hegel and the Human Spirit.* Translated by Leo Rauch. Detroit: Wayne State University Press, 1983.

PhG/PhS   *Phänomenologie des Geistes*, Bd 9 GW. Hamburg: Felix Meiner, 1980. *The Phenomenology of Spirit.* Translated by A. V. Miller. Oxford: Clarendon Press, 1977.

W1/GC   *Die Verfassung Deutschlands*–Bd1 in *Werke in zwanzig Bänden.* Frankfurt am Main: Suhrkamp, 1969–1991. "The German Constitution (1798–1802)." In *Political Writings.* Edited by L. Dickey and H. B. Nisbet. Cambridge: Cambridge University Press, 2004.

W2/Diff.   *Differenz des Fichteschen und Schellingschen Systems der Philosophie*–Bd2 in *Werke in zwanzig Bänden.* Frankfurt am Main: Suhrkamp, 1969–1991. *The Difference Between Fichte's and Schelling's System of Philosophy.* Translated by H. S. Harris and W. Cerf. Albany: State University of New York Press, 1977.

Adorno, T. 1993. *Hegel: Three Studies.* Translated by S. Weber Nicholsen. Cambridge, MA: MIT.

Ahrweiler, G. 1976. *Hegels Gesellschaftslehre.* Neuwied, Darmstadt: Luchterhand.

Arndt, A. 1985. "Zur Herkunft und Funktion des Arbeitsbegriffs in Hegels Geistesphilosophie." *Archiv für Begriffgeschichte* 39: 99–115.

Arthur, C. J. 2002. "Hegel's Theory of Value Form." In *New Dialectic and Marx's Capital.* Leiden: Brill.

Bienenstock, M. 1992. *Politique du Jeune Hegel 1801–1806*. Paris: Presses Universitaires de France.

Bourgeois, B. 1969. *La pensée politique de Hegel*. Paris: Presses Universitaires de France.

Caboret, D. 1998. "Economie marchande et classes sociales chez J. Steuart et G.W.F. Hegel." In *Sir James Steuart et l'économie politique*, Cahiers de l'ISMEA, Novembre–Décembre, 79–96.

Chamley, P. 1963. *Economie, Politique et Philosophie chez Steuart et Hegel*. Strasbourg: Dalloz.

———. 1965. "Les Origines de la pensée économique de Hegel." *Hegel-Studien* 3: 225–262.

Dickey, L. 1987. *Hegel: Religion, Economics and the Politics of Spirit*. Cambridge: Cambridge University Press.

Habermas, J. 1973. "Labor and Interaction." In *Theory and Practice*, translated by J. Viertel. Boston: Beacon Press.

Hartmann, K. 1982. "Linearität und Koordination in Hegels Rechtsphilosophie." In *Hegels Philosophie des Rechts. Die Theorie der Rechtsformen und ihre Logik*, edited by D. Henrich and R.-P. Horstmann. Stuttgart: Klett-Cotta.

Honneth, A. 1995. *The Struggle for Recognition: The Moral Grammar of Social Conflicts*. Translated by J. Anderson. Cambridge: Polity Press.

Hyppolite, J. 1983. *Introduction à la philosophie de l'histoire de Hegel*. Paris: Seuil.

Kervégan, J.-F. 1991. "Le citoyen contre le bourgeois. Le jeune Hegel et la quête pour l'esprit du tout." In *Rousseau, die Revolution und der Junge Hegel*, edited by H.-F. Fulda and R-P. Horstmann. Stuttgart: Klett-Cotta.

———. 2004. "Le droit du monde. Sujets, normes et institutions." In *Hegel: Penseur du Droit*, edited by J.-F. Kervégan and G. Marmasse. Paris: CNRS.

Koyré, A. 1971. "Hegel à Iéna." In *Etudes d'histoire de la pensée Philosophique*. Paris: Gallimard.

Lebrun, G. 1972. *La Patience du Concept*. Paris: Gallimard.

Luhmann, N. 1988. *Die Wirtschaft der Gesellschaft*. Frankfurt am Main: Suhrkamp.

Lukács, G. 1975. *The Young Hegel. Studies in the Relations between Dialectics and Economics*. Translated by R. Livingstone. London: Merlin Press.

Marx, K. 1976. *Capital: A Critique of Political Economy*, vol. 1. Translated by Ben Fowkes. London: Penguin.

Nakano, T. 2004. "Hegel's Theory of Economic Nationalism: Political Economy in Philosophy of Right." *European Journal of the History of Economic Thought* 11 (1): 33–52.

Priddat, B. 1990. *Hegel als Ökonom*. Berlin: Duncker & Humblot.

Schmidt am Busch, H-C. 2001. *Hegels Begriff der Arbeit*. Berlin: Akademie-Verlag.

Smith A. 1981. *An Inquiry into the Nature and Causes of the Wealth of Nations*. Indianapolis: Liberty Fund.

Sohn-Rethel, A. 1972. *Geistige und Körperliche Arbeit*. Frankfurt am Main: Suhrkamp.

Steuart, J. 1966. *An Inquiry into the Principles of Political Economy*. Edited by A. Skinner. Edinburgh: Oliver & Boyd.

Taminiaux, J. 1984. *Naissance de la Philosophie Hégélienne de l'Etat*. Paris: Payot.

Waszek, Norbert. 1988. *The Scottish Enlightenment and Hegel's Account of "Civil Society."* Boston: Kluwer.

2

Beyond Recognition in Capitalism

From Violence and Caprice to Recognition and Solidarity

KOHEI SAITO

Introduction

Recent work by Kurt Rainer Meist has convincingly demonstrated that Hegel's *System of Ethical Life* originated from the lecture course titled "Critique of Fichte's Natural Right," which, however, was canceled owing to an institutional issue.[1] Even if Hegel had modified a great deal of the original lecture notes in the process of preparing the book manuscript that Karl Rosenkranz later named *System of Ethical Life*, it is still reasonable to assume that he there elaborated many themes in conscious opposition to Fichte's system of natural right. In fact, the results of Hegel's reception of political economy are for the first time crystallized in this manuscript, which in other respects as well indicates a sharp contrast to Fichte's view. Both young German Idealists avidly studied political economy, precisely because they were keenly aware that the newly emerging economic system was radically transforming the nature of human material life. Nevertheless, they reached almost opposite solutions to the negative consequences of capitalism. While Fichte rejects the ideal of free commerce and legitimates state coercion against the alien force of the market, Hegel integrates without external coercion the commodity relations of the free market into his ethical system as the "system of needs."

In order to comprehend the reason for the dissimilar outcomes in their reception of political economy, this chapter first deals with Fichte's critique of capitalism in his *Closed Commercial State*. I argue that his demand for a "planned economy" and "closure of commerce within the state" is not an abrupt idea, but instead follows consistently from his central effort in the *Foundations of Natural Right* to secure the formal equality of rights for *all* rational beings based on the principle of "mutual recognition." Hegel continues Fichte's theory of mutual recognition but also transplants its transcendental account into a historical context. He also claims that the Fichtean form of mutual recognition, based as it is on the "person," inevitably turns into inequality and enslavement under a system of market exchange. Confronted with this contradiction, Hegel, instead of advocating for the abolition of free-market commerce like Fichte, attempts to incorporate the modern market as a component in the free and ethical unity of a people. He does this by developing a different form of recognition, one in which the antagonistic relationship inherent in the struggle for recognition becomes constitutive of freedom and equality in ethical life. However, the integration of the negativity of modern capitalism into ethical life forced Hegel to change his system conception and abandon the manuscript.

Fichte's Radical Critique of Capitalism

Famously enough, Fichte's *Closed Commercial State* (1800) argues for "planned economy" and "closure of commerce within the state." After the collapse of the Soviet Union and the establishment of capitalism as the globally dominant economic system, such a position now appears completely utopian, even absurd. Yet already during Fichte's lifetime, Adam Müller in his review rejected the work as "one of the most thoughtless plays in the century of enthusiasm" and claimed that it is full of presumptuous judgments by an author unacquainted with the subject.[2] In this context, it may appear astonishing that, despite harsh criticisms, Fichte remained convinced of the quality of this "best and most thoughtful work," as his son conveys, and basically repeated the same view in the 1807 *Addresses to the German Nation*.[3] One might thus be tempted to agree with Müller and accuse Fichte of being a naive idealist who simply superimposed abstract ideas, derived from his philosophical system of the "I," upon reality.

However, it is still necessary to ask why Fichte continued to vouch for the high quality of this problematic work even after his *Science of Knowledge* (*Wissenschaftslehre*) underwent enormous revision in his later years. It suggests that his confidence in the quality of the *Closed Commercial State* was deeper than his theoretical philosophy—a confidence based on his funda-mental practical belief in the value of freedom and equality of *all* rational beings. Though often neglected because of its provocative claims, the work does represent the consistent development of his political beliefs, some-thing that becomes apparent in his severe critique of modernity. Fichte was confronted with the brutal reality of commercial competition compelling people to pursue the maximization of profits, totally depriving them of the ability to autonomously regulate their own behavior according to the law of reason. Consequently, even if "closure of the state" and "planned economy" did appear absurd and illusionary to advocates of the free market, Fichte had to insist that state coercion is the only means to guarantee the freedom and equality of all rational beings against the arbitrariness of capitalism.

In order to understand Fichte's critique of capitalism, it is first neces-sary to clarify the distinction between "possession" and "property." In his early essay on the French Revolution, anonymously published in 1793, Fichte did not yet distinguish between these two concepts, maintaining simply that the activity of "formation" assigns an external object the status of property according to natural right.[4] In other words, he still equated natural right with something already *given* to all by nature. By contrast, the *Foundations of Natural Right*, published in 1796/1797, makes clear that natural right is something not given by nature but *established* through a collective contract among rational beings. According to this view, the prod-uct of labor is in itself a mere possession without any stipulations for a future use, one that others may still use for their own purposes. It is only through intersubjective practices of "mutual recognition" that possession is transformed into property, a transformation legitimizing its exclusive use for an individual's particular purposes. This recognition of possession takes place when each rational being freely agrees with others in a form of contract that he or she will not invade possessions held by others, those lying beyond his or her own sphere of freedom. In the act of voluntarily limiting one's own sphere of freedom lies a key element of recognition, according to which a rational being recognizes the contractual other as a "person," that is, as an equal subject entitled to rights to her own body and a part of the external sensible world.[5]

Nonetheless, Fichte adds that the property contract between pri-vate persons remains "problematic," not "categorical" because it can be annulled at any time by malicious will or negligence if one subject invades another's sphere of freedom. Once the property contract is violated, the relationship of recognition immediately collapses, and the contractors fall back into the Hobbesian state of nature, the "war of all against all."[6] It thus becomes evident that private contract alone is not a sufficient founda-tion for natural right. This experience of insecurity leads rational beings to seek the guarantee of rights through a "social contract," predicated on the establishment of a state based on the general will of the people. In this contract, individuals agree to surrender absolutely their use of violence to the state as a neutral third party; the state then assumes, with its absolute monopoly on violence, full and unconditioned responsibility for mediating conflicts and policing illegitimate behavior. Protected by the state, the possession of each person, provided that it is acquired by legitimate means, becomes a secured property via such mutual recognition. If acquired through theft or exploitation, the possession is not recognized, but immediately becomes a target of state sanction.

The uniqueness of Fichte's argument lies in his transcendental deduction of rights from a "free efficacy" of the I to "posit" itself. That is, he starts his discussion with the free activity of the I, deducing the physical world and other rational beings. In this process Fichte aims to demonstrate the reality of natural right as the condition of possibility for the coexistence of finite rational beings in an external world. Considering the historical context, the radical character of Fichte's transcendental deduction manifests itself in his demand that the state guarantee the right to property to *each* person. Rejecting the error of the dominant theory, which sees "original property in an exclusive possession of *a thing*," Fichte's *Closed Commercial State* argues rather that original property emerges from "*an exclusive right to a determinate free activity*"—more simply, the right to work.[7] While the former conception of property bestows the right to property only on "large landholders" and "nobles," and the state accordingly restricts citizenship or rights in general to them, Fichte claims that a legitimate state must provide every person with an equal right to property regardless of class, gender, or race, thus allowing all laboring subjects the ability to enjoy the fruits of their labor. In arguing for this requirement, Fichte transcendently deduces the right to property as an "original right," that is, as an essential condition for the free activity of all rational beings. Fichte denounces the land ownership of feudalism because its institutionalization of property justifies a merely passive possession of a piece of land (one without labor), thus excluding nonlandholders from the right to property. The feudal state cannot prove its legitimacy according to Fichte, as it fails to realize the equal rights of all rational beings. As a neutral third party, the state needs instead to protect the absolute equality of persons and to intervene if this equality is endangered. The absoluteness of this formal equality is therefore nothing but a critique of the feudal state, one through which Fichte speaks for those oppressed by an illegitimate conception of the "right to property."

One should note here that Fichte's critique of the feudal state does not merely represent a German version of the Enlightenment. Had he argued only for the formal equality of all persons, Fichte would not have differed greatly from Enlightenment thinkers. Yet he consistently emphasized that realization of natural right requires not merely its formal guarantee by the state, but also the equality of *material* life, something he deemed essential for human freedom. In fact, in his 1796 "Review" of Kant's *Perpetual Peace*, he supplements Kant's discussion by insisting that the realization of the Kantian ideal of a cosmopolitan right also requires "the equilibrium of possessions."[8]

In addition, Fichte's critical insight into modern equality and freedom developed further after 1796, even if, at first glance, his argument in *The Closed Commercial State* might seem to continue the "Review." Here he robustly attacks the intensification of market competition. He points out that the egoistic maximization of profits causes global competition, with the result that a majority of people suffer from "the most screaming injustice" and "great misery."[9] This occurs as the result of a logic of commerce that forces everyone, independently of their will, to sell commodities as cheaply as possible, often even below the original price. Poverty prevails among the losers in the competition and their families, who are not able to afford even daily necessities. This situation signifies nothing but a violation of the most fundamental interest of human beings, that is, "to be able to live from labor"—for Fichte, the "ultimate end" of human beings.[10] One might therefore conclude that Fichte argued for the state intervention in the market simply in order to secure the material equality of people. However, this judgment is premature, for obviously there are other ways to deal with the problem of economic inequality. The question remains why Fichte had to advocate the "closure of the state," seemingly the most difficult policy countermeasure to implement.

In fact, Fichte's real critique of capitalism goes much deeper than simply denouncing the market's tendency to cause economic inequality and dependence. He feared the dominance of commerce more because the magnification and multiplication of human desire through market activities triggers the deployment of a *direct form of violence*, one establishing domination of the stronger over the weaker, and thus completely annihilating the formal equality of persons.[11] Fichte even indicates the possibility for the reemergence, in the middle of civilization itself, of the Hobbesian state of nature, which should have been overcome through the social contract: "An unceasing *war of all against all*, of buyers and sellers, will arise among the trading public."[12] This state of nature in the market became more and more intensified and allowed for the domination of Europeans over the rest of the world in such diverse ways as "servitude of the colonies to the motherlands," and "slave trade."[13] This use of brutal violence is a particularly modern product brought about by the worldwide egoistic competition for the infinite accumulation of wealth. Because human desire was not properly restricted, Europeans pursued the satisfaction of their unbounded desires by any means possible. As a consequence, colonies were subjugated by cruel physical force. Fichte's critique of the capitalist state of nature is directed not solely to material inequality and the one-sided economic dependence of the weaker upon the stronger. Rather, he warns against Europeans' unrestricted desire for wealth under capitalism, one that negates formal equality and dominates the rest of the world through arbitrary will and violence.

Fichte recognizes that the unrestricted behavior of Europeans does not promote a path to realizing the vocation of the human being as a universal being, and that the reality of capitalism represents on the contrary a crisis in the foundation of natural right, deemed by Fichte the fundamental condition of freedom of all rational beings. In order to reestablish the principles of natural right and to establish an egalitarian relationship between Europeans and the inhabitants of the rest of the world, it is permissible to constrain the freedom of Europeans, whose desires are distorted by the penetration of market logic. More concretely, Fichte claims that commerce with any foreign country must be banned and that the state as a neutral agent must voluntarily restrict the sphere of Europeans to Europe itself. Clearly, the closure of the state is a surprising solution for Europeans, and Fichte is fully aware that it would be difficult for his idea to be widely accepted.[14] As he says in the Introduction to the *Closed Commercial State,* even if he could fully prove that the closure of the state is the only solution to the destructive tendency of world commerce, it would not change the behavior of Europeans; preferring instead to maintain the status quo, they would simply answer: "Let us then take advantage of this for as long as it continues, leaving it to the generations that are around when it finally comes to an end to figure out for themselves how they will cope."[15]

In the *Foundations of Natural Right,* Fichte was aware that a simple "ought" in the sphere of natural right is powerless in the face of those who do not desire coexistence with others, but he still hoped that a general will might emerge, one that would facilitate departure from a Hobbesian state of nature. Fichte now realizes, however, that the real state of nature in the midst of civilization cannot be overcome through the general will. It is only through the actual deployment of the physical force on the part of the European state against Europeans themselves that rationality over the egoistic will can be enforced on the latter. It is no wonder that Fichte thought that free trade advocates would not understand his claim and so did not concern himself with the reputation of the *Closed Commercial State* during his lifetime.

As is obvious by now, Fichte's critique of capitalism and colonization is more radical than his contemporaries. When Hegel, fearing tyranny, rejects

external coercion of individuals' activities and any absolute negation of
the market, it is questionable whether he fully understood Fichte's intent
in rejecting capitalism. In any event, Hegel's aim instead is to tame the
market, something he does through a different account of recognition.
Contrary to Fichte's transcendental theory of recognition, Hegel histori-
cizes recognition of the "person" in the context of market exchange. In
so doing, Hegel, to protect the formal equality among persons, seeks to
integrate positive aspects of the modern market itself into the system of
ethical life.

"Property," "Person," and "Recognition" in the *System of Ethical Life*

Influenced by Fichte, Hegel, in the *System of Ethical Life,* adopted Fichte's
theory of recognition with regard to the distinction between possession
and property. This is extremely important for the development of Hegel's
practical philosophy, not only because it shows the extension of its theoretical scope, but also because it prompts him to perceive the limit of this
abstract recognition in the market.

Hegel, during his Frankfurt period, mainly elaborated a notion of
mutual recognition based on "love." As Ludwig Siep points out, however,
the limitation of a natural relationship based on love derives from its
exclusivity and its inability to account for possession, property, and rights
in social institutions.[16] Hegel becomes fully aware of this problem in the
System of Ethical Life. When arguing for the mutual dependence and formative education (*Bildung*) in the "relation of parents and children," he
does speak of "a recognition which is mutual" and which attains "supreme
individuality and external difference."[17] Hegel thus esteems its potential to
realize an absolute equality. Yet he immediately adds that natural love and
feeling are not institutionalized in society, asserting that mutual recognition here does not attain a universal form but instead remains exclusive
to the parent-child relationship.[18] Hegel thus makes clear that the precise
limitation of recognition in love lies in the discrepancy between universal
content and exclusive form.

If one takes this background into account, it becomes clear how
Fichte's theory of recognition helps Hegel avoid the exclusive form recognition has in love. As seen earlier, Fichte differentiates possession and
property with use of a concept of mutual recognition in which every free
being becomes a subject of a contract. Hegel makes the same distinction,
regarding the direct product of labor as a mere possession. When he first
discusses possession, he explicitly states that "there can be no question at

all here of the legal basis or aspect of possession."[19] This is because the product of labor is analyzed only in terms of the laboring subject and the external physical object in abstraction from social interaction with others. By contrast, Hegel deals with the problem of property in part B, where he does consider property in terms of social interaction. This time Hegel writes that it is the "beginning of legal, and formally ethical, enjoyment and possession."[20] Like Fichte, Hegel's distinction implies that the right to property is not naturally given independently of social interaction, but only emerges through intersubjective social praxis. Yet while Fichte justifies the right to property in an a priori manner, Hegel focuses instead on a concrete social praxis that allows its emergence in a historical sense. According to Hegel, the universalization of the commodity exchange relations provides the modern foundation for the mutual recognition of persons.

In the first "Potent a)" in part B, Hegel describes a stable state where a possession is already recognized by others. Without relating to others, the subject sustains its connection to an external physical object through labor and through direct use. The subject appears as a "possessor" in this situation. Yet this tie between the subject and the object can also be recognized by others through social interaction, where it receives universal form: "[The subject] is a single individual with a bearing on others and universally negative as a possessor recognized as such by other."[21] Recognition by others entails their renunciation of free access to my possession. Their negative relation to my possession becomes fixed under the universal form of "the right to property" and "in this respect possession is property." The subject is also recognized as a proprietor, and "personality" is thereby given to each subject as a legal subject. It is clear that Hegel adopts the distinction between possession and property by way of an account of recognition.

Despite the similarity to Fichte, Hegel's originality becomes immediately apparent when he asks how such recognition actually takes place. In the first "Potent a)," Hegel does not precisely state how a possessor came to be recognized by others as a proprietor, as there remains a "legal right at rest [. . .], and therefore inwardly concealed and hidden." In the next "Potent b)," he employs the term *anerkennen* again in order to explain how "right emerges."[22] Here Hegel describes for the first time how modern market relations solve the problem of the exclusivity of recognition through love, demonstrating that mutual recognition manifests itself on a universal social level through the historical development of commodity exchange.

For the development of free commerce to be possible, the social division of labor and the process of mechanization play a significant role. As a result of these transformations in modern society's mode of production, labor becomes increasingly mechanical and segmented. Each individual is able to produce a large amount of the same product. Yet because individual consumption of one kind of product is quantitatively limited, individual labor inevitably produces a "surplus" that is not directly usable by the producer himself, even though he still has to obtain other kinds of products in order to satisfy his other needs. Hegel resolves this contradiction by pointing out that "[t]his sort of laboring, thus divided, presupposes at the same time that the remaining needs are provided for in another way, for this way too has to be labored on, i.e., by the labor of other men."[23] The inability of a surplus to satisfy one's own needs compels everyone to interact with others who possess a needed object. The material conditions of modern civil society, in which individuals are unable on their own to satisfy their wants, provide the historical condition for the constitution of property, as individuals are forced to engage in "exchange," or more precisely, commodity exchange.

In societies where a social division of labor develops, relations of mutual dependence emerge enabling members to satisfy their needs. These function as a material basis for universal equality, although this equality does not appear as such, but is "reflected in the thing" as equality of "value."[24] People are forced to engage in producing this form of equality through the exchange process, due to their lack of means to satisfy needs on their own. As the commodity relation extends throughout society, mutual recognition also develops through the exchange process via the mediation of value: "This is *exchange*, the realization of the ideal relation. Property enters reality through the majority of persons involved in exchange and *mutually recognizing one another*."[25] The ideal relation of equality presupposed by the right to property becomes "real" as value in the exchange process, in which possession is also transformed into a property. Before the exchange, one's possession may seem secured merely by accident. Engaging in exchange founded on mutual consent between free subjects, however, an owner of one commodity recognizes another who possesses a desired commodity. He or she does not threaten the other with violence or steal the commodity. Exchange proceeds only when both sides have freely agreed to the terms of the exchange, when they acknowledge their equality in the value of their commodities. Participating in this process, commodity possessors reciprocally recognize each other as the "proprietors" of certain pieces of property and thus as persons who have a right to property. It is only within modern civil society that this practice of exchange becomes universal, as does the conscious practice of individuals reciprocally recognizing one another as "persons."

The recognition involved in exchange goes beyond the scope of love in natural relations because it extends universally with the development of the social division of labor within capitalism. Contrary to Fichte's transcendental deduction, Hegel describes how mutual dependence, for the sake of the satisfaction of needs, forces individuals to engage in reciprocal recognition through exchange under the historical system of commodity exchange. As our daily experience confirms, however, market relations of recognition usually remain superficial, as individuals typically strive to satisfy their physical needs without much consideration of the exchange partner. This essentially egoistic form of recognition cannot replace the often self-sacrificing and nonutilitarian sort present in love. In fact, Hegel argues that the formal and abstract equality of person that negates all the "external differences" turns into real inequality, seriously threatening the ethical life of a people.

Because the equality of two commodities expressed in value is purely quantitative, their qualitative difference is completely abstract. The same characteristic applies to the equality of persons. As Hegel says, the person is "absolutely formal" and "the individual, considered under this abstraction, is the person."[26] In other words, person signifies nothing more than that which remains formally living after abstracting out all individual difference. This formal equality creates the legal equality of all, regardless of rank, gender, or wealth. Despite such abstraction, however, various differences and individual distinctions remain. The concept of person cannot accommodate all the important distinctions vital to the ethical life.[27] Because "the power of life is unequal" between individuals, the possibility of arbitrariness could destroy relations of recognition.[28] The relationship between two persons becomes a fixed relation of inequality owing to specific real differences in wealth, skills, gender, race, and that cannot be addressed with the category of person alone. Formal equality indifferent to individual distinctions turns into a relation of inequality and dependence, that is, "the relation between master and servant": the master "is in possession of a surplus, of what is physically necessary; the servant lacks it."[29] There emerges a possibility of arbitrariness because the stronger can profit more from the "nonrecognition" and "nonfreedom" of the weaker.[30] Yet this negative consequence of the exchange relation does not prompt Hegel to fall back on a view that absolutely negates market relations. He still values establishing the category of "person" in reality, not only because it enables the universally equal treatment of all, but because the material basis of commodity exchange facilitates realization of the free unity of a people as a "system of needs."

Struggle for Recognition as an Ethical Praxis

In the *System of Ethical Life*, Hegel esteems the physical mutual dependence within the market as the system of needs, even though he is certainly conscious of the danger that, owing to abstractions endemic to the intersubjective relations of persons, equality in exchange relations can be transformed into inequality and enslavement. This integration of market relations into the ethical life is quite distinctive compared to earlier ambiguity. In the *Natural Law* essay, written just before the *System of Ethical Life*, Hegel could soften the negative tendencies of civil society only by way of analogy to "tragedy": "*Tragedy* consists in this, that ethical nature segregates its inorganic nature (in order not to become embroiled in it), as a fate, and places it outside itself."[31] He was still unable to overcome the contradictions of the market and instead simply demanded that ethical life "sacrifice" one part of itself to the nonethical relation of the market. Hegel tacitly admitted the impossibility of removing the tension with the nonethical component and so could only strive to prevent the market from extending beyond what is necessary.[32] Because he sought to comprehend ethical life as the realization of the absolute identity of a people, any solution leaving market relations alien to the organic whole was obviously inadequate.

By contrast, Hegel's *System of Ethical Life* documents a substantial change from his earlier thinking on this issue. After studying political economy intensively, Hegel succeeds in *integrating*, via the system of needs, its positive aspect into ethical life owing to the fact that through the subjective practice of workers he found a way to limit market contradictions. This clearly contrasts to Fichte's argument for state intervention and a planned economy. Unlike Fichte, Hegel recognizes the necessity of preserving fundamental principles of the free market in constructing the free unity of a people.

As the social division of labor develops in modern society, the relation of mutual physical dependence becomes an independent universal system. Within the system of needs, no one controls production as a whole; every being produces privately without knowing *what* others need and *how much* they need. Consequently, overproduction and underproduction become normality. While Fichte tried coercively to regulate this unpredictable market dynamic with a planned economy, Hegel discerns that the modern economic system itself constitutes a historically new unity of free individuals. Members of this system are only able to satisfy their needs through exchange, so they are strongly driven to produce objects that satisfy the needs of others in order to obtain in return objects that satisfy their own needs. Because of this historically particular form of mutual dependence, each individual freely, even without the system forcing anyone to produce certain products, reflects on the needs of others, constantly creating new products and trying to arouse new desires in order to satisfy in return their own needs. The modern market organizes the free praxis of people as production by all and for consumption by all. Yet this relationship of mutual physical dependence mediated by commodities depends on unconscious natural drive, and its unforeseeable dynamics appears as a force alien to individuals.

In fact, the contradictions endemic to the abstract relations among persons extend in the system of needs to the entire society, thus enlarging the inequality between the rich and the poor. It transforms the mutual dependence of individuals into a one-sided dependence of workers upon capitalists. The problem expands as money arouses ideals of unlimited enjoyment and the strong desire for its acquisition. Money modifies human desire because it allows the accumulation of wealth far beyond the amount any individual can actually spend. Because the total sum of objects of enjoyment within a society is finite, for "the accumulation of possession at one place, possession must diminish at another," that is, "[t]he inequality of wealth is absolutely necessary."[33] This results in the deepest poverty of the working class, one tied to the intensified relation of master and slave. The harsh labor of workers for the sake of capitalists' profits degrades them to the "unmitigated extreme of barbarism." Not only is their wage reduced to the level minimally sufficient for bare subsistence, but working conditions worsen to an unbearable state due to the mechanization and segmentation of the labor process. Conversely, the tremendous wealth of the bourgeoisie grants them an autonomy and independence based on the reified power of money, and their egoistic pursuit for its accumulation makes them eschew respect for society as a whole: "The individual who is tremendously wealthy becomes a might; he cancels the form of thoroughgoing physical dependence, the form of dependence on a universal, not on a particular."[34] This necessary inequality endangers the unity of a people: "The absolute bond of the people, namely ethical principle, has vanished, and the people is dissolved."[35]

Confronting the contradictions of the system of needs, Hegel indeed asserts, like Fichte, the necessity of state intervention. Hegel recognizes the role of the state in the market in imposing taxes and satisfying the "most universal needs," such as the construction of infrastructure and temples. However, he also differs from Fichte decisively in that he attempts to preserve the freedom realized in the system of needs. Fichte argues for the necessity of centralized state control over production and commerce to prevent arbitrariness within the market. In order to protect formal equality and freedom, he could only counter the negative aspects of the market through the absolute negation of the free market itself. Hegel rejects Fichte's solution, because he believes that people would lose their free subjectivity if the state treated them as mere objects of a governing process.

Instead of relying on external state intervention to restrict the market's domination of private and public life, Hegel focuses on internal regulative praxis, claiming that "the inner constitution of the class" can overcome the abstract mutual dependence between persons. This is organized as a guild or craft union through which workers in an isolated and atomized state of existence attempt as a collective subject to regulate the force of capital. It aims to replace "the relation of physical dependence" based on the abstract logic of commodity production and exchange with "a living dependence and a relation of an individual to an individual, a different and an inwardly active connection, which is not one of physical dependence."[36]

In order to comprehend this "living dependence" of the "inner constitution" within civil society, one should refer to Hegel's analysis of "family." After pointing out the limit of formal equality among persons, Hegel regards natural ties within the family as "reason existing as nature" and finds in it an element that overcomes the "relation of master and servant." According to Hegel, marriage is "a negative contract which annuls just that presupposition on which the possibility of contract in general rests, namely, personality or being a subject." As a result, "there is no antithesis of person to person or of subject to object" and the "master and servant relation" becomes "only something qua external." The modern paradigm of the formal legal subject disappears through marriage, and "so too all contracts regarding property or service and the like fall away here because these things are grounded in the presupposition of private personality." The abstract mutual recognition as based on persons does not occur at all when commodity exchange is not necessary. Surplus products do not become commodities within the family, but are directly distributed to members whose full needs are already known, with the result that it is necessary only to distribute the required labor force to each sphere. This means that family members carry out labor communally, not privately, even if the father directs the entire labor process. Therefore, the product of labor is not an individual property, but "the surplus, labor and property are absolutely common to all." Hegel concludes that the distribution of the surplus within the family is "not an exchange, because the whole property is directly, inherently, and explicitly common."[37] Without exchange, the intersubjective relation within the family does not develop into an antithesis between persons, but retains an organic unity that carries out labor and consumption as absolutely one; the family proves to be the highest form of "reason" in nature. However, this rational unity of the family remains a natural one in which the negation of formal equality only occurs unconsciously. It confronts the same limitations as the parent-child relation encountered earlier. The natural relation based on love and emotion cannot be the basis of legal rights and property in society as it necessarily excludes nonmembers of the family.

In contrast to the natural and unconscious aspects of unity within the family, "the inner constitution of the class" reorganizes the living dependence as a social institution and aims to regulate formal recognition in the market. Within the inner constitution, the exclusivity of love no longer exists because it is institutionalized as the conscious praxis of the people. Counteracting the atomized state of the workers responsible for their one-sided dependence on capitalists, they unite in a guild or craft union, improving conditions of labor and establishing an educational system. The unification of the workers enables them to appropriate the means of production collectively; the inner constitution substitutes private labor with a more communal form, allowing workers to surmount their subordination to the alien process of production and attain more autonomy in their labor activity. The relation between workers is transformed from an abstract relation mediated by money and commodities into a conscious unity of living dependence mediated by "their will and their own activity." The constitution supplements the relation founded on the abstract quality of value with an ethical relation of "trust" and "respect."[38] As working conditions improve and as workers subjectively participate in the labor process, they can affirm their own activities as ethical ones contributing to the maintenance of the whole.

Even though a single individual alone cannot resist the alien force of the system of needs, the collective will of workers compels the wealthy individual "to modify his relation of mastery, and even [others'] distrust for it, by permitting a more general participation in it. The external inequality is diminished externally, just as the infinite does not give itself up to determinacy but exists as living activity, and thus the urge to amass wealth indefinitely is itself eradicated."[39] Here Hegel sees the prospect for modifying the distorted desire for wealth accumulation by adjusting the relations of production, as the production based on the corporation becomes institutionalized and gradually reorganizes the private character of labor. Accordingly, the chaotic character of commodity exchange would be much milder and the market would acquire stability.

The successful negation of contradictions within the market, such as improvement of working conditions and the limitation of the infinite desire for wealth, are not guaranteed in advance. Workers must strive to convince the rest of society of the legitimacy of their demands. Here emerges a struggle for recognition considerably different from the formal recognition of persons in the market. This struggle aims to supplement the equality of persons in the market, whose abstractness is unable to reflect the fundamental interests of many individuals. Through this process, the depoliticized economic life of the bourgeoisie becomes politicized as workers confront the rich. Yet this antagonistic relationship in the system of needs is no longer the Hobbesian state of nature feared by Fichte. Here the struggle is always already conditioned by law and social norms, although it consists in the conscious activity of changing the existing constellation of power and normativity. While the negation of freedom in Fichte's state resulted from a coercive attempt on the part of the state to achieve directly an abstract universal, Hegel construes the tension in the economic relations differently, arguing that the continuous process of mediation rooted in the subjective practice of consciously changing and supplementing existing social norms itself sustains the organic unity of the system of needs.

This new insight as advanced in Hegel's "critique of Fichte's natural right" should not be underestimated. Recognizing the regulative role of workers' collective action, Hegel was later able to include civil society, in addition to the family and the state, as an essential component of ethical life. In the *Philosophy of Right* he maintains that the experience of overcoming the negativity of market relations, rooted in the conscious praxis of individuals positing law and rights in the political domain, contributes to the cultivation of a people. In the face of the ever-growing wealth disparity under today's capitalism, it remains an open question whether Hegel's solution could actually tame the alien force of the market or whether Fichte's stern measures must be deployed after all.[40]

Notes

1. Cf. Meist 2002, xxxv–xxxviii.
2. Müller 1801, 439.
3. Fichte 1971, xxxviii. Cf. Fichte 2008, 171.
4. Fichte 1964, 267.
5. Fichte 2000, 53.
6. Ibid., 136.
7. Fichte 2012, 130, emphasis in original.
8. Fichte 2001, 321.
9. Fichte 2012, 145.
10. Fichte 2000, 185.

11. David James misunderstands the core of Fichte's critique in the *Closed Commercial State* as "the possibility of one-sided forms of economic dependence" and "an indirect form of coercion" (James 2010, 63, 66). As a result, he also misleadingly emphasizes the theoretical gap between the *Foundations of Natural Right* and the *Closed Commercial State*. After all, his interpretation of Fichte's critique of capitalism is based on the standpoint of Fichte's 1796 "Review."

12. Fichte 2012, 145, emphasis added.

13. Ibid., 85.

14. One notable exception is Karl Rosenkranz's lecture titled "Japan und die Japaner" (1875), in which he affirmatively identifies the Japanese political and economic system with the idea of Fichte's closed commercial state.

15. Fichte 2012, 86–87.

16. Cf. Siep 1979, 40.

17. Hegel 1979, 111.

18. Ibid.
19. Ibid., 107.
20. Ibid., 120.
21. Ibid., 118.
22. Ibid., 120.
23. Ibid., 117.
24. Ibid., 121.
25. Ibid., emphasis added.
26. Ibid., 124.
27. In a previous section Hegel writes: "It is laughable to regard everything under the form of this abstraction as legal right; right is something entirely formal, (α) infinite in its variety, and without totality, and (β) without any content in itself." (Hegel 1979, 118).
28. Ibid., 125.
29. Ibid., 126.
30. Ibid., 124–125.
31. Cf. Hegel 1975, 105.
32. Ibid.
33. Hegel 1979, 170.
34. Ibid.
35. Ibid., 171.
36. Ibid.
37. Ibid., 127–128.
38. Ibid., 171.
39. Ibid.
40. This does not at all mean that Hegel has overcome for good all the contradictions of the civil society. As Frank Ruda convincingly shows, its negative tendency and destructive force haunts Hegel's system in the problem of the "rabble." Cf. Ruda 2011, 32–34.

Works Cited

Fichte, I. H. 1971. "Vorrede des Herausgebers" to *Fichtes sämmtliche Werke*, unveränderter Nachdruck, Bd. III, v–xliii. Berlin: Walter de Gruyter.
Fichte, J. G. 1964. "Beitrag zur Berichtigung der Urtheile des Publikums über die französische Revolution." In *J.G. Fichte-Gesamtausgabe*, Reihe I. Bd. 1, edited by R. Lauth and H. J. Jacob, 201–404. Stuttgart: Frommann-Holzboog.
———. 2000. *Foundations of Natural Right*. Edited by F. Neuhouser, translated by M. Baur. Cambridge: Cambridge University Press.
———. 2001. "Review of Immanuel Kant, *Perpetual Peace: A Philosophical Sketch* (Königsburg: Nicolovius), 1795." Translated by D. Breazeale. *The Philosophical Forum* 32: 311–321.
———. 2008. *Addresses to the German Nation*. Translated by G. Moore. Cambridge: Cambridge University Press.

———. 2012. *Closed Commercial State.* Translated by A. C. Adler. Albany: State University of New York Press.

Hegel, G.W.F. 1975. *Natural Law.* Translated by T. M. Knox. Philadelphia: University of Pennsylvania Press.

———. 1979. "System of Ethical Life." In *System of Ethical Life and First Philosophy of Spirit,* edited and translated by H. S. Harris and T. M. Knox, 99–177. Albany: State University of New York Press.

James, D. 2010. "Fichte's Reappraisal of Kant's Theory of Cosmopolitan Right." *History of European Ideas* 36: 61–70.

Meist, K. R. 2002. Einleitung *System der Sittlichkeit [Critik des Fichteschen Naturrechts],* by G.W.F. Hegel. Hamburg: Felix Meiner, ix–xxxix.

Müller, A. 1801. "Ueber einen philosophischen Entwurf von Hrn Fichte, betitelt: 'der geschlossene Handelsstaat.'" *Neue Berlinische Monatsschrift* 6: 436–458.

Rosenkranz, K. 1875. "Japan und die Japaner." *Neue Studien von Karl Rosenkranz. Erster Band. Studien zur Culturgeschichte.* Leipzig: Erich Koschny, 326–359.

Ruda, F. 2011. *Hegel's Rabble: An Investigation into Hegel's Philosophy of Right.* New York: Continuum.

Siep, L. 1979. *Anerkennung als Prinzip der praktischen Philosophie.* Munich: Karl Alber.

3

Anonymity, Responsibility, and the Many Faces of Capitalism

Hegel and the Crisis of the Modern Self

ARDIS B. COLLINS

In 1985–1986, Václav Havel created a memoir in the form of a long-distance conversation with a Czech journalist. At one point in the conversation, the journalist asks, "How would you describe your present ideas regarding a more meaningful way of organizing the world." In response to this and several follow-up questions, Havel speaks of "the current crisis that the world finds itself in." He identifies the crisis as a conflict between "an impersonal, anonymous, irresponsible and uncontrollable juggernaut of power" and the "elemental and original interests" of concrete human individuals.[1] According to Havel, this conflict has its roots in something much deeper than the way modern societies organize their economic or political systems; and no fine-tuning of these structures will address the real problems. Whether the impersonal, anonymous, irresponsible power operates as the clash of large, privately owned economic power structures or as a central governmental authority, it still transforms real human beings into cogs in a mechanism "for which no one is responsible and no one understands."[2] Participants in the system get their rewards and punishments by adapting more or less well to the impersonal dynamics of the system. In the process, they lose all contact with what their work means, all sense of responsibility for its character and consequences, all power to determine or challenge the direction it takes.

The crisis begins, Havel says, with the development of science, technology, and human knowledge accompanied by an "arrogant anthropomorphism" convinced that human intelligence can know everything and human ingenuity can control everything. Modern man has lost all sense of responsibility to something higher than himself. Havel calls this something higher by many names—metaphysical certainties, the experience of the transcendental, a super-personal moral authority, some kind of higher horizon, the order of nature or the universe, the absolute. He is apparently open to any way of speaking that can name our experience of being responsible to something that transcends the mundane concerns of modern man. According to Havel, when we lose this sense of responsibility, we lose the very self that makes us human; and only a change in human consciousness, a deeper sense of who we are, can save us from this mega-suicide. A new state of mind must emerge in which human beings show themselves capable of taking responsibility for something eternal, something that does not immediately concern their private interests, capable of relinquishing private concerns for the sake of the community. Without this transformation, no reorganization of economics or politics can produce an environment in which work becomes meaningful, workers act as responsible persons, and the workplace becomes a place of personal relationships.[3]

Wilfred Cantwell Smith, writing in the 1970s and 1980s, also talks about a modern crisis in which human society has lost its relation to the transcendent. He, too, expands the notion of transcendence to include ways of thinking and living that do not express themselves in terms of a God concept. He notes especially the tradition of ancient Greek metaphysics, which conceived reason not as a human construct but as a transcendent order.[4] Like Havel, Cantwell Smith claims that the dominance of the impersonal emerges in the development of the empirical sciences. According to Smith, the method of detached objectivity, which is characteristic of these sciences, distorts the true reality of a human being, because it dismisses the subjectivity in which a human being experiences and owns his or her reality. To know the truth of human affairs, we must know not only the objective facts but also how a human being feels in the objective situation, what it means to him or her, how he appropriates it, how she forms her life in terms of it.[5]

Cantwell Smith has developed a verification principle that makes it possible for knowledge projects to include the subjectivity dimension of human reality in their study of human affairs. Those whose subjectivity has committed itself to a tradition, those who live it as their own, must be able to recognize themselves in the way the work of detached critical observers represents them.[6] Hegel's experience principle functions in a similar way.

According to this principle, every knower has the right to acknowledge as true only what his or her experience attests to as true. Hegel insists, however, that personal conviction cannot by itself justify a truth claim. Truth must be public. It must command assent from every knower. If, therefore, an individual's own experience does not acknowledge the truth of a proposed point of view, the individual in this experiential position has a right to demand that the truth of this proposal be demonstrated in a way that exposes its presence at the heart of this individual's own self-consciousness.[7]

The project developed in this essay uses Hegel's *Phenomenology of Spirit* as a resource for creating an encounter between the personal, responsible dimension of human life and the alienating dynamics of capitalist and socialist economic systems. The *Phenomenology* is especially appropriate for a study of this personal element, because the phenomenological project begins within the consciousness of a singular self, and examines the necessities that emerge in the way this consciousness tests itself in the reality of human experience.[8] The *Phenomenology* shows us how those committed to certain truth expectations experience themselves, their world, and other self-conscious individuals. Moreover, Hegel explicitly defines the task of the *Phenomenology* in terms of the experience principle. As Hegel represents it in the Preface, the *Phenomenology* honors the right of an individual self situated within the truth expectations of experience to have the truth conceived by philosophy revealed as the true essence of this self's experience. Finally, the demonstration developed in the *Phenomenology* follows a disciplined proof procedure whose necessity can command the assent of every knower.[9]

We begin, therefore, with a brief analysis of this procedure, based on the way Hegel himself interprets it in the introductions to his major works. With this analysis in place, we examine the way this procedure operates in those forms of knowing that situate human affairs in the context of a truth that transcends the mundane concerns of human life. The examination focuses on those forms that are most effective for putting capitalism and socialism in their place.

Hegel's Dialectical Proof Procedure

Hegel's dialectical procedure begins with a concept or experience structure that identifies a subject matter to be investigated. In the *Phenomenology*, this beginning is a certain way of defining what a form of consciousness takes the truth to be. The proof proceeds by exposing in the beginning definition of the subject matter a necessary connection to its opposite.

The proof concludes from this that the subject matter must be reconceived as the unity of these opposites. In order to preserve the necessity
in this procedure, the new concept or truth criterion preserves the necessary connection as an opposition relation, and conceives the unity only
as a dynamic between the opposites. The unifying principle identifies the
opposites as differences within the same dynamic truth, and it determines
these differences as necessarily different from each other.

Although Hegel calls this new concept a self-contradiction, he does
not represent it as asserting and denying exactly the same claim.[10] And
he explicitly and repeatedly distinguishes it from the kind of dialectic that
disproves and dismisses a position by manipulating it into an assertion that
speaks against itself.[11] In Hegelian dialectic, self-contradiction expands the
beginning definition to include its necessary connection to its opposite.
Contradiction negates the way the initial definition cuts off the subject
matter from its connections and context, but preserves the content of the
beginning concept within a larger, more inclusive concept.

Hegel describes dialectical proof procedure as a retreat into a ground.
The demonstration begins with something accessible and accepted as true.
It proceeds to show that this truth depends on a ground from which it has
been derived and by which it has been determined. In the order of knowing, therefore, knowledge of the ground depends on, is mediated by, the
proof provided by the derivative truth. The demonstration proves, however,
that in the order of being the derivative truth depends on the ground.
Hegel concludes from this that a dialectical proof requires a shift into a
knowing that asserts the ground in its immediacy, since the proof demonstrates that the ground is the origin not the result of the evidence that has
retreated into it. The dialectical development of the ground preserves the
dynamics involved in the evidence leading up to it, but transforms these
into manifestations of the ground.[12] In the introductory essays of the *Science
of Logic,* Hegel explicitly and repeatedly says that this procedure operates
not only in the philosophical system but also in the *Phenomenology.*[13]

In the transition from self-consciousness to reason, the *Phenomenology*
retreats into reason as the ground of the dialectical moves developed in
object-dominated consciousness and subject-dominated self-consciousness.
Reason expects the truth to be a unifying ground that diversifies itself
and reunites with itself in the dynamics between the independence of the
objective world and the independence of self-consciousness.[14]

Reason as Impersonal Objectivity

Reason-as-observation looks for the rational in the given reality of the
world confronting it. The examination of reason in this form, however,

demonstrates that observed particulars do not manifest the necessary connectedness and relational integrity that reason expects the rational to be. Their association manifests nothing more than a contingently given pattern. In the life sciences, rational observation finds relational integrity in the generic form of the organism. But this form manifests itself in various species whose differentiation is not determined by the genus, but by contingently given configurations of particulars; and it is situated within an environment of contingent and destructive forces that do not operate organically, like storms, earthquakes, floods, drought, and fire. Reason shifts its focus, therefore, to look for rationality in self-consciousness and the natural world's relation to it.[15]

As the observation of self-consciousness, reason fares no better. The relations between self and world involve a given set of particulars that identify this self's individual character and the various ways in which this character expresses itself—body language, behavior, speech, work, handwriting, even the inert shape of the skull. All these external manifestations are contingently related to the self-consciousness they signify, and hence none of them presents to observation self-consciousness itself. Either self-consciousness becomes absorbed into the world's conditions and succumbs to the world's unintegrated divisions, or it remains hidden behind the signs in which it expresses itself, or it is reduced to the externality of a physical thing.[16]

Hegel explicitly identifies these contingency elements as the irrational (*Unvernunft*): as nature released from the control of the concept, its independent otherness made manifest; as self-consciousness reduced to a thing, its very rationality presented as its opposite. Hegel concludes from this that the domain of independent objectivity, including self-consciousness itself presented as an object, negates its own claim to truth and refers itself to the subjectivity of the rational self as the unifying principle in relation to which it becomes rational.[17]

This analysis and critique applies not only to the observational sciences that focus on the psychology of self-conscious individuals but also to those, like economics, that focus on social relations among individuals. Economics, like other observational sciences, reduces the human self to the contingent ways in which the self manifests itself to a detached, objective observer. Economics completely preoccupied with itself, therefore, loses its orientation to the subjectivity of the human self, detaches itself from the unifying purpose that gives its contingent associations a rational order, and thus becomes irrational. I call this state of affairs economic narcissism, and I suggest that the modern crisis described by Havel and Cantwell Smith qualifies as this kind of pathology.

The first form of practical reason exposes another aspect of this pathology. This form of reason preserves the independence of the objective

domain, and simply expands it to include the way the objective domain
refers itself to the self by giving pleasure. By becoming identified with
the enjoyment of the world, the individual finds his or her self defined
in terms of this world, absorbed into it, subject to whatever fate the ways
of the world impose upon him or her.[18]

The rhetoric of neoclassical economic theory shows how the dominant theory of contemporary capitalism manifests this loss of self in the
impersonal objectivity of economic narcissism. This theory defines the
human self as a singular self completely absorbed by the pursuit of its
own preferences, in no way determined by the concerns of others or by
any "value" or norm that identifies what one ought to prefer. Rationality is
conceived as a kind of shrewdness for discerning the most effective strategy for looking after the self's own interests. Proponents of neoclassical
theory claim that free market economics best serves this vision of the self,
because it offers a wide variety of resources for satisfying each individual's
particular desires, allows each individual to freely choose those products
that best serve his or her preferences, and rewards most those who contribute most to this distribution of pleasures throughout the system. This
reasoning supposedly demonstrates that free market economics effectively
serves society at large, without any micromanagement by ethical norms.
The reasoning assumes, however, that the good of society at large can be
adequately defined by the dynamics of desire and preference satisfaction,
and that the independent contingencies of the free market adequately
identify and serve the true self of the individual. It also ignores the fact
that the individual's desires and preferences are significantly determined
by participation in the market, and hence the market serves the self by
making the self adapt to the market.[19]

The examination of reason-as-observation, however, has demonstrated
the necessity of conceiving the rational with the self's subjectivity in the
dominant role. Hence, the self of desire and pleasure, absorbed into a
relation of dependence on the independent ways of the world, does not
identify the true self of a rational individual.

Self-Confident Individuality

The second and third versions of practical reason develop the context for
examining the complex structures at the heart of the capitalism-socialism
debate. As the law of the heart, the rational self asserts itself as a law that
overrules the independent dynamics of the objective world, and imposes
its own felt law as this world's true spirit. The self finds itself challenged,
however, by other individuals imposing their own law of the heart on the

same world. Hegel calls this result the law of individuality. The world dissolves in an opposition dynamic between different individual spirits. This demonstrates the necessity of conceiving the self as a rationality detached not only from the self's desires and pleasures but also from the exclusivity of the self's individuality. The self asserts itself as a virtuous self called to act against the divisiveness of individuality and to expose the true at-oneness that lies hidden in it.[20]

Virtue, however, cannot become actual without acting on the powers, capacities, and talents that belong to the virtuous self's individual character. Without these concrete interests, virtue has no content other than its negative stance toward the divisiveness of individuality. Thus, virtue shows itself necessarily connected to its opposite. It cannot become actual without becoming identified with the diversity played out in the law of individuality, which is the way of the world.[21] This result demonstrates the necessity of shifting to a new form of practical reason, which I call *self-confident individuality*. This form of practical reason expects to find the universality of the rational embedded in the individuality dynamic of the actual world, and it expects to find this world explicitly oriented toward the self's own individuality and determinate character.[22]

For example, a talented musician finds herself involved in a world full of music—concerts, recordings, orchestras, and music schools. In order to make this world show itself as her world, her element, she becomes actively involved in it—as a music student, performer, composer, or teacher. The individual's active involvement, however, exposes the limitations of the self's determinate nature. The world in which the musical individual becomes active also exists as a world of literature, painting, sculpture, and architecture. The world of the arts is also a world of trade, industry, finance, communication, farming, medical care, and sports. The music produced by the violinist or composer becomes a tax write off for a wealthy entrepreneur, a form of relaxation or entertainment for a physician, an environment for dining out. The individual's work becomes absorbed into the world's orientation to the concrete interests of others.

In this encounter with the complex world of different determinate natures, the individual's action disintegrates into contingently associated factors. What the individual sets out to do, the means employed for doing it, and the result produced by it do not preserve the integrity of the individual's determinate nature. A conductor of a famous orchestra finds his musical nature entangled in public relations activities that in no way reflect his musicianship. A farmer involved in the work of producing food finds his production entangled in the gamesmanship of the futures market. Health professionals find their talent for healing entangled in the power play of a presidential election. Since, however, this form of practical reason accepts the law of individuality as a necessary condition of the actual world, the individual self shifts to a broader point of view. It claims for itself the whole dynamic of action, including the breakup of its action in a diversity of contingent relations, and the orientation of its work to the special interests of others. The acts of others belong to my action and responsibility because my action operates as a provocation for theirs, or because I rush in to help with their causes, or because I take an interest in or have an opinion about their projects.

Thus, the responsibility factor enters the experience of practical reason as responsibility claimed not only for the immediate results of an individual's action but also for the way the actions and interests of others are connected to and involved in the world's being for this self. This responsibility claim, however, finds itself challenged by the protests of others, who insist that their projects and causes are their own action and responsibility. Yet these others do not hesitate to claim as their own the work of this and other individuals involved in their world.[23]

Before proceeding further, let us look at what the examination of self-confident individuality reveals about the dynamics and tensions of capitalism. First, self-confident individuality exposes the way a rational individual's active engagement in the world inevitably appropriates for itself the actions and purposes of others and thus asserts itself as the dominant factor that defines the whole relation. Since other individuals act in the same way, the agents become involved in a dynamic that shifts back and forth between the dominance of one and the dominance of other active individuals. Second, self-confident individuality introduces group interests into the dynamics of practical reason. The world presents itself as a world appropriate to the specific interests of the individual's determinate character, for example, a music world, an agricultural world, a business world. Hence, the self claims the world as its own not only as a singular self but also as one who shares a set of interests with others who are active in this world.

Capitalist economics involves three primary interest groups: private owners of production resources; workers whose skills actively transform these resources into useful products and services; financiers and investors who provide investment capital for production. The dynamics of self-confident individuality shows how individuals whose determinate character finds itself matched by the interests and concerns of one group are necessarily connected to the shared determinate nature of the other groups. The same dynamic exposes the way each group asserts its shared determinate nature as the primary truth of the relational system, and reduces the determinate nature of the other groups to a factor in service to their own. The truth implicit in this dialectical development calls for a consciousness in which the very subjectivity of the singular self, and its identification with the group interests of its own determinate nature, must know itself as a self identified with and responsible to others. And yet this sense of self must hold on to its status as a self whose individuality and particular determinate nature embodies and actualizes the rational. As such, the self must be able to experience itself as one in whom the world becomes rational and meaningful. Applied to capitalism, this means that workers as well as corporate executives and investors have the same right to experience their personal individuality as a self in which the world fulfills its true purpose.

Rational Individuality Universalized

Reason as lawgiver conceives the truth implicit in self-confident individuality. It takes the truth to be a system of determinate laws that emerge from the actions of different individuals engaged in a relational dynamic with each other. By acting according to a law, the individual identifies his or her self with a principle that grounds the claims of other individuals as well, and thus acknowledges that this individual's self belongs to the relational whole and is responsible to its other members. Hegel offers two examples of such laws: tell the truth and love your neighbor. Since we are examining issues related to capitalism, we add here the law according to which individual freedom identifies the fundamental value of human life. The content of these laws, however, does not preserve the sameness required for responsible action. The individual tells the truth as he or she interprets it, which may or may not correspond to what others take it to be. The active love of one's neighbor may be defeated or distorted by the overwhelming power of the social world, so that its content in the agent's purpose may not be matched by the way this purpose becomes actual in the world.[24] So also, the way each person individually determines his or her free action may or may not be realizable in a world full of other persons with their own very different free choices.

Reason, therefore, distinguishes the unity of the rational form from the diversity displayed in the content of determinate laws. A law qualifies as a rational law only if it remains self-same in the individual self and in the world of other rational individuals. Hegel examines reason in this form by applying the noncontradiction norm to laws governing ownership relations.[25] He formulates three different versions of ownership laws: nonownership, private property, and communal ownership. The testing of all three laws shows that all three satisfy the norm in their formulations, because each posits itself by itself as the same law for all. If, however, we consider each one as a law activated in the agency of self-conscious individuals, all three become self-contradictory, because the law must operate within the opposition dynamic between the singular subjectivity of the self and the universality of the world.[26]

The law of nonownership separates the world of things from the subjectivity of the self, and makes the self dependent on the independent
operations of the world. The individual gets what he or she needs only if
the dynamics of the world at large happen to provide it. The individual's
needs, however, belong to the continuous life of a conscious self, and the
subjectivity of rational thought is embodied in this life. Hence, nonownership contradicts the status of the singular self as a rational subjectivity that
gives the world its true purpose.

Private property treats a thing existing in the world at large as something belonging exclusively to one individual or one group of investors.
Its exclusivity contradicts its reality as a thing situated within the dynamics
of the natural world and the world's dynamic relations to other persons.
The way owners appropriate and use the resources of the world affects
the natural environment on which other persons depend and restricts
or controls the availability of resources for the projects of these others.
Moreover, the individual's appropriation of these resources depends on the
willingness of others to acknowledge and respect the individual's ownership, which transforms exclusive ownership into the action and responsibility of everyone.[27] In capitalist production, the exclusivity of the property
owner contradicts the universality of production itself, which operates in
a natural world that belongs to everyone's life, actively produces goods
and services through the organized actions of a workforce, and depends
on the consumer's willingness to buy.

We see this ambiguity reflected in the different versions of capitalism
actualized in the contemporary world. In the early days of capitalism, the
unregulated activity of private owners provoked violent, destabilizing reac-
tions from labor. Out of this anarchy emerged various forms of managed
capitalism in which government regulation imposes restrictions required
for stabilizing the market.[28] Thus, the universalizing interests of the government were added to the dynamic played out between the particular
interests of private property, labor, and finance. Three versions of contemporary capitalism exemplify significantly different ways in which these
various interests play off each other.

In Swedish capitalism, employers, labor, and government have emerged
as strong, organized, well-coordinated factors in the nation's economy. In
the United States, capitalism reflects the individualism of U.S. culture,
which tends toward a reduced role for the government, and allows the
stronger particular interests, those of employers and large stock market
investors, to dominate the economy. In Japan, capitalism has developed
as a dynamic between strong government and strong companies, with the
welfare of labor integrated into the company's interests, and the interests
of the company protected from the pressures of stock market investors.

All these forms of capitalism manifest the way the universal interests of society, represented by the government, and the competing interests of individuals and groups pull against each other in the dynamics of private property.[29]

Communal ownership fares no better. The law of common ownership requires a law determining how the resources of the world should be distributed; and this gets the universality of communal ownership involved in the opposition dynamic played out between exclusive individualities and the competing priorities of different interest groups.[30] David Schweickart's theory of market-based socialism provides a good example of how this dynamic might affect a socialist system more attuned to the individuality and diversity dimension of human affairs than the central planning systems of Havel's time.

According to Schweickart's theory, the resources for production belong to society. The communal ownership of productive resources takes the form of a capital assets tax, which operates as a leasing fee charged to enterprises for the use of social capital, with all revenues reinvested in the economy. Investment funds are distributed to individual industries through local public banks. The distribution to regions and communities is based on per capita fair share, not on the investment funds collected by each region. The distribution to individual banks is not determined by fair share, but by the bank's performance in serving the general goals of investment, namely profitability and employment. Enterprises in this system operate as worker-controlled economic democracies, with the creativity of entrepreneurs integrated into the work system. Industries compete in a free market economy. Their income must cover costs, including a depreciation fund and the capital assets tax. Workers get all that remains after these costs have been covered. Workers in this system, therefore, have the status of a residual claimant. Their income is not represented as a wage, nor as a factor in the cost of production. Hence, their work is not represented as a commodity surrendered in an exchange.[31]

Although Hegel examines a rather simple version of communal ownership, his critique of it identifies certain tensions that show up even in Schweickart's more complex version. Hegel points out that "to each an equal share" does not acknowledge the diversity of determinate natures in which rational subjectivity is embodied. An individual finds his or her self represented as an abstract sameness indistinguishable from others.[32] On the other hand, economic democracy, like other democracies, tends to favor the majority, which fails to preserve the equal rights of individuals to have their rationality reflected in their world. And the dynamics of a free market system, whether capitalist or socialist, preserves the dominance of the objective system. Individuals and groups must adapt to the dynamics of the market, which fails to actualize the rational self as the true essence of the objective world.

What exactly does all this prove? It exposes a self-contradiction in practical reason. Rational principles actualized as the self-actualization of a singular self inevitably become entangled in an opposition dynamic with the universalizing dynamics of the natural and social world. No economic system can avoid the tensions and conflicts involved in this dynamic, since these tensions belong to the necessary conditions of rational action. The negation exposed in this dynamic calls for a revised concept of the rational. The singular subjectivity of the rational agent and the universal objectivity of the social world must be reconceived as the same social spirit, the same social self-consciousness, identified with the singular self-consciousness of individuals and the objectively articulated self-consciousness of the social whole. Hegel explicitly calls this result a retreat into a ground.[33]

The Spiritual Transformation of the Human Self

Since we are looking at issues related to capitalism, we look first at Hegel's account of the social spirit that takes as its fundamental value the absolute freedom of the individual. This spirit reproduces the individuality dynamic as a social dynamic in which the individual asserts his or her exclusive individual will as the will of society itself, only to be challenged by other individuals acting in the same world and claiming the same unrestricted, universal status. This shows that the individual will of the citizen, whether governing or governed, is not the true spirit of the social world. Its true spirit is a unifying moral spirit that governs the necessary connections played out in the individuality dynamic.[34]

The examination of the moral spirit, however, shows that moral action identifies the universality of duty with the exclusivity of the individual agent and the contingency of natural determinations. In the God postulate, the moral view distinguishes the true selfsameness of the moral spirit from the compromises of moral action. The God postulate conceives the uncompromised selfsameness of a holy will identified with the independent conditions of objective existence. The spirit of conscientiousness conceives this divine spirit identified with the individuality of the moral agent and its self-actualization in objective existence.[35]

In the spirit of conscientiousness, we see the dynamics of practical reason transformed into the interpersonal dynamics of speech. Conscientious individuals speak to each other about their shared commitment to conscientiousness. Each individual seeks from others explicit acknowledgment of her or his conscientiousness, and protests when this acknowledgment is refused.[36] Thus, responsibility to others becomes actual in real I-you relations to other persons.[37] In these relations, however, the spirit of conscientiousness shows itself trapped in the unification-diversification dynamic of an integrated whole. Beautiful soul conscientiousness clings to the tranquil at-oneness of its communality and preserves it by refusing to tolerate or acknowledge the conscientiousness of moral action. Since action reproduces the self-concerned dynamics of individuality, the beautiful soul dismisses the agent's claims to conscientiousness as hypocrisy. Conscientious agents, however, defend their involvement in self-satisfying causes by insisting that these projects are motivated by the agent's concern for what is right and good. They accuse the beautiful soul of hypocrisy, because its conscientiousness does nothing but talk, and its talk divides the community by excluding from the communal spirit those engaged in actualizing the moral spirit in the reality of the objective world.

Thus, the spirit of conscientiousness dissolves in a unification-diversification dynamic played out between the unification of the moral fellowship in the conscientiousness of the beautiful soul and its diversification in the individuality of conscientious agents, the particularity of their projects, and the independent contingencies of the natural element. This calls for and justifies a new concept that defines the moral spirit as the unity of these opposites. In the dynamics of conscientiousness, this unity appears as confession, forgiveness, and surrender. Conscientious agents acknowledge the hypocrisy and divisiveness of their agency, and thus acknowledge the legitimacy of the beautiful soul's negative judgments, which calls them back to the unity of the moral fellowship. The beautiful soul surrenders its self-righteousness by acknowledging the necessity of actualizing the moral spirit in the diversity and tensions of real action, and by forgiving the hypocrisy and divisiveness of conscientious action for the sake of the conscientiousness embodied in it.[38]

In the transition from the spirit of conscientiousness to the concept of religion, the spirit of conscientiousness retreats into the selfsameness of a ground. Religion knows the diversified world of secular social relations as a world unified by its being for religious self-consciousness.[39] Hegel says explicitly that revealed religion represents the unifying spirit of the divinity in a form that meets the requirements of the negation exposed in the dynamics of conscientiousness.[40] The doctrine of the Trinity represents the divine spirit as divine being expressing itself in a word that communicates its very self and thus surrenders its self into an other in which it knows itself.[41] The doctrine of the Incarnation represents the divine spirit as the divine word surrendered into a world that is this spirit's absolute opposite, a world divided against itself in the opposition between self and nature, and between self and self.[42] The death of God and the indwelling Holy

Spirit represents the death of God's transcendence and the complete surrender of the divine spirit into the dynamics of human conscientiousness.[43]
The actualization of the divine spirit in the human world becomes our act
and our responsibility, conscientiousness is transformed into the spirit of
complete, unconditional self-sharing, and the divine spirit becomes identified with the tensions and divisions of the human world, including the
irrational contingencies of the natural element.[44]

Economic Relations Reconceived

Hegel's *Phenomenology* completes its dialectical examination of human
experience by showing us the transcendent ground that lives at the heart
of the human self, a self-sharing spirit that becomes actual in the conflicting dynamics of self and nature, self and self, and remains faithful
to the other throughout. This spirit is completely personal, conceived as
a word that gives the self away to others and lives in them. Whether we
live this spirit as the call to participate in the life of a transcendent God
or as a commitment to the highest aspirations of the human spirit, it
calls us to a purpose that the mentality of economic narcissism, whether
capitalist or socialist, cannot fathom. Suppose, however, that we situate
economics within the domain of this spirit, and acknowledge participants
in economic relations as persons called to its higher purpose. How does
this transform these relations? I offer three suggestions as an answer to
this question. First, the objective science of economics would identify the
regular patterns that appear in the contingencies of the natural element,
but would acknowledge that norms derived from humankind's higher purposes must determine how this information is used.[45] Second, participants
in economic relations would acknowledge Cantwell Smith's verification
principle. By this I mean that each individual self or interest group would
have the right to find its self recognizable in the way each is represented in
the words and actions of the other participants. Finally, different interests
identified as essential by the proof procedure of the phenomenological
project would learn to forgive the way each becomes absorbed by and
subordinated to the others, since this inevitable dominance shift belongs
to the necessary conditions of real action. They would also acknowledge
by words, laws, and economic action that this dominance shift cannot be
right and rational unless it is mutual. The universalizing function of government, the diversifying function of special interests, the individualizing
function of the singular free self must all be acknowledged as essential to
the system and to each other, and as responsible to the self-sharing spirit
of humanity's true self.

Notes

1. Havel 1990, 10.
2. Ibid., 13.
3. Ibid., 10–18.
4. Cantwell Smith 1997, chapter 3, especially 36–49.
5. Ibid., chapter 8.
6. Ibid., 123–125.
7. Hegel, *Enz* 7+A, 8, 12+A, 38A, 64A, 67–68+A; *PhG* 429–430/M para. 802. For a fuller discussion of the experience principle, see Collins 2013, chapter 4 §1, 5 §1–3, 18 §3–7.
8. Hegel, *PhG*, Introduction.
9. Hegel, *PhG* 22–24/M para. 26–27; 29–30/M para. 36; 429–430/M para. 802.
10. Hegel, *WL* 21:37–38/M 53–54.
11. Hegel, *Enz* §81A+Z1, *PhR* §31+A, *WL* 21:40/M 56.
12. Hegel, *PhR* §2+A, 31+A; *Enz* §17, 36A+Z, 50A, 65–67, 81A, 82A; *WL* 21:8/M 28, 21:27/M 43, 21:29–31/M 46–47, 21:32–34/M 48–49, 21:39–41/M 55–56, 21:54–56/M 68–69, 21:57–59/M 71–72; *PhG* 56–60/M para.79, 80, 82, 84–87. For an in-depth study of Hegel's proof procedure, based on the introductory essays of Hegel's major works, see Collins 2013, chapter 3 §3, 76–77, 104–105, chapter 7 §4–6, chapter 9 §3, §6.
13. Hegel, *WL* 21:8/M 28; 21:32–34/M 48–49; 21:54–56/M 68–69; 21:47–49/ M71–72.
14. Hegel, *PhG* 132–135/M para. 231–235. For a discussion of the thing-in-itself issue, see *PhG* 135–137/M para. 236–238. For a careful interpretation of the way Hegel analyzes Idealism here, and the way he justifies the transition from Idealism to "actual reason," see Collins 2013, chapter 13 §7.
15. *PhG* 139–142/M para. 246–248, 144–146/M para. 253–255, 154/M para. 275, 163–166/M para. 291–297, 189–190/M para. 341.
16. Hegel, *PhG* 171–180/M para. 310–322; 183–188/M para. 331–338.
17. *PhG* 185–186/M para. 335, 187–188/M para. 339. See also *WL* 12:39\M 607–608. For fuller discussions of the irrationality element, see Dudley 2003–2004, Collins 2000, Collins 2013, Part Seven, introduction, chapter 14 §1–3, chapter 16 §4, chapter 18 §1–2.
18. *PhG* 199–201/M para. 362–365.
19. DeMartino 2000, 4–7, 38–43, 49–52, 54–56, 77–79, 83–85. Finn 2006, chapter 2. See also Friedman 1962, Buchanan 1975, Hayek 1948.
20. Hegel, *PhG* 201–208/M para. 367–381.
21. *PhG* 208–214/M para. 381–389.
22. *PhG* 198/M para. 359; 212–213/M para. 389; 215–217/M para. 396, 398–399.
23. *PhG* 216–227/M para. 399–418.
24. *PhG* 227–230/M para. 418–425.
25. *PhG* 231–233/M para. 426–429.
26. *PhG* 231–234/M para. 429–431.

27. *PhG* 232–234/M para. 430–431.

28. Fulcher 2004, 38–41, 46–47.

29. Ibid., 58–80.

30. Hegel, *PhG* 233–234/M para. 230.

31. Schweickart 2011, 48–58.

32. Hegel, *PhG* 233–234/M para. 230.

33. *PhG* 193–195/M para. 347–350, 234–236/M para. 436, 238–239/M para. 438–439.

34. *PhG* 314–324/M para. 582–595.

35. *PhG* 325–342/M para. 599–634.

36. *PhG* 350–353/M para. 652–654.

37. *PhG* 349–350/M para. 647.

38. *PhG* 350–62/ M para. 651–671.

39. *PhG* 364–367/M para. 677–680.

40. *PhG* 361–362/M para. 671; 419–420/M para. 786.

41. *PhG* 409–411/M para. 769–772.

42. *PhG* 404–407/M para. 758–761, 414–415/M para. 779–780.

43. *PhG* 414–419/M para. 778–785.

44. *PhG* 419–423/M para. 787–789, 424–427/M para. 793, 795–798, 431–433/ M para. 804–808. For a fully developed defense of the interpretation summarized here, see Collins 2013, chapter 15 §5–9, chapter 16 §1–8.

45. See Hegel's discussion of the relation between philosophical science and the empirical sciences (*Enz* §6A, 7+A, 9, 12+A, 16+A.) and my discussion of it in Collins 2013, chapter 4 §2. See also Hegel's position on the normative function of philosophical concepts in relation to representations established in the culture (*PhR* §2A) and my discussion of it in Collins 2013, chapter 3 §2.

Works Cited

Abbreviations for Works by G.W.F. Hegel

Enz   *Enzyklopädie der Philosophischen Wissenschaften im Grundrisse.* In *Gesammelte Werke*, Band 20, edited by W. Bonsiepen and H.-C. Lucas, 1992 [1830]. Cited by §n with *A* (*Anmerken*) for Remarks, and *Z* (*Zusatz*) for Additions.

PhR   *Grundlinien der Philosophie des Rechts.* Edited by J. Hoffmeister. Hamburg: Felix Meiner, 1955 [1830]. Cited by §n with *A* (*Anmerken*) for Remarks.

PhG   *Phänomenologie des Geistes.* Edited by H.-F. Wessels and H. Clairmont, according to the text of *Gesammelte Werke* Band 9, edited by W. Bonsiepen and R. Heede (1980). Hamburg: Felix Meiner, 1988. Abbreviation is followed by the page numbers from Band 9 of *Gesammelte Werke*.

WL 12   *Wissenschaft der Logik: Die Lehre vom Begriff.* Edited by H.-J. Gawoll, according to the text of *Gesammelte Werke* Band 12, 1981, edited by F. Hogemann and W. Jaeschke. Hamburg: Felix Meiner, 1994 [1816]. Cited as *WL* 12:n.

WL 21   *Wissenschaft der Logik: Die Lehre vom Sein* [1832], Band 21 *Gesammelte Werke.* Cited as *WL* 21:n.

Buchanan, J. M. 1975. *The Limits of Liberty: Between Anarchy and Leviathan.* Chicago: University of Chicago Press.

Cantwell Smith, W. 1997. *Modern Culture from a Comparative Perspective.* Edited by J. Burbidge. Albany, NY: State University of New York Press.

Collins, A. B. 2000. "Hegel's Unresolved Contradiction: Experience, Philosophy, and the Irrationality of Nature." *Dialogue: A Canadian Philosophical Journal* 39: 771–796.

———. 2013. *Hegel's Phenomenology: The Dialectical Justification of Philosophy's First Principles.* Montreal and Kingston: McGill-Queen's University Press.

DeMartino, G. F. 2000. *Global Economy, Global Justice: Theoretical Objections and Policy Alternatives to Neoliberalism.* London and New York: Routledge.

Dudley, W. 2003–2004. "Impure Reason: Hegel on the Irrationality of the Rational." *The Owl of Minerva* 34 (1–2): 25–48.

Finn, D. K. 2006. *The Moral Ecology of Markets: Assessing Claims about Markets and Justice.* New York: Cambridge University Press.

Friedman, M. 1962. *Capitalism and Freedom.* Chicago: University of Chicago Press.

Fulcher, J. 2004. *Capitalism: A Very Short Introduction.* Oxford: Oxford University Press.

Havel, V. 1990. *Disturbing the Peace: A Conversation with Karel Hvížďala.* Translated by P. Wilson. New York: Knopf.

Hayek, F. A. 1948. *Individualism and Economic Order.* Chicago: University of Chicago Press.

Hegel, G.W.F. 1968ff. *Gesammelte Werke,* Rheinisch-Westfälischen Akademie der Wissenschaften and Hegel-Archiv der Ruhr-Universität Bochum. Hamburg: Felix Meiner.

———. 1969. *Hegel's Science of Logic.* Translated by A. V. Miller. London: Allen and Unwin; New York: Humanities Press. Cited with citations of the German text as M n.

———. 1977. *Hegel's Phenomenology of Spirit.* Translated by A. V. Miller. Oxford and New York: Oxford University Press. Cited with citations of the German text as M *para.* n.

———. 1991. *Elements of the Philosophy of Right.* Edited by A. W. Wood, translated by H. B. Nisbet. Cambridge: Cambridge University Press. This translation reproduces the section numbers of the German edition, and hence is implicitly cited with all citations of *PhR.*

———. 1991. *The Encyclopaedia Logic.* Translated by T. F. Geraets, W. A. Suchting, and H. S. Harris. Indianapolis: Hackett. This translation reproduces the sections numbers of the German edition, and hence is implicitly cited with all citations of *Enz.*

———. 2010. *The Science of Logic.* Translated by George di Giovanni. Cambridge: Cambridge University Press. This translation reproduces the page numbers of the German edition, and hence is implicitly cited with all citations of *WL.*

Schweickart, D. 2011. *After Capitalism.* 2nd ed. Lanham, MD: Rowman & Littlefield.

4

The Purest Inequality

Hegel's Critique of the Labor Contract and Capitalism

It is difficult to determine Hegel's position on capitalism. Hegel seems reluctant to endorse a system he doubts can create general prosperity,[1] or even provide universal opportunity (distributing wealth according to merit).[2] Yet, Hegel defends in principle the legitimacy of egoistic action and the consequent inequality in civil society.[3] And, he provides an explicit defense of the labor contract[4] (the practice most essential to capitalism in which money is exchanged not for a commodity of a fixed value, but instead for the power to create value). This vacillation leaves many with the impression that Hegel felt capitalism to be severely flawed, yet still legitimate, that is, that his ambivalence amounted to being emotionally uncomfortable with the conclusions of his thinking.[5]

However, there is a thoroughly philosophical indictment of capitalism in Hegel's work that has previously been overlooked. Let me begin by stating clearly that I claim neither that Hegel univocally condemned capitalism, nor that he worked out an alternative, nor even that Hegel himself was necessarily fully aware of the critique of capitalism contained in his work. I claim only that by reading the *Philosophy of Right*'s civil society section together with the *Phenomenology of Spirit*'s culture section, one can discern a hidden critique of the labor contract—and by extension of capitalism itself. Despite these section's differences, they contain

71

a single, consistent analysis of a new form of social organization arising in modernity.[6] In modern "civil society" and "culture" individuals strive to overcome their particularity and render themselves universal (to replace already existing, idiosyncratic modes of action with standardized, conventional behavior)[7] to acquire value, to count for something, and thereby to receive back and satisfy their particularity through the rewards to which this valorization entitles them.[8]

Thus in the *Phenomenology* the individual "noble-minded consciousness" strives to shed his individuality in service of the state, becoming a general image (*Bild*) of the culture (*Bildung*) and receiving in exchange honor and wealth. Similarly, civil society integrates people by compelling each, for honor and wealth, to educate or acculturate (*bilden*) herself, refining her raw individuality and making herself into a generalized image of what is required for the satisfaction of the other's needs. In both culture and civil society, failure to universalize oneself renders one valueless, counting for nothing, and consequently deprived of honor and wealth. Accordingly, people in civil society use others as means for private ends;[9] and, if one is not useful for the achievement of any of another's ends, then one counts for nothing.[10] Similarly, in culture one who fails to universalize oneself does not count (*gilt*) for anything;[11] or to put it differently, such a person has no value. As in English "validity" is related to "value," so in German *gelten* means "to be valid" or "to count [as valid]" when intransitive, but when transitive expresses the *value* of something (like "to be worth" in English). Hegel plays on this word frequently in the culture section to underscore his point that what "counts [*gilt*]" in culture is ultimately what one is worth (*gilt*) in money (*Geld*).

Though some are rewarded and others deprived, this way of distributing honor and wealth appears justified because the criterion for value is universalization, making oneself amenable to the needs of society at large. Thus the egoism of one who does what this arrangement requires only for honor and wealth is tempered by the fact that what is required is *giving up* one's particularity (at least initially). Accordingly, Hegel says states should allow particularity free rein to satisfy itself in civil society partly because everyone's interests still *should* be satisfied indirectly through each pursuing her own individual interests.[12]

However, this arrangement actually causes widespread misery rather than universal benefit. Moreover, this wretchedness is not caused only by the failure to universalize oneself: it can actually be the result of a person's *successful* universalization. This devalorization occurs when money replaces recognition of honor in the estates as the form of mediation between persons and the expression of their value, or (what turns out to be the same thing) when labor is sold on the market for money like any other good. An estate is an institutionalized social class, established on a political foundation rather than through market forces. In fact, estates provide the structure within which the market may operate, integrating economic agents and activity into the more comprehensive ends of the state. That this devalorization of persons follows the undermining of the estates and the consequent abandonment of the economy to the market means that it is only in capitalism that worth is transformed into worthlessness.

In this chapter I first leave aside money's disruption of social integration through the estates, examining only (1) the universalization process in civil society and how it at once gives the individual value and deprives her of value, (2) turning next to *Phenomenology* to see the more critical account of how money compels the alienation of personality—that is, of the labor contract. Finally, (3) returning to the *Philosophy of Right*, I identify a similar critique of money-based social relations and the labor contract that is present there in nascent form.

Valorization and Devalorization

Hegel knew from observation and philosophical speculation that civil society, left alone, is not only unlikely to accomplish what it should, but actually engenders the opposite: people render themselves *worthless* and impoverished not only through failure to develop skills and thereby "universalize" themselves, but even through universalization itself. In the *Philosophy of Right* this problem seems confined to the "reflective" estate (those involved in manufacture and sale of goods). Standardizing work makes the worker's position unstable, rendering her replaceable by another worker, or a machine. And, more efficient work increases the supply, which decreases the value of the products, and thus of the worker's labor.[13] Accordingly, the more the worker satisfies the criteria for valorization in civil society, the more worthless she becomes. The dynamics of civil society thus produce not universal enjoyment, but rather the enjoyment of some, alongside the misery of others as wealth is concentrated in a few hands while many are abandoned to poverty and exclusion, as a permanent underclass. This underclass (the "rabble") suffers not only physically, but morally: even if it is sustained by charity, its members will still lack the honor and self-respect of providing for themselves. The modern capitalist nation-state thus produces within itself a class that not only suffers unjustly, but that is animated solely by a radical contempt for and rebellion against this entire society.[14]

To go by the *Philosophy of Right* alone, it would appear that Hegel doubts the problem can be solved,[15] or even that it is a genuine injustice, rather than merely something unfortunate. He candidly recognizes that the nation-state cannot eradicate systemic poverty but only displace it through war (colonization): colonies provide a captive market for domestic goods that would otherwise be in surplus, impoverishing part of the population (because a surplus renders their labor worthless). Thus the nation-state avoids producing a rabble within itself only by making another country into its rabble.[16] Yet, because civil society should not be suppressed, the *Philosophy of Right* implies that despite the dismal prospects for universal satisfaction, even civil society's defects must be accepted.[17] In this work there appears to be no truly critical examination of the absurdity of civil society, which is supposed to be justified in principle, despite destroying the end it is supposed to promote. Yet the *Phenomenology* concerns identical problems in culture (which is structurally similar to civil society) and Hegel does offer there a thoroughgoing critique. Moreover, this critique is implicit even in the *Philosophy of Right*, such that we can reconstruct a radical and genuinely Hegelian critique of the problems of civil society.

The key point made clearly in the *Phenomenology* but obscurely in the *Philosophy of Right* is that the network of relationships characterizing both culture and civil society subsists only because the participants suffer from a certain delusion: contrary to their beliefs, the universality they strive to approximate has no existence apart from these individuals themselves,[18] whose personality or innermost self brings about through its labor the transformation of their "original determinate natures" into something universal. And, because this universalization creates value, the source of value is one's personality (not a separately existing universality to which one must adapt).[19] Unemployable individuality appears valueless only because people in culture wrongly identify the source of value as "state-power," that is, the "universal work" of everyone, the origin and the end of all labor, produced by all yet falsely thought to exist independently of each individual's contribution.[20] Culture therefore involves a "*double* actuality," with the individual personality as the "*true* actuality" and state-power as "the [ostensible] *true*, which *counts* [*gilt*]."[21]

Money and the Alienation of Personality

As in civil society one counts only through giving up one's particularity and taking on a universal character in work, so in culture one "counts" or has value only by transcending one's original determinate nature and approximating a universal cultural standard, a feat measured quantitatively.[22] And as in civil society the failure to universalize oneself deprives one of employment, so in culture what fails to become universal "is an *espèce* [something merely particular] that strives ludicrously and in vain *to put itself to work.*"[23] Culture is not as obviously focused on work as civil society, but it is concerned with the same process of valorization through universalization and the expression of the value in honor and money. The economic significance of culture is obscured only because Hegel draws his images not from economics but from the social world of early modern France, when the nobility, the bourgeoisie, the clergy, and the monarch all vied for power. Since Hegel's *Phenomenology* is not historiographical, he speaks not of the nobility as such but of the "noble-minded consciousness,"[24] alluding to a French social class while still including anyone striving to approximate a universal standard, regardless of class (or century). Yet the history of the French nobility clarifies Hegel's point that the relation between the cultural universal and the individuality (which alone generates and sustains them and yet mistakes itself as dependent on them for its value) has two important consequences, both of which express the concealed dependence of cultural standards on the individual personality.

First, culture undermines itself when the person strives *too* earnestly to universalize himself, since annihilating *all* individuality would also annihilate the universal (culture itself): if the nobleman is *too* sincere in his military service to the state, disregarding his own individuality to the point of dying in battle, he at once gives culture concrete existence (in his total devotion) and destroys it (in perishing).[25] Second, the universal standard only possesses what the individual puts into it: if the nobleman holds back, supporting the state only when it is in the interests of his own estate (class), state-power will be only apparently universal, but covertly the interest of this estate or another.[26]

For example, if the nobleman does not sacrifice himself, but instead maintains his being-for-self (interiority, personality), giving only counsel, then culture would remain unactualized: his counsel (which purportedly seeks the ends of the state) would really seek only the good of his own estate; and, the state will lack subjectivity, a private will by which it could parse the counsel it receives.[27] The only way for the state to gain being-for-self, in virtue of which it becomes more than a plaything of contending classes, is for the "noble-minded consciousness" to alienate *everything* in the state, even his own being-for-self. To show total devotion in action (military service) would entail the agent's (and culture's) destruction. However, in flattering the monarch the courtier alienates his identification with a particular estate (which becomes irrelevant in the absolute monarchy), and even one's own being-for-self, thereby giving culture an enduring actuality and self-consciousness. Here the noble consciousness' innermost self (the "I," or personality) enters into audial externality.[28] In this exchange state-power (as monarch, the object of the speech) acquires this alienated self-consciousness, while the nobleman continues to exist and to provide flattery.

The noble-minded consciousness receives from the monarch in return political power in the form of money, which is thus revealed as the true form of state-power.[29] The noble-minded consciousness always received wealth as a reward for service, but before the primary motivation was the *honor* received from the other members of his estate. In contrast, by alienating himself through flattery, he dishonors himself, receiving only wealth in return. Wealth (*Reichtum*) is the true political authority (*Reich*) because like state-power, wealth is the result of the work of all, but in wealth the aspect of "being-for-another" is explicit: money is nothing in-itself, only something to be surrendered for the sake of something else, and is not mistaken for something existing and having legitimacy apart from one's actions. In fact, state-power was always implicitly being-for-another (i.e., wealth): noble-minded consciousness takes state-power for something independent of his action promoting it and efforts to transform his own character into something universal, but culture is nothing apart from these actions on the part of individuals. And, just as state-power (as monarch) had to receive being-for-self externally, through flattering speech, so the noble receives it externally in wealth.

The fraudulence of culture is now apparent. In accordance with the demands of culture, the nobleman universalized himself completely. He alienates his own personality, that which *creates* value, receiving in return only money, which has no qualitative character, only greater or lesser quantity, and thus is the truth of culture (the transformation of any given quality into a greater or lesser quantity). But possessing state-power as wealth is unsatisfying: it is insubstantial, not an end in itself. Even worse, unlike the noble-minded consciousness' more certain possession of honor in his estate's eyes through noble deeds, he only receives wealth (regaining his alienated personality) through the arbitrary fancy of its bestower. This loss of oneself, and the arbitrariness with which the rich man may or may not allow one to regain it in wealth, transforms gratitude into the radical rejection of the whole world of culture. The world of culture is rejected because successful acculturation, universalization through flattery, the process by which the individual hoped to *attain* himself ends by reducing his personality to a thing received externally, if indeed it is received at all.[30]

Flattery thus becomes cutting barbs of *wit*. If in culture everything in transformed into its opposite (in-itself into for-another, noble service into flattery, and even abject wretchedness, the innermost self into a contingent, external thing), then wit is speech uniting both sides of the opposition.[31] Thus wit mercilessly mocks the vanity of the world of culture, how the reputedly noble is in fact base, and the ostensibly base is in fact noble, such that wit is the only true speech in culture, the only speech actually expressing (externally) what it means (internally).[32] Wit is true because in wit "every *Gleiche* is dissolved; for the *purest* Ungleichheit is present there."[33] *Gleiche* is translated as "identity" or as "equality," and *Ungleichheit* as "nonidentity" or "inequality." The dissolution of every identity in the face of the purest nonidentity refers to how in culture every "fixed essence" (good, bad, noble, base) is also its opposite, because in culture the most radical loss of identity has occurred (the reduction of personality to an external thing received arbitrarily). The dissolution of every equality in the face of the purest inequality refers to how the determinate values assigned to people in culture (as a function of their successful acculturation), a value to which the person is supposed to be equal, is rendered absurd insofar as the purest inequality obtains, that is, personality itself, the source of all value is held to be equal to a determinate sum of money.

Hegel also says wit is the identity in the judgment where the same personality is subject and predicate, though these are indifferent entities (or, entities of equal value, *gleichgültige Seiende*).[34] A judgment for Hegel expresses both the identity and nonidentity of a subject and its universal character (its predicate),[35] because a judgment immediately unites a singular thing and some universal predicate, without explaining how a singular thing can "be" a universal.[36] Being subject and predicate in a judgment means that personality is identical and nonidentical to itself—just as in culture personality is "torn apart,"[37] separated from itself. By saying that subject and predicate (i.e., personality and wealth) are *gleichgültige Seiende*, Hegel is saying: first, that they are "indifferent" (as *gleichgültige* is commonly translated), that is, separate and cannot be identified, for one is the source of all value and the other is a determinate value; but second, and despite their difference, in culture the two are equally (*gleich*) valued (*gültige*). Thus here Hegel gives a genuine critique of the labor contract, condemning the absurdity of a social system based on exchanging value-creating power for a determinate value. Moreover, critique was always present in nascent form in the *Philosophy of Right*, as becomes clear when one knows what to look for.

Critique of the Labor Contract in the *Philosophy of Right*

Thus the *Phenomenology* shows that the universalization acculturation requires, which promises to valorize the individual, ends by depriving him of his estate, and subjecting him to the humiliation of exchanging value-creating power, which is hence priceless, for a determinate sum of cash (the material expression of being-for-another, intrinsic worthlessness). Culture leads noble-minded consciousness to this base condition because in culture the universal is mistaken for an in-itself bestowing value, when in truth it is for-another, and without intrinsic value. Wit emerges as the resulting rejection of the entire cultural order. Bearing this in mind, it is clear how in civil society, too, the use of money to mediate relations between people undermines the division into estates, renders most people wage-laborers and produces a "rabble," which rejects the social world wholesale.

Estates can be undermined by money only because money is initially only *one* form of wealth (*Vermögen*) in civil society. The peasantry's wealth is the "fruitful ground and soil." The reflective estate, which is divided into three subgroups, has two different forms of wealth. The craft and manufacturing subgroups their "social wealth" in the network of contingencies involving the skills, talents, understanding, and industry of individuals; and the commercial subgroup has its own expression of value in "money [*Geld*]."[38] In each case, wealth expresses the value an estate finds given. However, these forms of wealth are not mutually indifferent: the peasantry's wealth is the raw material for manufacturers, whose finished products are the raw material for merchants.[39] Thus nature's product has value only for what it can be crafted into; and these goods have value only if they can be sold for money. Money, however (which is valuable only when surrendered), is supposed to be valuable in-itself.

Money thus seems to order the relations between estates, but in truth it renders the activity of all estates absurd, because the goods of all estates have value only insofar as they can be exchanged for money, which has no value in-itself. Moreover, money's universality renders even the distinctions between estates meaningless. While money originates as a form of wealth peculiar to the commercial subgroup of the reflective estate, money is the medium "in which the abstract value of *all* goods is actual,"[40] extending beyond commerce strictly speaking throughout civil society. Because money is an expression of value that is thus "universal" each person's work becomes *labor generally*, correlated with a determinate sum of cash. Estate membership thus becomes insignificant because the value of all work is expressed in a single (monetary) form. Thus in modernity the peasantry becomes bourgeois, working not for satisfaction, but for profit: the farmer produces products that require the least labor, because the people in his employ are no longer regarded as his family.[41] The bonds of estate thus count (*gilt*) for nothing. The proliferation of money is therefore the de facto abolition of estates, the reduction of most people in civil society to wage-laborers, who sell not a particular kind of good, but labor generally—that which creates value rather than an item of a determinate value—though this valorizing power is nonetheless accorded a definite price.

Money thus functions in culture as it does in civil society: the nobleman and the craftsman suppose value to exist independently (whether as
a cultural standard or as "social wealth"). But in each case value comes
to be only through the efforts of individuals to actualize it. This mistake
compels both nobleman and craftsman to give up their estate and alienate
their personalities (which alone create value) to give culture or work a
truly universal form, which is only received back in the money he receives
in return.

As in culture this alienation constitutes the tearing apart of personality, so in civil society the loss of estate is catastrophic. One's estate is,
after all, one's ethical life: estate membership gives life meaning by giving
purpose and support to work and repaying it with the "honor of one's
estate,"[42] the recognition of one's value from other members of one's
estate. The expression of value through honor differs from its expression
in money (though money may also be received) firstly because money is
indifferent to estate (and helps to undermine differentiation in estates)
whereas honor is bound to one estate's particular ethos, such that there
is no honor except the honor of this or that estate; and secondly because
whereas the honor of one's estate is qualitative, an end in-itself, money
is merely quantitative, "subject to no qualitative limit."[43] In other words,
whereas recognition from one's peers in the estate is attainable and satisfying, wealth is a "bad infinite"[44]: one could always be richer, so one who
looks to wealth to express his value is never satisfied.

Capitalism thus involves not only misery for the poor, but also meaninglessness for rich and poor alike. To lack an estate (*Stand*) is to lack
standing or validity (*Geltung*) in society. In an attempt to gain recognition
as having value, even the rich man can only flaunt "external manifestations
of success," that is, hollow conspicuous consumption.[45] As Hegel says in
the *Phenomenology*: "Wealth stands at the brink of this innermost abyss, of
this bottomless depth in which all stability and substance have disappeared.
It sees in this depth nothing but an everyday thing, a play of fancy, an
accident of whim. Its spirit has become a belief quite without essence,
a superficiality forsaken by spirit."[46] This nihilism extends also to one's
political identity: for those lacking an estate, even the laws appear to be a
"play of fancy," an "accident of whim." A law can appear as justified only if
it is possible for it to be applied by a jury of one's peers,[47] that is, by the
fellow members of one's estate, who share one's ethical life.[48] Indeed, the
estates are meant to mediate between the government and the people by
justifying the former in the eyes of the latter, such that individuals become
integrated into the larger nation-state.[49] The loss of estate is thus not only
the loss of honor, of recognition by one's peers, it is also the deprivation of
any peers at all. In a social system based on according a determinate value
to what alone creates value (i.e., in one based on "the purest inequality

[*die reinste Ungleichheit*]"), one is deprived of any peer (*Gleiche*), reduced to an atom in a heap of alien atoms. Thus even for the rich man, to lose one's estate is to share the nihilism, if not the material deprivation, of the rabble (who are defined by their lack of estate).[50] If one attends not to the material poverty but to the poverty of spirit characterizing the rabble, then whether rich or poor, everyone in capitalism is part of the rabble, since even if they work, the proliferation of money deprives them of the honor of their estate, and thus of a meaningful expression of their value.[51]

Yet though the rich and poor in capitalism suffer from the same meaninglessness, only the poor know this, and thus enjoy a more adequate perspective insofar as the very misery of the poor prevents them from sharing the delusions of the rich (who vainly seek value in conspicuous consumption). Rather, the poor are like the "mocking laughter," the "echo, audible to itself, of the confusion of the whole [society]."[52] The rabble have lost their estate, and the honor proper to it; not because they have failed to live up to the demands of civil society, but because they have lived up to them *too well*. The rabble have universalized themselves to the point of rendering their labor worthless; they have an excess of *Tüchtigkeit* (capability, or power), and a consequent deprivation of *Vermögen* (wealth, or power).[53] The "purest inequality" of pure power and pure powerlessness is concretized in the labor contract, in which valorizing power is exchanged for a determinate quantity of money unless, due to the contingencies of the market or the whim of a capitalist, it is unable to be redeemed at all. To analyze civil society, and to find that the only true thing in it, given this purest of inequalities, is the rabble's total rejection of it, cannot be interpreted as anything other than a critique and rejection of the labor contract (and by extension, a rejection of capitalism) on Hegel's part.[54]

Yet if hidden beneath the surface of these texts there is a powerful critique of the labor contract (and thus of capitalism itself), it remains to be shown why Hegel so explicitly endorsed the selling of labor in the section on abstract right. He says there that one can legitimately alienate not only individual products, but also particular mental and physical skills, provided that it is only sold for a limited period. To alienate the whole of one's time, or (what is the same thing) the totality of one's productive power made actual through work, would be to render work, which is normally a limited externalization of personality, into something substantial (because the entire use of a good is the good itself[55]); and, because personality is inalienable,[56] the whole of my productive power cannot be alienated.[57] But, Hegel says, alienation of only a portion of my time in work does not mean enslaving myself, and so is not forbidden; and what is the sale of labor for a limited period (e.g., eight hours) if not a labor contract?

First of all, I repeat that I do not claim that everything in Hegel's work is consistent with the critique of capitalism that genuinely belongs to Hegel, and that I have reconstructed in this essay; and §67 of the *Philosophy of Right* certainly seems to contradict this critique. Second, the foregoing exposition shows that this critique of the labor contract is more closely bound to (if not immediately apparent in) Hegel's social philosophy generally, and should be given more weight than §67, a single paragraph of abstract right.[58] After all, the labor contract (if it is legitimate) can only be understood as taking place in civil society, and so any attempt to show that it agrees with the general thrust of Hegel's social philosophy would have to integrate it into his account of civil society (and not just his openly abstract account of the relation between society-less "persons" and "things" in abstract right).

Moreover, recall that that wit, the consciousness of culture's absurdity, is the identity of both sides of the judgment in which personality is (individual) subject and (universal) predicate.[59] Indeed, civil society and culture generally are "judgments" in Hegel's technical sense, immediately identifying individual persons with a universal standard of value to which the person *ought* to be equal. To solve this problem would be to identify the particular term mediating between the extremes opposed in this judgment. Now, consider that the two principles of civil society are: (1) the *individual* person with her needs and who is her own end; (2) the form of *universal* mediation (i.e., interdependence) whereby the person gives herself value (*sich geltend macht*) and gains satisfaction (*befriedigt*).[60] People in capitalism misunderstand that only the labor of individual persons creates value, and persons labor for *self-valorization and satisfaction*—these constitute the particular term mediating between individual and universal, and rendering this judgment a syllogism.[61]

If this is true, a social system that valorizes goods only through devalorizing persons and withholding satisfaction from them violates the very concept of civil society. That is, accepting the concept of civil society as legitimate does not mean accepting capitalism, which is rather a perversion of civil society. Understanding civil society correctly involves seeing that labor's valorization of things is legitimate only to the extent that it also valorizes the person and provides satisfaction. The capitalistic labor contract appears justified in abstract right only because there persons and things are considered abstractly. Yet a thorough analysis of civil society shows that while labor is the source of value in things, *labor itself* cannot be made into a mere *thing* with a determinate value (this would be to collapse the syllogism once again into a judgment).

The endorsement of the labor contract in §67 must be discounted therefore because everything in abstract right is presented abstractly and inadequately relative to the more concrete study of civil society, where more factors are accounted for. Even if Hegel himself failed to notice that what he says about the labor contract in §67 is incompatible with his own elucidation of personality's creation and sale of value and valorizing power in his analysis of culture and civil society, it would still be true that Hegel's philosophy, according to its own principles and complete exposition, offers a denunciation rather than a defense of the labor contract, and indeed of capitalism.

Notes

1. Hegel 1991, §§185, 195.

2. Ibid., §§200, 237, 241.

3. Ibid., §§185R, 186–187, 200R.

4. Ibid., §67.

5. This is the conclusion of two eminent scholars, Wood 1995, 250, and Williams 1997, 242–245.

6. To be sure, the "culture" section of the *Phenomenology* concerns social relations in pre-modern, feudal Europe, but it concerns these insofar as they are undermined and replaced in the transition to modern capitalism.

7. Hegel 1988, para. 488; 1 Hegel 1991, §§186–187. Indeed, Hegel even calls the process of assimilation in civil society "acculturation [*bilden*]" or even simply "culture [*Bildung*]" 1991, §187, 1923, §525, among other places.

8. Hegel 1988, para. 491; Hegel 1991 §§187, 189.

9. Hegel 1991, §§187, 189, 192–193, 197.

10. "In civil society each individual is his own end, and all others are nothing to him" (Hegel 1991, §182 Addition, amending Nisbet). See also §§187, 189, 197.

11. Hegel 1988, para. 488–489, 504.

12. Hegel 1991, §§187, 195R.

13. Ibid., §§204, 198, 245; 1923 §526. That skill development decreases labor's value is a point usually attributed to Marx, who did make it (1975, 283–295), but it belonged to standard economic theory at least since Adam Smith.

14. Hegel 1991, §§185, 244–245. See also Hegel 1995 §118 and Addition.

15. See Avineri 1972, 147–154, and Wood 1995, 247–250.

16. Hegel 1991, §245–248. See also Hegel 1995, §120 and Addition.

17. Wood 1995 takes this to be Hegel's final position, 250.

18. Hegel 1988, para. 491.

19. That is, value does not exist apart from the *persons* who bring it about by their universalizing labor.

20. Hegel 1988, para. 494.

21. Ibid., para. 504.

22. "The universal, which counts [*gilt*] here, is that which has *become*, and is therefore *actual*. That whereby the individual has validity and actuality, is culture" Hegel 1988, para. 488–489.

23. "*sich ins Werk zu setzen*" (para. 489, my emphasis).

24. Hegel 1988, para. 503.

25. Ibid., para. 503, 506.

26. In French this ambiguity would be more apparent. Social classes under the *ancien régime* were called *états*, usually translated into English as "estates." This translation is not inaccurate, but état also means simply "state." The calculating hypocrisy of the nobleman who only serves the state so long as it agrees with the interests of his estate (his class) can thus hide behind the technically true claim that in any case, he is always a loyal servant of his état.

27. Hegel 1988, para. 505–506.

28. Ibid. 1988, para. 508. This paragraph uses the terms "I [*Ich*]" and "*individuality existing for-itself* [*fürsichseiende Einzelheit*]" to refer to what undergoes alienation (*Entfremdung*), but this process must be the same as what he calls later the abdication of personality (*Persönlichkeit*) (para. 513). Indeed, the "abdication [*Entsagung*]" is necessarily a surrender accomplished through *speaking sagen, dic-*).

29. Hegel 1988, para. 512.

30. Ibid., para. 516–517.

31. Ibid., para. 521. See also where Hegel describes wit in a way that hints at its role in both culture (*Bildung*) and in civil society (*bürgerliche Gesellschaft*), calling it the height of "social culture [*gesellschaftlichen Bildung*]" Hegel 1923, §394A.

32. Hegel 1988, para. 521.

33. Ibid., para. 517.

34. Ibid., para. 520.

35. Hegel 1923, §166R.

36. Judgment's instability is resolved only in the syllogism, by positing a middle term whereby the universal (predicate) determines itself, and can exist in singularity, Hegel 1923, §§179–180. At the end of the chapter I note where I think Hegel identifies the middle term for this judgment.

37. Hegel 1988, para. 519.

38. Hegel 1991, §§203–205; 1923, §528.

39. Hegel 1995, §104. See also Hegel 1991, §§299 and R, 63A.

40. Hegel 1991, §204, my emphasis. See also §299 and R.

41. Hegel 1995, §104A; see also 1991, §203A.

42. Hegel 1923, §527; Hegel 1991, §207.

43. Hegel 1995, §104. See also Hegel 1991, §253R.

44. See Hegel 1923, §§94–95.

45. Hegel 1991, §253R.

46. Hegel 1988, para. 519, amending the Hegel Translation Groups' version slightly.

47. Hegel 1991, §§220, 228.

48. Hegel (1991) says there must be *Gleichheit* between the accused and his jury (§228). See also in the first edition of the *Philosophy of Right* where Hegel says that difference in estate must result in difference in how the law is understood in its judicial application (§115A), and that jury members must be "of equal birth" as the accused, who must be "confident that they have the same interests and the same circumstances that he has," (§116A)—that is, that trial "by one's peers" means that the jury must belong to the same estate as the accused.

49. Hegel 1991, §§301 & R-302 and R. To be sure, Hegel says though rectitude (one's having shaped oneself through education and acculturation so as to

be adequate to the tasks typical of one's position in society) "is ethical life in the sphere in question"—that is, in civil society—"it is not yet ethical life as such" (Hegel 1995, §107A). However, as he goes on to explain, he means by this only that human beings have "higher aims" and one accomplishes these aims by *fulfilling* not neglecting the duties of one's estate.

50. Hegel (1991) §207. Hardimon 1994, like Neuhouser 2000, 114, distinguishes between subjective alienation (failing to grasp the rationality of the world) and objective alienation (living in a world not completely rational) (119–120); and Hardimon charges that Hegel did not grasp that the poor were objectively alienated, and so restricted himself to trying to alleviate the subjective alienation of the bourgeoisie (246). Although I agree that the *Philosophy of Right* does give the impression that Hegel did not fully appreciate or think through the problem of poverty and the consequent alienation, Hegel was keenly aware of the alienation resulting from the mediation of social relationships by money (for both the rich and the poor), as I hope to have shown.

51. Admittedly, that all in capitalism share the rabble's nihilism (insofar as all lose their estate, and thereby a meaningful expression of their value) is a conclusion that Hegel does not draw in the *Encyclopedia* or *Philosophy of Right*. However, close attention to the account of culture in the *Phenomenology* and his undeveloped remarks on the effect of money in the Heidelberg and Berlin versions of the *Philosophy of Right* legitimate this conclusion, as I have shown. Indeed, I underline in this essay just how important estate membership is for Hegel, and thus to argue against Neuhouser 2000, who objects to the prominent place Hegel gives to the estates as illiberal, but pardons Hegel, calling the estates "a relatively expendable part of Hegel's social theory"(205). Regarding the so-called expendability of the estates, I simply note that if the estates are lost, the person in civil society loses her ethical life, and all meaningful expression of value—hardly a negligible loss. Moreover, regarding the alleged illiberality of the estates, we should keep in mind that Hegel defends the estates not from a reactionary desire to resurrect medieval guilds or feudal institutions generally. After all, Hegel rarely did anything to conceal his disdain for the middle ages. However, he was very concerned about the form of the modern body politic that would replace the medieval social patchwork. Above all, he wanted to ensure that people would be united organically with each other and with state institutions, and this required mediating organs such as the estates. Accordingly, he hoped to preserve what was best about the medieval estates while leaving out what was objectionable (namely, their independence from the state, the way they entrenched feudal privilege). See Lee 2008, 630. If the estates are abandoned, and no alternative mediating organ is created, it is unclear how anything but poverty and nihilism can result. The corporation (*Korporation*) cannot step in to take the place of the estate, as it is only meant to supplement what the estate does in the case of the second estate (the estate of craft, manufacture and trade) (*Philosophy of Right* §250), and in fact is more restrictive in its membership, not including everyone even in this estate (*Philosophy of Right* §252R). Indeed, Cullen 1988 argues convincingly that for Hegel wage-laborers do not meet the criteria for corporation membership (32).

52. This is how Hegel describes wit 1988, para. 525, amending the Hegel Translation Group's version slightly.

53. Just as overproduction of goods leads to their devalorization and the consequent poverty of some in civil society, an absurdity that led Hegel to remark that "despite an *excess of wealth,* civil society is *not wealthy enough*" Hegel 1991, §245 (Hegel's emphasis), so despite an excess of "power," the poor are not powerful enough.

54. Again, I do not claim that Hegel univocally condemned capitalism, but only that the critique I have outlined here is present in Hegel's work. I would further add that if this criticism of capitalism bears strong similarities to that of Marx, it is only because the former was the inspiration for the latter, whether Marx acknowledged or even realized the extent to which this is true. In fact, in volume one of *Capital* (1977), which more than any other work of Marx's articulates the "Marxist" indictment of capitalism, there is actually an oblique reference to the culture section of Hegel's *Phenomenology.* In explaining how the value of a commodity is expressed in terms of other commodities, he says: "Determinations of this kind are altogether very curious. For instance, one man is king only because the other men stand in the relation of subjects to him. They, on the other hand, imagine that they are the subjects because he is king," 149n.

55. Hegel 1991, §61.

56. Ibid., §66.

57. Ibid., §67; Hegel 1995, §37.

58. And, although the claim that selling one's labor is a legitimate concretion of right does appear in the Berlin and Heidelberg editions of the *Philosophy of Right,* it ought to count for something that Hegel declined not once, nor twice, but three times to include it in the *Encyclopedia* (leaving it out in the editions of 1817, 1827, and 1830, presumably because he did not consider it a central feature of the concept of right).

59. Hegel 1988, para. 520.

60. Hegel 1991, §182.

61. See Hegel 1923, §§179–180. An analogy may help: just as a particular conception of happiness is the middle term between the (universal) will and its (singular) impulses, such that "free spirit" wills a certain impulse only insofar as it promotes and can be integrated into the particular conception of happiness (which the will wills always in all of its impulses) (§480), so the (singular) person in civil society should participate in its system of (universal) interdependence only insofar as by these means the person is thereby valorized and gains satisfaction. The mediating, particular term here is the pair self-valorization and satisfaction. When civil society is grasped in this syllogistic way, the sale of personality, valorizing power for a determinate value becomes absurd.

Works Cited

Avineri, S. 1972. *Hegel's Theory of the Modern State.* Cambridge: Cambridge University Press.

Cullen, B. 1988. "The Mediating Role of Estates and Corporations in Hegel's Theory of Political Representation." In *Hegel Today,* edited by B. Cullen. Brookfield: Gower.

Hardimon, M. O. 1994. *Hegel's Social Philosophy: The Project of Reconciliation*. Cambridge: Cambridge University Press.

Hegel, G.W.F. 1923. *Enzyklopädie der Philosophischen Wissenschaften im Grundrisse*. 1830. Hamburg: Felix Meiner Verlag.

———. 1986. *Grundlinien der Philosophie des Rechts*. *Werke* Band 7. Frankfurt: Suhrkamp Verlag.

———. 1988. *Phänomenologie des Geistes*. Hamburg: Felix Meiner Verlag.

———. 1991. *Elements of the Philosophy of Right*. Translated by H. B. Nisbet. Cambridge: Cambridge University Press.

———. 1995. *Lectures on Natural Right and Political Science: The First Philosophy of Right*. Translated by J. Michael Stewart and P. Hodgson. Berkeley: University of California Press.

———. 2001. *Spirit: Chapter Six of Hegel's Phenomenology of Spirit*. Edited by D. Shannon. Translated by the Hegel Translation Group. Indianapolis: Hackett.

Lee, D. 2008. "The Legacy of Medieval Constitutionalism in the Philosophy of Right: Hegel and the Prussian Reform Movement." *History of Political Thought*. 29 (4/1): 634.

Marx, K. 1975. *Early Writings*. Translated by R. Livingstone and G. Benton. New York: Vintage Books.

———. 1977. *Capital*. Vol. 1. Translated by B. Fowkes. New York: Vintage Books.

Neuhouser, F. 2000. *Foundations of Hegel's Social Theory: Actualizing Freedom*. Cambridge, MA: Harvard University Press.

Williams, R. R. 1997. *Hegel's Ethics of Recognition*. Berkeley: University of California Press.

Wood, A. 1995. *Hegel's Ethical Thought*. Cambridge: Cambridge University Press.

5

Hegel's Notion of Abstract Labor in the *Elements of the Philosophy of Right*

GIORGIO CESARALE

Hegel introduces the concept of "abstract labor" in a very dense paragraph of the *Elements of the Philosophy of Right*:

> The universal and objective aspect of work consists, however, in that [process of] *abstraction* which confers a specific character on means and needs and hence also on production, so giving rise to the *division of labour*. Through this division, the work of the individual [*des Einzelnen*] becomes simpler, so that his skill at his abstract work becomes greater, as does the volume of his output. At the same time, this abstraction of skill and means makes the *dependence* and *reciprocity* of human beings in the satisfaction of their other needs complete and entirely necessary. Furthermore, the abstraction of production makes work increasingly *mechanical*, so that the human being is eventually able to step aside and let a *machine* take his place. (*Rph* §198)

The beginning of the passage might well have appeared in works by Ferguson and Smith: the simplicity of labor and the growing ability to perform it are issues that can be easily found in their descriptions of the outcomes of the division of labor.[1] However, the Scottish Enlighteners seem to be far less aware than Hegel of the connection between the results of the division of labor and what Hegel himself calls "abstraction" of the medium (i.e., human activity and tool) of the teleological syllogism of labor. It is precisely the philosophical foundation of the division of labor that undergoes a deep revision in Hegel.

On a more attentive reading of Hegel's paragraph, the same note appears to run through the three remarkable advantages of the division of labor he highlights (growing simplicity, a higher skill level, and larger amount of production), namely the reduction of quality to quantity. Let's start by analyzing the growing simplicity of labor. Labor becomes simpler, as it is limited to one or few acts. In addition, its connection with other activities resides outside it, whereas labor is complex in so far as it combines different gestures, procedures, and competences.[2] We face, therefore, a "quantitative" reduction of multiplicity to homogeneity. Yet labor is simple not only in so far as it abstracts from the totality of social labor, but also because it abstracts from the totality of the worker's needs. Only *one* single need of the worker is satisfied by his own work, and he has to rely on the work of others to satisfy his other needs. Moreover, the one need the worker can satisfy by means of his own work is actually oversatisfied, because he produces more goods of the same type than he can possibly consume.

Moving on to skill, we need to make similar observations: the division of labor promotes a higher skill level and an increasing productive specialization, which boost the "quantitative" outcome of labor. Thus, as soon as the division of labor is introduced into the production process, it has the effect of increasing the volume of the output. But because in Hegel demand is deeply influenced by supply, the output volume also increases as an effect of the higher degree of the division of labor and of the simplicity of work on the process of multiplication and differentiation of needs. In the *Philosophy of Right* this nexus between the simplicity of labor determined by the division of labor and the multiplication and refinement of needs is less emphasized than it is in the Jena writings. But the text offers all the elements we need to infer it: it is clear that with the increasing of the division of labor, not only a larger amount of the same product, but also more and more refined products will be available to an increasing number of consumers. Consumers' taste is gratified, stimulated to discover new properties of the products and helped to enjoy the goods, which are made ready for use. The consumer "is *cultivated* as naturally enjoying [them]" (*JR1*: 243; *HHS*: 139), accustomed as he is to what Hegel in his lectures, drawing from the English people, calls the "comfortable" (*Rph Ilting 1822–1823*: 593).[3] The more refined consumers' taste becomes, the stronger is the pressure on the sphere of production, which is obliged to enrich and increase supply.[4]

On the other hand, the domination of abstract labor, and the reduction of quality to quantity related to it, is still more pervasive than this. The "abstraction of ability and means" turns the dependence and reciprocity of human beings in the satisfaction of their needs into *gänzlichen Notwendigkeit*,[5] into entire necessity. With "entire necessity" Hegel hints at a horizon in which the satisfaction of everyone's needs is entirely affected by the universal *continuum*; or, better, he hints at the fact that everyone's labor for the satisfaction of his own needs is, in itself, a universal labor. Because the worker cannot satisfy, through his own labor, the totality of his needs, he works to satisfy the society's needs. Consequently need becomes as abstract as labor. Individual labor "is for *need* [in general], it is for the abstraction of a need as universally suffered, not for his need" (*JR*: 322; *SEL*: 247). But because this universal continuum does not realize itself according to the "concept" but rather according to necessity, the appearance remains of differentiated needs and labors. Hegelian necessity is the universal continuum underlying the phenomenal differentiation, in this case the differentiation of needs and labors. Necessity determined by civil society is, however, another form of necessity when compared to what the individual experiences when he is immersed in the immediacy of natural passions and drives. It is a social necessity grown out of natural necessity.

Thus, abstract labor has revealed its great potential for the construction of social relations. But it is, at the same time, the origin of their necessity, because it is split in itself. Abstract labor is both labor immersed in the differentiation of the means and the needs and, as Adam Smith called it, labor commanded, labor able to produce a quantity of commodities that "command" the exchange with the same quantity of other commodities. Therefore, necessity originates from the lack of internal mediation between labor commanded (universality) and labor that distinguishes means and needs (particularity), so that the universal continuum promoted by labor commanded does not exhaust in itself the manifold and indefinite differentiation of means and needs. It leaves it out.

On the other hand, Hegel's conception of abstract labor is affected by the lack of differentiation, first introduced by Marx, between the technical division and social division of labor.[6] The Hegelian division of labor encompasses both the division among individuals cooperating in specific kinds of labor within the same company (the Smithian pin factory) and professional specialization. But, in this way, Hegel overlooks that the specialization within the same labor, on the one hand, and the differentiation of the labor process in a series of productive operations completely homogeneous in themselves, on the other, are situated on different levels of abstraction. In the first case, individual labor is still a synthesis of different productive procedures; in the second, labor coincides with the realization of a unique productive gesture. In this latter case, the synthesis is situated at the level of the company.

The domination of abstraction over the production process makes labor increasingly mechanical. On this point, Hegel's words create some discomfort. We have to deal here with a regression in the dialectical development. If labor is, in its essence, as Hegel stressed in §189 of the *Philosophy of Right*, a teleological activity, hence purpose, then it is paradoxical to affirm, as Hegel does in this paragraph, that labor, if left free to unfold, leads to mechanization. The teleological goal turns itself into what dialectically precedes, into mechanism. If the "abstraction of production" transforms the teleological goal into mechanism, this means that subjectivity plays no role in the development of the particular purposes and in the use of the means. As Hegel affirms in the Jena lectures on the philosophy of spirit (1803–1804), mechanical labor loses its so-called formal activity, which consists in adjusting his activity to a purpose.[7]

Thus, entire necessity gives shape to every single productive procedure: it adjusts its purposes to the tasks set by the dependence and reciprocity of human beings and prescribes the form of its objective performance. A *Trieb* (drive) remains, as it does in the mechanism, which sets it in motion; but it is a *Trieb*, again like in the mechanism, which is hidden from the subject. As it happens in the mechanism, then, the movement propagates to the objects, yet its complex articulation remains unknown. The automatism of labor process develops, but its moments ignore finalism and direction.

At this point, it can be useful to turn our attention to Hegel's observations on this topic in one of his Jena manuscripts, *System of Ethical Life*. In an obscure language, which is barely understandable, especially for those who are not familiar with the Schellingean terminology that he adopted in the first years of his philosophical apprenticeship, Hegel writes: "The particular, into which the universal is transferred, therefore becomes ideal and the ideality is a partition of it. The entire object in its determinate character is not annihilated altogether, but this labor, applied to the object as an entirety, is partitioned in itself and becomes a single laboring; and this single laboring becomes for this very reason more mechanical, because variety is excluded from it and so it becomes itself something more universal, more foreign to [the living] whole" (*SS*: 297; *SEL*: 117). We find ourselves in a state of affairs in which, although particularity and universality are related to one another, universality does dominate. Yet, referring to particularity, universality causes changes in particularity itself. In Hegel's language, this is expressed through the notion that, once particularity has come into contact with universality, it becomes ideal. What Hegel means is that particularity has assumed a quality that makes it different from what it used to be. In this passage, labor functions as particularity, and its ideality consists in the loss of its original, so to speak, consistency. Confronted with the object as a whole, labor is partitioned, which means that it becomes a single laboring. Yet this single laboring, which is the simplicity of labor we have met before in the *Philosophy of Right*, coincides, for Hegel, with mechanization, because—and this is decisive—*variety* is excluded from it. Thus, Hegel offers a theoretically stimulating interpretation of the necessity that leads the division of labor to become the basis for a system of social organization dominated, first, by the mechanization of human production and, second, by the machine.

This necessary transition from division of labor to machine, which Steuart and Smith had already pointed out, is determined by the inability of simple and individual labor to treat the object with the aim to make it match labor's own purposes without recurring to the help of other workers. It is in this sense that variety is excluded from single and simple labor: the multiplicity of procedures, gestures, and competences that labor has to actualize in order to mould the object and make it functional to the satisfaction of human needs is transferred onto the level of the entire system of social organization: this is one of the conditions for the birth of the machine: "This sort of laboring, thus divided, presupposes at the same time that the remaining needs are provided for in another way, for this way too has to be labored on, i.e., by the labor of other men. But this deadening [characteristic] of mechanical labor directly implies the possibility of cutting oneself off from it altogether; for the labor here is wholly quantitative without variety, and since its subsumption in intelligence is self-cancelling, something absolutely external, a thing, can then be used owing to its self-sameness both in respect of its labor and its movement" (*SS*: 297; *SEL*: 117).

Labor without variety, deprived of the qualities it should have as a teleological figure, and reduced to the performance of a specific operation, is, Hegel says, *ganz quantitativ*, labor in which what matters is only the influence over its quantitative dimension rather than over its qualitative expression. However, the deficit of variety produces deadening, *Abstumpfung*,[8] the dulling of the mental faculties and the rigidity of the body. Mechanical labor can be replaced, now, without interruption, by the machines themselves. Because quantity—Hegel here argues—cannot structurally contain within itself qualitative variations, it is immediate self-sameness. But immediate self-sameness belongs, in Hegel's philosophy, to the lower strata of being, especially to inorganic objects. Something absolutely external can, therefore, replace human labor. The only difficulty is to find a dead principle of movement, which activates such an absolute external element. Hegel tackles what can carry out this function in a restless natural power, water or wind.

Does this labor without multiplicity relate to the labor done by the *Klasse*, as Hegel calls people working in a society "internally occupied with expanding its population and industry," that is to say in that economic and social condition sketched in §243 of the *Philosophy of Right*, in which the accumulation of wealth firmly occupies the center of civil society, as its secret driving force? I believe this is the case: indeed, in the same paragraph Hegel maintains that the *Klasse*'s labor in a more developed capitalistic condition is "particular." It is particular because, specialized and limited as it is, it cannot link up to the universality represented by that system, the system of the social division of labor, which comprises in itself all partitioned and divided labors. This is what generates the "dependence" and the "distress" of the *Klasse* that is linked to such work, its impossibility to "enjoy the wider freedoms, and particularly the spiritual advantages, of civil society."

Therefore, if the *principium individuationis* of this labor is the obtuse particularity, there is no possibility that it organizes itself in estates and then corporations, which require that their members share not only the same occupation and interests, but also a certain awareness of their own work and place within the social division of labor. Yet, if the *Klasse* cannot escape its fate—it cannot, indeed, for the specialization and limitedness of labor are so extreme as to bring to light the machine—it cannot but degenerate into *Pöbel*, rabble. On the other hand, the link between the establishment of the machine and the production of the rabble is explicitly expressed by Hegel in his lectures.[9]

Because we have touched on the question of nature, we have the occasion here to illustrate the link between the reasons for the rise of abstract and mechanical labor and the specific objective form of such necessity, that is, precisely, the machine. Hegel, like large part of the philosophical tradition,[10] finds the principle of the machine in movement, that is, in the combination of space and time, which constitutes, in short, the first stage of his philosophy of nature, that is, mechanics. Space and time are, as Hegel clearly states in the Jena lectures on the philosophy of spirit (1805–1806), what corresponds to the figure of abstract labor.[11] If we bear in mind the characteristics of abstract labor I have listed before, it will become easier to highlight the reasons that lead to find in the machine its adequate objective correlative. So far, I have pointed out at least three aspects of abstract labor: the analytical differentiation of the overall process of social reproduction in a serial sequence of simple labor procedures; the fact that labor increasingly makes itself homogeneous, surrendering to what Hegel calls *Abstraktion des Producierens*, the abstraction of production; the domination of quantity rather than quality as constitutive principle of labor. Now, space and time, and their combination—that is, movement—reproduce, although at the level of nature, these dimensions of abstract labor. Space and time are for Hegel "self-externality in its complete abstraction" (*EN* §253), the juxtaposition of moments that are different from one another and whose unity is indifferent to them.[12] Certainly, this consideration holds especially with regard to space, because time stresses the subjective and negative dimension of the serial sequence of moments. Yet, it is equally true that time itself cannot do without the monotonous and indefinite flow of instants. Thence a second aspect: space and time consist of moments that are homogeneous with themselves and with the others. Each point and each instant are nothing but the reproduction of the previous ones and there is no internal "depth" that differentiates them from all other moments. Lastly, space and time are the main locus of determination of the category of quantity. It will suffice here to mention that the objects of the sciences of quantity, geometry and arithmetic, are space and time respectively.[13]

As is apparent now, space and time correspond, at the level of nature, to what the machine represents within social relations.[14] And it is for this reason, too, that the emergence of abstract labor demands the concurrent emergence of the machine.

It is necessary, at this stage of our theoretical discourse, to pay attention to a question of remarkable importance, even within this issue of the relationship between abstract labor and natural powers. That is to say: one cannot neglect that the emergence of the machine demands the formation of a new figure of subjectivity. This has nothing to do, at least directly, with the *Abstumpfung* of labor, with the deadening ensuing from the domination of mechanical labor and the machine. Rather, this has to do with the structure of subjectivity as needed to "sustain" mechanical labor, given that subjectivity proper realizes itself within the full unfolding of the teleological position. It is necessary, in other words, to know what sort of destiny hangs over a subjectivity that no longer has the possibility, included in the medium of the teleological syllogism of labor, to *translate* its purpose into objectivity, and can only formally posit the purposes.

With regard to this, we can find some indications in the Jena lectures on the philosophy of spirit (1805–1806). Hegel begins describing the relation the I establishes with itself as inorganic nature, that is to say, as subject of needs:

> The things serving to satisfy those needs are worked up (*verarbe-itet*), their universal inner possibility posited [expressed] as outer possibility, as form. This processing (*Verarbeiten*) of things is itself many-sided, however; it is consciousness making itself into a thing. But in the element of universality, it is such that it becomes an

abstract labor. The needs are many. The incorporation of their multiplicity in the I, i.e., labor, is an abstraction of universal models (*Bilder*), yet [it is] a self-propelling process of formation (*Bilden*). The I, which is for-itself, is an abstract I; but it does labor, hence its labor is abstract as well. The need in general is analyzed into its many aspects—what is abstract in its movement is the being-for-itself, activity, labor. (*JR1*: 225; *HHS*: 120–121)

Thus, to abstract labor corresponds an abstract I, capable only of containing an indefinite multiplication of elements freed from the analytical differentiation of the needs. What we have now is not a subjectivity committed to reunify the *disjecta membra* produced by the analysis of the needs, but a subjectivity, which is like a neutral box of elements with no reciprocal bond among them. It is a subjectivity, Hegel himself concludes in this passage, that has transformed itself into thinghood, losing its own character. In the *Philosophy of Right*, and especially, I think, in §7, Hegel is even more explicit in outlining the fundamental traits of what is subject, of what turns an individual into a subject. Hegel is following here a somewhat Kantian trajectory: for Kant, "subject" means to be self-conscious while being at the same time aware of one's own interior and exterior determinacies; it means, in other words, the impossibility to know the (exterior and interior) determinacies of the objective world, without a center that accomplishes such knowledge experiences and is a unitary reference point. In the same way, for Hegel the individual is a subject any time it brings the particularity, all particularities, to a unitary horizon, the horizon of universality.[15] But in order to do so and to be a proper subject, the individual must break up with anything that appears in the forms of unrelated multiplicity, of determinacies to which he can only be indifferent. Subjectivity is such only when it poses itself in the determinacies, and poses them in itself. This is the reason why it necessarily becomes degraded when it poses itself as a neutral container of determinacies.

But if subjectivity transforms itself into a neutral box of elements indifferent to one another, it turns itself into something that reproduces the mechanics: space, time and their combination, movement. Subjectivity is, therefore, structured according to the mode of quantity. This happens because, as Hegel states in the *Logic*, subjectivity contains quantity within itself: "more graphic examples of pure quantity can be drawn from space and time, also from matter in general, from light, and so forth, even from the 'I'" (*WL*: 178; *SL*: 156); and he soon adds: "the determination of pure quantity extends to the 'I' as well, for the 'I' is an absolute becoming-other, an infinite distancing or all-around repulsion that makes for the negative freedom of the being which, however, remains absolutely simple continuity—the continuity of universality, of self-abiding-being interrupted by manifold limits, by the content of sensations, of intuitions, and so forth" (*WL*: 179; *SL*: 156–157). We said before that Hegelian subjectivity is such insofar as it is self-determination, that is the ability to universalize the particular determinacies, which cannot therefore be assumed in their unrelated multiplicity. Hence, subjectivity as such cannot be quantity. Nonetheless, it is necessary for subjectivity to include in itself quantity, as we know from the *Logic*. If it were not, modern subjectivity would not contain what Hegel terms "indeterminacy" in §5 of the *Philosophy of Right*, that is the "absolute possibility of abstracting from every determination in which I find in myself." This "possibility of abstracting from every determination" is what Hegel in the same paragraph calls "negative freedom," the basis of the modern individual's juridical and civil freedom. This means, at least in this regard, that the generalization of abstract labor is not only cause of the subjection to social necessity, but even of the emergence of those characteristics of subjectivity that render it more able to participate freely in the social life.

Now the problem caused by the emergence of mechanical labor and the machine is that the I reduces itself to mere quantity; it cannot gain more mature and richer determinations, and in case it already has these determinations it has to give them up. But if the abstract I is thinghood, we cannot but notice a strong naturalization of the I.

This conclusion is somehow surprising. For Hegel, too, is persuaded that the transition from the tool to the machine is nothing but an intensification of that estrangement from nature, which is immanent to the teleological syllogism of labor process itself. Hegel vividly expresses this conviction in the Jena lectures on the philosophy of spirit (1805–1806): if it is true that thanks to the tool, between "myself and the external [world of] thinghood, I have inserted my cunning—in order to spare myself, to hide my determinacy and allow it to be made use of," it is equally true that "what I spare myself is merely quantitative; I still get calluses. My being made a thing is yet a necessary element—[since] the drive's own activity is not yet in the thing." The subject is still prey to reification when it uses the tool. Only when "the tool's activity" is "placed in the tool itself," Hegel continues, can the subject avoid reification, the "consumption" of his body (*JR1*: 206; *HHS*: 103). It is the machine, therefore, that radicalizes the estrangement from nature, the denaturalization of the worker. Nonetheless, the consequences are weighty and result in the quantitative transformation of the constitution of subjectivity.

Moreover, the naturalization of the I, which culminates in the emergence of mechanical labor and the machine, can be also investigated from another point of view: the more mediating terms exist between human being and nature in its infinite variety, the more human being's relation to nature becomes "not living" and mechanical. Thus, the naturalization of the I does not concern only the structure that the I has gained through mechanical labor and machine, but it also invests the character of its relation to nature's alterity. Nature, in the totality of its manifestations, is no longer grasped by the subject, because mechanical labor and the machine analyze the concrete world and dissect it into its many abstract aspects.[16] On the other hand, if the I's relation to nature's alterity becomes increasingly external, the consequences will be remarkable even for the I itself.[17] Moving from these considerations, the problem of the "revenge" (*JR*: 321; *SEL*: 247) of nature over labor teleology and its development becomes even more acute. The degradation of labor due to its separation from nature translates, as the machine appears, into the transformation of the constitution of subjectivity, into its stiffening according to quantitative and mechanical modes, which should actually belong to a lower stage of its definition. Hegel thinks therefore that the development of abstract labor, from mechanical labor to the machine, might fatally debase the subjectivity's content and form. On the other hand, especially in Heidelberg and Berlin, he does not abandon the hope that man's enslaving machine could turn into the possibility of a freer and more dignified life. Both in the 1817–1818 and in the 1822–1823 lectures,[18] he insists, as a matter of fact, that machines provide an occasion for man to be occupied in higher activities than those carried out through mechanical labor. This is, however, just a wish, because the economical conditions of his times, especially in England, showed him rather that machines were not used according to "humanistic" considerations. This results in a tension, which is difficult to solve, between the hope in a new evolutionary leap in the form of human activities and the capitalistic economic-productive relations' resistance to make use of the emancipative potentialities offered by the machine.

This conception of abstract labor keeps Hegel far from an objectivistic and positivistic conception of the machine. Whereas the latter considers the machine as a tool, as a mere facilitator in the relation between subjectivity and objectivity, ignoring the countereffects of the machine on the subjectivity, Hegel focuses precisely on the consequences for subjectivity resulting from the introduction of the machine into the labor process. This is not, therefore, a "neutral" conception of the machine. And it is for this very reason that Hegel stays away from a promethean vision of the relation between subjectivity and the labor process dominated by the machine—a vision characterizing those conceptions that reduce the machine to the tool. By mistaking the machine for the tool, one promotes the idea that man's control over the production process is something that can be achieved without much difficulty.

Hegel's complex and profound reflection on the link between abstract labor and the machine forces us to revise, I believe, a perspective—widely disseminated in many twentieth-century philosophical currents—according to which Hegel would simply nullify the relation with the alterity of nature in the constitution of spirit. It was a conviction held, for example, by Adorno, who—while appreciating the homology between the notions of spirit and of "social labor"—objects to the negation of nature implied in the Hegelian concept of spirit; nature, Adorno argues, continues to play a fundamental role in the labor process.[19] But, as I have tried to show, Hegel's idea of modern capitalism's abstract labor does not imply a negation of nature: if, on the one hand, the spirit is, in virtue of the tool's mediation, excluded from nature's variety, on the other, it becomes itself nature, something immersed in inorganic thinghood, owing to the emergence of the machine. The unfolding of more mature forms of capitalistic development led Hegel to further elaborate on his vision of the relationship between spirit and nature: spirit appears as such—that is, as the overcoming of nature—only by becoming nature itself, by acquiring *some* of the being's forms of organization that belong specifically to nature or, to put it in a more Hegelian way, to "first" nature. Yet for Hegel spirit can incorporate nature only as "second nature," as objectivity penetrated by reason and freedom. It is precisely this that abstract labor does not ensure: its naturalization seems not susceptible to being "recaptured" by spirit. From a Hegelian perspective, therein lies the problem.

Notes

1. See Ferguson 1773, 272–273; Smith 1963, vol. II: 7–8. In these pages of the *Wealth of Nations* we can also find the famous example of the jump in the production of pins associated with the growth of the division of labor. Hegel refers to it from Jena on, and especially in his mature lectures on philosophy of right. Curiously enough, Hegel quotes from Smith always incorrectly, with the exception of the 1817–1818 lectures. For the Jena period, see *JR*: 323; *SEL*: 248 and *JRI*: 224; *IIIS*: 121. For the Heidelberg and Berlin periods see *Rph Ilting 1817–1818*: 118 translated in *LNRPS*: 176; *Rph Ilting 1818–1819*: 314; *Rph Henrich 1819–1820*: 159; *Rph Ilting 1822–1823*: 609; *Rph Ilting 1824–1825*: 502. On this issue in general see Waszek 1988: 131–132.

2. At this stage, Hegel does not deal with the "perverse" effects of the simplification of labor yet. Neither does he touch on the greater or smaller "intelligence" of simple labor compared to complex one. Similar to Adam Smith, Hegel deals with this latter topic later in the text.

3. It appears in French, not in English, in the *Nachschrift*. It is a Smithian idea that the refinement of needs does not only lead to the production of new

goods, but also to the improvement of existing ones (see Smith 1978, vol. V: 487).

4. *Rph Ilting 1822–1823*: 593. It is the lust for money of *Fabrikanten* and businessmen, Hegel says here, that stimulates the *Erfindung*, the invention, of new needs. This invention has, along with the usual "educational" benefits that derive from any process of multiplication and differentiation of needs, a counterpart: each comfort has, in a process *ad infinitum*, its discomfort. It is again Smith who saw in the *opulence*, that is in the affluent consumption and in the differentiation of the needs, one of the most important impulses behind economic growth (Smith 1978, vol. V: 487 and ff.).

5. *Rph* §198 *GW*, XIV, 169.

6. Marx 1976, 471.

7. *JR*, 321; *SEL*, 247.

8. From what has been said so far, it is evident that Hegel first reflects on the *Abstumpfung* of mechanical labor without referring to any moral conceptions. What first interests him is the analysis of the mechanism that leads from instrumental labor to the machine. Reading these passages, however, it becomes possible to question some interpreters' assessment that Hegel's vision of the productive specialization is much more idyllic than Fichte's (see Jermann 1987, 170).

9. Cf. *Rph Henrich 1819–1820*, 193.

10. In his description of mechanics, Hegel refers to the Cartesian tradition, although he considers it not entirely satisfactory (see *EN* §251 Addition). He also had in mind the materialistic continuation of the Cartesian mechanism in the French philosophy of the eighteenth century, as his *Lectures on the History of Philosophy* prove (see *LHP*, 508–509; *VGP*, 393).

11. *JR1*, 225; *HHS*, 121.

12. *EN* §254.

13. *EN* §259 Remark.

14. Connecting the structure of labor with the Hegelian concept, A. Kojève especially insisted—drawing on some Heideggerian ideas—on the temporalizing nature of labor. The premise of his reasoning is that the Hegelian concept, on which labor relies, is time. According to Kojève, in Kant time is a schema and a passive intuition, whereas in Hegel it is action and movement. Therefore, concept in Kant is a notion that allows man to conform to reality; in Hegel, on the contrary, concept is a project that allows man to transform reality in order to make it conform to the project itself. Thus, there is no concept as long as there is no labor. If on the earth animals were the only living creatures, Kojève continues, Aristotle would be right: concept would be embodied in the eternal species, eternally identical to itself. But, for the separation between concept and object to be possible, one has to presuppose labor. On the other hand, for this to be thinkable, being has to be temporal. The natural object does not manifest temporality; only the object of labor does. It is labor, thus, which temporalizes the natural world and makes *Begriff* possible (see Kojève 1980, 141–142). Even if one can agree with Kojève on the connection between concept, time, and labor, the general horizon within which he inscribes his theoretical-interpretive discourse is less convincing. What really matters for Hegel is not to underscore the characteristics of labor as

a general human activity, but to reveal them as form determinations within the concrete development of the labor process throughout history. In other words: the transition from the tool to the machine indicates the capitalistic form determinations within the teleological syllogism of labor process itself. The latter deserves attention only in so far as it is embodied in history.

15. Pinkard 2002, 30.

16. Despite what some interpreters hold (see Fornaro 1978, 84), Hegel does not express any nostalgia, neither in the Jena period nor in the Berlin period, for an organic reconciliation with that nature from which mechanical labor and the machine have cut off the individual.

17. *JR*, 321; *SEL*, 247.

18. See *Rph Ilting 1817–1818*, 118; *LNRPS*: 177 and *Rph Ilting 1822–1823*, 613.

19. Adorno 1994, 20.

Works Cited

Abbreviations for Works by G.W.F. Hegel

EN   *Enzyklopädie der philosophischen Wissenschaften im Grundrisse* (1830). English translation: *Hegel's Philosophy of Nature*. Translated by M. J. Petry. New York: Humanities Press, 1970. Cited by paragraph number.

GW   *Gesammelte Werke*. Edited by the Rheinisch-Westfälischen Akademie der Wissenschaften, Hamburg 1968 ss.: Felix Meiner.

HHS   *Hegel and Human Spirit. A Translation of the Jena Lectures on the Philosophy of Spirit (1805–6)*. Translated by L. Rauch. Detroit: Wayne State University Press, 1983. Cited by page number.

JA   *Sämtliche Werke. Jubiläumsausgabe in zwanzig Bänden*. Edited by H. Glockner. Stuttgart: Frommann, 1927.

JR   *Jenaer Systementwürfe*, in *GW*, VI. Cited by page number.

JR1   *Jenaer Systementwürfe 1*, in *GW*, VIII. Cited by page number.

LHP   *Lectures of the History of Philosophy*. Vol. III. Translated by E. S. Haldane. Lincoln: University of Nebraska Press, 1995. Cited by page number.

LNRPS   *Lectures on Natural Right and Political Science. The First Philosophy of Right* (Heidelberg 1817–1818 with additions from the Lectures of 1818–1819). Translated by J. M. Stewart and P. C. Hodgson. Berkeley, Los Angeles, London: University of California Press, 1995.

Rph   *Grundlinien der Philosophie des Rechts* (1821). In *GW*, XIV. English translation: *Elements of the Philosophy of Right*. Translated by H. B. Nisbet, edited by A. Wood. Cambridge: Cambridge University Press, 1991. Cited by paragraph number.

Rph Henrich   *Philosophie des Rechts. Die Vorlesung von 1819/1820.* Edited by D.
1819–1820   Henrich. Frankfurt a. M.: Suhrkamp, 1983. Cited by page number.

Rph Ilting   *Die Philosophie des Rechts. Die Mitschriften Wannenmann (Heidelberg
1817–1818*   *1817–18) und Homeyer (1818–19).* Edited by K.-H. Ilting. Stuttgart:
         Klett-Cotta, 1983. Band I, pp. 229–351, cited as *Rph Ilting 1818–1819*;
         Band III cited as *Rph Ilting 1822–1823*; Band IV cited as *Rph Ilting
         1824–1825*. Cited by page number.

SEL   *System of Ethical Life and First Philosophy of Spirit.* Translated by H. S.
         Harris. Albany: State University of New York Press, 1979. Cited by
         page number.

SL   *The Science of Logic.* Edited by George di Giovanni. Cambridge: Cam-
         bridge University Press, 2010. Cited by page number.

SS   *System der Sittlichkeit*, in *GW*, V, pp. 279–361. Cited by page number.

VGP   *Vorlesungen über die Geschichte der Philosophie*, in *JA*, XIX. Cited by page
         number.

WL   *Wissenschaft der Logik*, in *GW*, XI, pp. 237–409, XII, XXI. Cited by
         page number.

Adorno, T. W. 1994. *Hegel: Three Studies*. Translated by S. Weber Nicholsen. Cam-
    bridge, MA: MIT Press.
Ferguson, A. 1773. *An Essay on the History of Civil Society*. London-Edinburgh: A.
    Millar-T. Caddel.
Fornaro, M. 1978. *Il lavoro negli scritti jenesi di Hegel*. Milan: Vita e Pensiero.
Jermann, C. 1987. "Die Familie, Die bürgerliche Gesellschaft." In *Anspruch und
    Leistung von Hegels Rechtsphilosophie*, edited by C. Jermann, 145–182. Stuttgart-
    Bad Cannstatt: Frommann-Holzboog.
Kojève, A. 1980. *Introduction to the Reading of Hegel: Lectures on the Phenomenology of
    Spirit*. Ithaca: Cornell University Press.
Marx, K. 1976. *Capital: Volume 1*. Translated by Ben Fowkes. Harmondsworth:
    Penguin.
Pinkard, T. 2002. *German Philosophy. 1760–1860. The Legacy of Idealism*. Cambridge:
    Cambridge University Press.
Smith, A. 1963. *The Works. In five volumes*. Reprint of the edition 1811–1812. Aalen:
    Otto Zeller.
———. 1963. *An Inquiry into the Nature and Causes of the Wealth of Nations*. In *The
    Works*, I–IV. Cambridge: Cambridge University Press.
———. 1978. *Lectures on Jurisprudence*. In *The Glasgow Edition of the Works and Cor-
    respondence of Adam Smith*, vol. V, edited by R. L. Meek, D. D. Raphael, and
    P. G. Stein. Oxford: Clarendon Press.
Waszek, N. 1988. *The Scottish Enlightenment and Hegel's Account of "Civil Society."* Dor-
    drecht: Kluwer.

6

Hegel's Torment

Poverty and the Rationality of the Modern State

C. J. PEREIRA DI SALVO

In his discussion of civil society in the *Elements of the Philosophy of Right,*[1] Hegel declares that the "important question of how poverty can be remedied is one which agitates and torments modern societies especially" (§244A). After considering and dismissing various proposed solutions, he concludes that "despite an *excess of wealth*, civil society is *not wealthy enough*— i.e. its own distinct resources are not sufficient—to prevent an excess of poverty and the formation of a rabble" (§245).

Some have taken these candid remarks as an admission of failure.[2] They claim that, by Hegel's own lights, poverty constitutes an insurmountable obstacle to the speculative proof that the modern state is rational, or, as he puts it, that it is the "actuality of concrete freedom" (§260). This challenge has not gone unanswered,[3] and it has spawned a lively debate on the significance of the problem of poverty for Hegel's project.

It would be impossible to examine here the manifold arguments that have been advanced in the literature on Hegel and poverty, both by Hegel's critics and by his defenders. My aim in this chapter is much more modest. I focus on Hegel's answers to the following two questions: (1) What is poverty? (2) Why is it a problem *for individual members of the modern state?*

I defend the thesis that Hegel's answers to these questions follow systematically from his account of the relationship between personality and property in the "Abstract Right" division of the *Philosophy of Right.*

If my thesis holds water, then it readily suggests a method for investigating the significance of the problem of poverty for Hegel's project. Specifically, my suggestion is that, if we can get clear on Hegel's answers to (1) and (2), we will be in a better position to understand (or, when deemed necessary, to reconstruct) his answers to two further questions that arise downstream, in the "Civil Society" section of the *Philosophy of Right*: (3) What kind of problem does poverty pose *for the modern state*? (4) Does poverty have a solution that is consistent with the principles of that state?

The debate between Hegel's critics and his defenders turns on this second set of questions. Critics maintain both that the problem of poverty impugns Hegel's claim that the modern state is rational, and that none of the proposed solutions Hegel considers is adequate to the task. Defenders fall into either of two camps. Some simply deny that poverty calls the rationality of the modern state into question. Others are prepared to agree with Hegel's critics that poverty *would* call the rationality of the modern state into question were none of the proposed solutions Hegel considers adequate to task; however, they maintain that at least one such solution is in fact adequate.

The chapter is divided into three sections. In the first and second sections, I lay out the accounts of poverty provided by Kant and Hegel respectively. I begin with Kant's account because it allows me to highlight what is distinctive about Hegel's. In particular, I show that, whereas for Kant, poverty is problematic because it constitutes a condition in which a *person* stands in a wrongful relation of dependence to other persons, for Hegel, poverty is problematic for a much more fundamental reason: namely, because it constitutes a condition in which a *human being* is prevented from realizing her capacity for personality in the first place. In the third and concluding section, I argue that Hegel's account of poverty has two important implications for understanding (or reconstructing) Hegel's answers to (3) and (4).

Poverty as Wrongful Dependence on the Choice of Another

My aim in this section is to present Kant's account of poverty. I am interested not only in his answers to questions (1) and (2), but also in his systematic justification for those answers. It is therefore not sufficient to turn to the few instances in the "Public Right" division of the *Metaphysical First Principles of the Doctrine of Right*,[4] in which Kant discusses the problem of poverty. Rather, we have to locate that discussion in the context of

Kant's overall justification for a state. This, in turn, requires that we turn
to his account of external freedom and his justification of property rights
in the "Private Right" division.[5]

Kant's point of departure in the *Doctrine of Right* is a state of nature
characterized by two principles, both of which are contained in the following passage:

> *Freedom* (independence from being constrained by another's
> choice), insofar as it can coexist with the freedom of every other in
> accordance with a universal law, is the only original right belong-
> ing to every man by virtue of his humanity. (6:237)

The main clause in the passage expresses the "principle of innate
freedom" (6:237), on which more in a moment. The subordinate clause
expresses the "universal principle of right," which Kant elsewhere formulates thus: "Any action is *right* if it can coexist with everyone else's freedom
in accordance with a universal law" (6:230).

Kant's formulation of both of these principles relies heavily on technical terminology, so it is important to get clear on some of it before moving
forward. We can gloss *choice* as the capacity to deploy *means* in order to set
and pursue *ends*.[6] *Action* is the exercise of that capacity. Finally, *coercion* is
any interference with the choice of another (see 6:231).

Kant's two principles exhaust the rights to which individuals are entitled in the state of nature. If the universal principle of right delimits the
sphere of ends we may rightfully pursue, the principle of innate freedom
tells us what means we rightfully have at our disposal in the state of nature
in order to do so. In particular, as a human being I have an original right
to "what is *internally* mine" (6:237). Because my right to what is internally
mine requires no positive act for its establishment (6:237), it consists of
nothing but my right to my physical and mental powers—in short, to my
body.[7] Furthermore, because the universal principle of right entitles me to
exercise my choice whenever doing so is consistent with a like exercise of
choice by others, I am entitled to use my powers to prevent others from
wrongfully coercing me. In doing this, I hinder their hindrance of my
freedom, as Kant puts it (6:231).

Rights in the state of nature are not restricted to rights in my body,
but also to whatever things I happen to have in my physical possession. To
use Kant's own example, if I have my hand around an apple, I alone am
entitled to use it in ways that are consistent with right. I may, for instance,
eat it. The reason is that, in order for you to use that apple as a means
to your ends, you would have to violate my external freedom; literally, you
would have to *move* my body (6:247–248). But, by the universal principle

of right, such an action would be wrongful, and thus authorize my use of physical force to frustrate your attempt.

The next step in Kant's argument is generated by a puzzle: May we acquire rights to external objects over and above those that are in our immediate physical possession?[8] Acquisition of external objects, a pedestrian experience to us as members of organized states, is puzzling in the state of nature because it is not obvious that a unilateral action on my part could place you under a duty of right not to use some external object.[9]

Kant has a twofold answer to this puzzle, each part of which is a premise in his argument for the duty to leave the state of nature and enter a state. The first part of his answer is that it *must*[10] be permissible for any external object to belong to someone (6:246). The second part of his answer is that external objects may belong to someone only in a rightful condition—that is, in a state (6:255–256). The first and second parts of Kant's answer entail that all (physically interacting) persons have a duty of right to enter a state.

Both premises of Kant's argument are controversial, especially the first one. Here, I follow Kyla Ebels-Duggan's strategy for reconstructing the argument for the first premise.[11] The universal principle of right has the form of a constraint on the external freedom of each. As Ebels-Duggan puts it, that principle does not assign anyone unlimited freedom, but rather limits each to the freedom that can simultaneously be enjoyed by all. But it does entitle us to the *maximal freedom* that we can have subject to this restriction.[12]

Hence, if we can show, first, that private property is consistent with right, and, second, that it affords *greater* external freedom to each than the state of nature does, then we will have shown the first premise for Kant's argument for the duty to enter a state.

The argument for the first step is complicated, so I merely assume this step here.[13] The argument for the second is more straightforward. In the state of nature, each of us is dependent on the choice of others for the use of any external object in pursuit of a complex end. If I am hungry and want to feed myself, then holding an apple is sufficient to entitle me to its rightful use in my pursuit of that end. But if I want to use the same apple for a more complex end, such as the painting of a still life, then I am dependent on the choice of all others. Anyone may rightfully seize the apple mid-painting, thus frustrating my end.

Matters are quite different if private property is permissible. Having external objects as my own makes a whole set of complex ends available to me, in pursuit of which I may not be interfered with—at least not rightfully. It follows that private property in external objects decreases my dependence on the choice of others, and thus affords me greater external freedom than the state of nature does. Therefore, the universal principle of right *demands* the establishment of a system of private property.

So much for the first premise of Kant's argument for the duty to enter a state. The second premise is also controversial, but the line of reasoning is easy to follow. Kant's claim is that no individual in the state of nature can rightfully acquire *conclusive* property rights in an external object (6:256–257). There are three reasons why this is so, but I only focus on what seems like the central reason. The central reason is that no *unilateral* act on my part could entitle me to use coercion to prevent others from using an external object. For, as Kant argues,

> a unilateral will cannot serve as a coercive law for everyone with regard to possession that is external and therefore contingent, since that would infringe upon freedom in accordance with universal laws. (6:256)

Kant's point is simple. In the state of nature, my use of coercion to prevent others from using some object to which I lay claim is indistinguishable, from the standpoint of right, from my attempt to constrain the physical possession of another. Indeed, so long as we are in the state of nature, it is the other person who is entitled to use coercion to prevent *me* from regaining physical possession of some object to which I lay claim.

The inability of a unilateral will to establish conclusive property rights is what Ebels-Duggan calls the *problem of unilateralism*.[14] Kant's solution to this problem is a "united" or "omnilateral" will—the will embodied in the institutions of the state (6:263). An onmilateral will is one that represents the will of all. Because it does not act unilaterally, it has the authority to bind all those who are subject to its power. In particular, it has the authority to determine the extent of each individual's property rights, to enforce those rights, and to adjudicate among conflicting rights claims (6:312). The suggestion, which I do not pursue here, is that only people acting in accordance with law (or within the authority proper to their office) could embody such a will.[15]

Now that we have seen the rough outline of Kant's argument for the duty to enter a state, we are in a position to inquire into his account of poverty. We have to begin by distinguishing poverty from physical deprivation—for example, from starvation. That someone is starving does not suffice to make her poor. An individual can fast voluntarily, or a castaway can starve on a sandbank at sea, but in neither case would we say that the individual in question is poor. These examples point to the fact that poverty is a relation between individuals. In particular, poverty—like property—is a relation between individuals with regard to external objects. For

Kant, a person is impoverished when she lacks the means to satisfy her "most necessary natural needs" (6:326) *and* when those means are the property of another.

The far more interesting question is why, according to Kant, an individual's poverty is problematic. A common intuition is that poverty is problematic because it consists in the extreme frustration of an individual's well-being. But, for Kant, the well-being of individuals is irrelevant from the standpoint of right.[16] All that matters here is the *external* form of their relations (6:230)—in particular, what matters is that they enjoy independence from the choice of others under universal law.

To begin to see why poverty counts as problematic for Kant, we have to realize that poverty is made possible by the establishment of conclusive property rights in a state. If all external objects (in particular, all land) may be rightfully owned, then it is possible that some individuals, through no fault of their own (or because of imprudent choices), might become propertyless.[17] But now consider the predicament of any such individual. She is in an even worse position in terms of external freedom than the denizen of the state of nature. The latter is certainly dependent on the choice of others for her pursuit of any complex ends, but at the very least she may not be prevented from pursuing simple ends such as nutrition. If there is some apple tree in her vicinity, she may help herself to its fruit, so long as no one else physically obstructs her access to it. By comparison, the poor person in a system of conclusive property rights may only gaze at my apple trees from afar, and I can rightfully call on the state to use coercion to prevent her from helping herself to my apples.

In short, the poor person is, as Arthur Ripstein puts it, "entirely dependent upon the generosity of others."[18] But no condition that made such dependence possible could be rightful. The possibility of poverty arising from a system of conclusive property rights shows that Kant's argument for the duty to enter the state is subject to a nontrivial constraint. Not just *any* system of private property will guarantee each person a degree of external freedom greater than she would have enjoyed in the state of nature; rather, only a system of private property that guarantees each person rightful title to a minimum of property does so. It follows that the authority to guarantee this minimum is not a separate power that the state enjoys by virtue of the fact that it must embody the united will of all;[19] it is rather part and parcel of any system of private property rights capable of generating the duty to enter a state in the first place.

It remains only to say a word about Kant's proposed solution to the problem of poverty. Kant suggests that the state must tax the wealthy in order to provide for the poor, and that this provision must be in the form of direct transfers (6:326, 367). Both of these suggestions flow immediately from Kant's account of the problem of individual poverty. First, if the state must guarantee a certain minimum of property in a context in which all assets are privately owned, it can do so only by redistributing assets from those who own more than the minimum (the wealthy) to those who own less than it (the poor). Second, Kant suggests that a policy of direct transfers by the state is the solution most consistent with the universal principle of right. According to him, poor houses and foundations "severely limit" the external freedom of the poor (6:367), presumably by setting conditions on the receipt and use of benefits.

Poverty as Socially Frustrated Personality

Hegel's account in the *Philosophy of Right* begins from the concept of the free will, and aims to show how this concept becomes "Idea"—in other words, how it realizes itself in the world (§§1, 4). In the process of advancing toward full realization, the free will takes various shapes. One of the earliest of these shapes is *personality*, which is the subject of the first major division of the work, "Abstract Right."[20]

It is true that Hegel's most extensive discussion of poverty does not take place until a much later stage in the unfolding of the concept of the free will in civil society. Nevertheless, I claim that his account of the relationship between personality and property in "Abstract Right" explains the distinctiveness of his account of what poverty is and why it is a problem for individual members of the modern state.

I begin, then, by looking at abstract right. For Hegel, the fundamental principle of abstract right is "*be a person and respect others as persons*" (§36). This principle contains two demands. On the one hand, the second demand, "respect others as persons," is very much in line with Kant's discussion in the "Private Right" division of the *Doctrine of Right*. Abstract right consists of a series of permissions (strict rights) and correlative obligations (duties of right) that govern persons' behavior toward one another as owners of property (§§38 and 40). On the other hand, the first demand, "be a person," represents a radical departure from Kant. Unlike Kant, Hegel does not think that human beings get personality for free, merely by virtue of their humanity (§35R and A, and §57R and A). It follows that Hegel must reject Kant's principle of innate freedom, even if his principle of respect for persons embodies some of the elements of Kant's universal principle of right.

Because Hegel does not think that we get personality for free, he is faced with the task of specifying the conditions under which a human being realizes her personality.[21] In order to become a person, Hegel argues, a human being must *at a minimum* take possession of her body and acquire property in external things. For him, only a human being who meets both of these conditions realizes her personality, and is thereby entitled to respect by other persons.[22] Let us consider each of these requirements in turn, beginning with the second.

The concept of personality is closely connected to the concept of an arbitrary will (see §15). "Personality," Hegel says,

> begins only at that point where the subject has not merely a consciousness of itself in general as concrete and in some way determined, but a consciousness of itself as a completely abstract "I" in which all concrete limitation and validity are negated and invalidated. (§35R)

The most important moment in such a will is the moment of abstract subjectivity. Such a will withdraws from the various drives and needs of its internal nature and regards them with indifference. It can choose to pursue some drive, but it can as well choose to pursue another.

Hegel's claim that an individual can realize her personality only if she acquires property in external things just is the claim that the free will can give itself existence only by reference to an external "sphere of freedom" (§41)—a collection of external objects over which it alone has power. Since, for Hegel, external objects are soulless and the will can therefore impose its own ends upon them (§44R), a human being who owns property thereby embodies her will in her possessions (§45). She does this by coming into a concrete relationship with external things that mirrors the relationship that her will has to the different determinations of her internal nature.[23] So, for instance, if she owns an apple, she may decide to paint a still life, or she may decide to eat it, but she is under no external compulsion to put it to any particular use. Hence, in her relationship to the apple, she has a concrete experience of herself as a free will—that is, as independent of both internal and external nature, even if ultimately determined in particular ways.

The first requirement of personality is a bit more elusive than the second. When Hegel rejects Kant's claim that we have personality merely by virtue of our humanity, he rejects in particular the claim that we have an exclusive right in our bodies by mere accident of birth. As "a person," Hegel claims, "I . . . possess my life and body, like other things, *only in so far as I will it*" (§47). Nevertheless, the *capacity* to become a person is something each of us has innately and must realize:

> The human being, in his immediate existence in himself, is a natural entity, external to his concept; it is only through the *devel-*

opment of his own body and spirit, *essentially* by means of *his self-consciousness comprehending itself as free,* that he takes possession of himself and becomes his own property as distinct from that of others. Or to put it the other way around, this taking possession of oneself consists also in translating into *actuality* what one is in terms of one's concept. (§57)

The process of taking possession of one's body and spirit is the subject matter of Hegel's famous dialectic of mastery and servitude in his *Phenomenology of Spirit.*[24] This is no place to venture into that thicket, so I only suggest that Hegel considers labor in the service of another's need a necessary moment of that dialectic.[25] My suggestion, in other words, is that for Hegel the discipline and education to which a human being must subject herself in labor is a necessary condition of taking possession of her body.[26]

With this brief and admittedly cursory look at Hegel's account of the relationship between personality and property behind us, we can now turn to his discussion of poverty in the "Civil Society" section of the *Philosophy of Right.* Civil society is the sphere in which abstract right finds its realization. Hegel characterizes this sphere by means of two principles: "The *concrete person,* who, as a *particular* person, as a totality of needs and a mixture of natural necessity and arbitrariness, is his own end, is *one principle* of civil society" (§182, first emphasis added). The second principle of civil society is the "all-round interdependence" of each upon the activity—and, in particular, upon the needs and labor—of others (§183).

The second principle of civil society implies the possibility that Kant considers with regard to poverty. Once property rights are made conclusive in the state, it is possible for all external objects—and, in particular, for all land—to be privately owned. If such a condition is realized, further property acquisition can be rightful only if it takes place through contract (see §217A). If, in conjunction with this, there is a proliferation of needs and an attendant refinement of the division of labor, then a member of civil society has to satisfy her needs either through her own property, or through labor in service of the needs of others (§189). Hegel defines poverty as a condition in which individuals can do neither. "Impoverished is he," he states in his lectures of 1817–1818, "who possesses neither capital nor skill."[27] This same thought is echoed in the *Philosophy of Right* when Hegel describes the poor as those from whom society has taken "the natural means of acquisition" (§241). Thus, while Hegel agrees with Kant that poverty entails deprivation of that minimum of property sufficient to afford the "necessary" standard of living of a society (§244), he adds a further condition to the Kantian account: poverty entails an inability to acquire such property through labor.

While Hegel partially agrees with Kant about what poverty is, he disagrees with him about the nature of the problem poverty poses for the individual:

> The poor man feels excluded and mocked by everyone, and this necessarily give rise to an inner indignation. *He is conscious of himself as an infinite, free being, and thus arises the demand that his external existence should correspond to this consciousness.* . . . Self-consciousness appears driven to the point where it no longer has any rights, where *freedom has no existence.* In this position, where the existence of freedom becomes something wholly contingent, inner indignation is necessary. (n. 1 to §244, emphasis added)

For Hegel, what is problematic is not just that the impoverished individual is dependent on the arbitrary wills of the wealthy. Rather, poverty is problematic because those who are subject to that condition are rendered *incapable of realizing their personality.* It is what we might call a condition of *socially frustrated personality.*

Hegel's account of poverty as socially frustrated personality follows directly from his account of the conditions of possibility of that shape of the free will. First, we saw that the impoverished individual is deprived of a necessary minimum of property. It follows for Hegel that she lacks the sphere of freedom that is necessary for reflecting and thereby giving existence to the free will. Second, the impoverished individual is also deprived of the opportunity to work for a living by the very dynamic of civil society, in particular by the simplification of labor and the eventual replacement of the worker by machines (§§198, 243). As a consequence, she is rendered incapable of taking possession of her body.

A striking upshot of Hegel's account of poverty is that, according to it, the poor in modern society find themselves in a condition not unlike what he calls "savagery" or "barbarism." They are reduced to their most immediate needs, which they, unable to labor, must satisfy immediately (say, by consuming what they manage to obtain through begging). This is comparable to savagery, as he conceives of it:

> a condition in which natural needs as such were immediately satisfied would merely be one in which spirituality was immersed in nature, and hence a condition of savagery and unfreedom. . . . (§194R)

Furthermore, on Hegel's account the poor individual is like a "barbarian" in that she fails to experience what he calls "the moment of liberation which is present in work" (§194R), and which distinguishes the barbarian from the "educated man" (§197 and R).

We can see, then, that Hegel's account of the relationship between personality and property grounds a damning account of what he calls the "evil" of poverty (§245). On the Kantian account, poverty is problematic for the individual member of the modern state because it places her in a wrongful relation of dependence on the choice of other persons. But Hegel's poor cannot even stand on their rights as persons, because poverty consists in their inability to realize their personality in the first place.

Poverty and the Rationality of the Modern State

In the previous section I argued that Hegel's answers to the first set of questions (What is poverty? Why is it a problem for individual members of the modern state?), follow systematically from his account of the relationship between personality and property in "Abstract Right." For Hegel, the poor individual is like a savage among (civilized) persons, whose condition prevents her from raising herself to their level of freedom. In this section, I flesh out some implications that my thesis has for understanding (or reconstructing) Hegel's answers to the more pressing second set of questions (What kind of problem does poverty pose for the modern state? Does it have a solution consistent with the principles of that state?).

The first implication concerns Hegel's discussion of proposed policy solutions. Hegel's account of poverty constrains the set of policies that can count as adequate solutions to that problem. If poverty is socially frustrated personality, then any acceptable remedial policy must *at the very least* make it possible for the poor to realize their personality. Call this the *personality constraint*. This constraint entails that any acceptable policy must make it possible for the poor to express their will in a sphere of external objects under their control, and to take possession of their body. This, in turn, entails that the poor must be enabled to acquire a minimum of property, and to do so through their own labor.

The personality constraint not only flows from Hegel's account of poverty, but also seems to guide his own assessment of proposed policies. This is clearest in his brief discussion of Kant's preferred policy: taxation of the rich to support direct transfers to the poor. Hegel claims that such a policy runs afoul of "the principle of civil society and the feeling of self-sufficiency and honor among its members" (§245).

Because Hegel highlights that transfers serve to maintain the poor "without the mediation of work," he is sometimes understood as appealing to the *second* principle of civil society in the foregoing passage.[28] He is thus represented as primarily concerned with the integration of particularity into the (limited) universality of the market. But his invocation of the feeling of self-sufficiency and honor harkens back to something even more fundamental: concrete personality, or the *first* principle of civil society. According to that principle, the individual who does not labor, who does not submit herself to the discipline involved in regulating her productive activity in the service of another's need, does not come into possession of her body. As a consequence, she does not realize her personality, even if whatever means she needs to meet her basic needs are made available to her for her immediate consumption.

The personality constraint also explains why, oddly, Hegel seems to consider transfers in the context of membership in a corporation as an adequate remedial policy. A corporation is analogous to a trade group. It is a voluntary association based on a certain branch of the social division of labor, which unifies the particular interests of its members and raises them to the status of a more general interest (§254). "Within the corporation," Hegel says, "the help which poverty receives loses its contingent and unjustly humiliating character" (§253R). Hegel's reason for thinking this is that the corporation replaces the need for concrete individuals to realize their personality through labor with the recognition of their skills and training in meeting certain membership standards (§253). The suggestion seems to be that transfers to the poor in this context do not run afoul of the personality constraint because, though not mediated by particular acts of labor, they are mediated by the recognition of the individual as a *laborer.*

Because my aim here is not to assess whether Hegel ultimately identifies an adequate solution to the problem of poverty, I will not comment on whether his suggestion that corporations provide such a solution is warranted.[29] Rather, what I have tried to show by considering his discussion of two policy proposals is that he is committed to evaluating them on the basis of a criterion that is ultimately based on his account of the relationship between personality and property in "Abstract Right."

I want to end by considering a second implication of my thesis, this time with respect to the far thornier question: What kind of problem does poverty pose for the modern state? Whether poverty calls the rationality of the modern state into question, and thus signals the failure of Hegel's project, seems to depend on at least two considerations. The first is the status of Hegel's claim—expressed in his lectures of 1819–1820, and implicit in this discussion in the *Philosophy of Right*—that "[t]he emergence of poverty is in general a consequence of civil society, and on the whole it arises *necessarily* out of it" (n. 1 to §244, emphasis added). Those who agree with Hegel's assessment of the relationship between civil society and poverty generally think that the latter constitutes a major, perhaps insurmountable, problem for Hegel's project of demonstrating the rationality of the modern state.[30] Those who aim to defend the ambition of Hegel's project either reject his judgment that poverty arises *necessarily* out of the normal operation of civil society,[31] or deny that poverty *necessarily* has consequences that call the rationality of the modern state into question.[32]

Wherever an interpretation falls with regard to this first consideration, it seems clear that it is subsidiary to a second. The most ambitious aim of Hegel's *Philosophy of Right* is to show that,

> The state is the actuality of concrete freedom. But *concrete freedom* requires that personal individuality and its particular interests should reach their full *development* and gain *recognition of their right* for itself (within the system of the family and civil society), and also that they should, on the one hand, *pass over* of their own accord into the interest of the universal, and on the other, knowingly and willingly acknowledge this universal interest even as their own *substantial spirit*, and *actively pursue* it as their *ultimate end*. (§260)

The paramount question—not only with regard to the present discussion, but also more generally with regard to the *Philosophy of Right*—is what, precisely, the kind of "reconciliation" (§141A) that Hegel envisions in the foregoing passage requires. In particular, the question is: What is required for the reconciliation of "personal individuality," or what he elsewhere calls "principle of subjective freedom" (§185R), with the substantiality of the state?

If my thesis holds water, then Hegel's account of poverty as socially frustrated personality has an important implication with respect to this question. In particular, I think it places the burden of proof on anyone who would deny that in order for the modern state to count as rational, it must guarantee *each* of its members the *possibility* of achieving personality.[33] For how could the modern state guarantee that "personal individuality and its particular interests should reach their *full development* and gain *recognition of their right* for itself" unless it could, at the very least, guarantee its every member the possibility of realizing the most basic shape of the free will?

Naturally, my move here is in part driven by a normative individualist interpretation of the principle of subjective freedom. But I think that there is evidence in Hegel's own argument in the *Philosophy of Right* to support it. For instance, I think that it would be hard to draw as sharp a distinction between the ancient and modern worlds as Hegel wants to draw (see §§124R, 185R, and 258) if it turned out that some of the irrationality of the former lingered on in the latter in the form of *socially* frustrated personality for some. It is not for nothing that Hegel declares that the "important question of how poverty can be remedied is one which agitates and torments *modern societies especially*" (§244A, emphasis added). Poverty would not agitate and torment us unless we saw reflected in it the possibility that the promise of modernity has *not yet* been fulfilled.

Notes

I am grateful to Mark Alznauer, Hannah Kovacs, and the participants of the twenty-second biennial meeting of the Hegel Society of America for their helpful comments on earlier drafts of this paper.

1. Hegel 1991. I cite the sections of this work, along with their accompanying remarks (R) and additions (A), parenthetically. I also quote from Wood's excerpts from Hegel's 1819–1820 lectures on the philosophy of right in the editorial notes. When doing so, I provide the note number and the section to which it corresponds.

2. See, for instance, Avineri 1972, 154; Teichgraeber 1977, 63–64; Wood 1990, 255; and Neuhouser 2000, 174.

3. For two recent defenses of Hegel on poverty see Hardimon 1994 and Franco 1999.

4. Kant 1996. I cite Kant parenthetically, following the standard practice of providing the volume and page numbers of the *Akademie* edition (Kant 1907).

5. Kant's argument in the *Doctrine of Right* is notoriously obscure, so any presentation of it requires considerable reconstruction. My own presentation of that argument relies considerably on interpretations by Arthur Ripstein and Kyla Ebels-Duggan. For Ripstein's interpretation see Ripstein 2004 and 2009. For Ebels-Duggan's interpretation see Ebels-Duggan 2009.

6. Ripstein 2009, 40–42. For Kant's definition, see 6:213.

7. Cf. Ripstein 2009, 40, and Ebels-Duggan 2009, 2.

8. Kant uses the term "external object of choice" ambiguously between non-personal corporeal objects (e.g., a stone), performances by persons (e.g., gardening services), and statuses with regard to persons (e.g., parental custody) (6:247). In order to avoid some difficulties that arise because of this ambiguity, I reconstruct the argument in "Private Right" with regard to nonpersonal corporeal objects alone.

9. On this puzzle, Ebels-Duggan 2009, 3.

10. Due to the structure of the argument Kant presents, this "must" has the force of a duty of right. See 6:256.

11. This strategy is also suggested, but not fully developed, in Pippen 1999 and Westphal 2002.

12. Ebels-Duggan 2009, 4. Emphasis added.

13. Briefly, the argument involves showing that a *res nullius*—an external object that, by right, everyone would be forbidden from using—is contrary to right (6:246). It follows that it must be rightful for any external object to be usable by some person. The argument is completed by the observation that a system of private property rights meets this requirement.

14. Ebels-Duggan 2009, 4. The other reasons no individual can acquire conclusive property rights in the state of nature are what Ebels-Duggan calls the "*problem of indeterminacy*" and the "*problem of assurance*." Cf. Chapter 6 in Ripstein 2009.

15. See Ripstein 2009, 191.

16. It is by no means irrelevant, however, from the standpoint of virtue. See 6:453.

17. Cf. Ripstein 2009, 277.

18. Ripstein 2004, 33. Kant never says explicitly that this is the problem with individual poverty, but this is strongly suggested by his remarks at 6:367.

19. Ripstein 2004, 33–34.

20. Here I follow Dudley Knowles. See Knowles 1983, 48–49.

21. I follow Alan Patten in reading "Abstract Right" as an attempt to specify these conditions. See Patten 2002, 144.

22. It is not my claim that these conditions are, for Hegel, jointly sufficient for the realization of personality. Rather, my claim is that they are both necessary. This is compatible with the view that, on Hegel's account, there is a recognitive condition on the realization of personality *in addition to* the ones that I discuss. If I do not discuss that condition here, it is only because my aim is to build my argument on a minimalist interpretation of Hegel's account of the relationship between personality and property. I thank Ardis Collins and Andrew Buchwalter for pressing me to make this aspect of my argumentative strategy explicit.

23. Cf. Patten 2002, 148–149.

24. Hegel 1977.

25. Ibid., 117–119 (§§195–196). "Labor" here does not mean just any kind of purposive activity, but rather the imposition of form on external nature for the purpose of satisfying a need, physical or otherwise.

26. This claim is strongly supported by §§45, 194R, and 197.

27. Hegel 1983, 160 (§118R). The translation is my own.

28. See, for instance, Hardimon 1994, 243.

29. For a view that answers this question in the affirmative, see Houlgate 1992. For a dissenting view, see Teichgraeber 1977, 60–61.

30. See n. 3.

31. See Hardimon 1994, 248, and Houlgate 1992, 14.

32. See Franco 1999, 271.

33. Hardimon 1994, 248–249, explicitly rejects this. I find his brief defense of that position inadequate. For him, the question, whether the modern social world is a home or not, seems ultimately to turn on poverty being "the condition of the few." But I find it exceedingly difficult to believe that such a momentous claim could, for Hegel (or for us), ultimately hinge on a simple matter of numbers.

Works Cited

Avineri, S. 1972. *Hegel's Theory of the Modern State*. Cambridge: Cambridge University Press.

Ebels-Duggan, K. 2009. "Moral Community: Escaping the Ethical State of Nature." *Philosopher's Imprint* 9 (8): 1–19.

Franco, P. 1999. *Hegel's Philosophy of Freedom*. New Haven: Yale University Press.

Hardimon, M. O. 1994. *Hegel's Social Philosophy: The Project of Reconciliation*. Cambridge: Cambridge University Press.

Hegel, G.W.F. 1977. *Phenomenology of Spirit*. Translated by A. V. Miller. Oxford: Oxford University Press.

———. 1983. *Vorlesungen über Naturrecht und Staatswissenschaft*. Edited by C. Becker, W. Bonsiepen, A. Gethmann-Siefert, F. Hogemann, W. Jaeschke, Ch. Jamme, H.-Ch. Lucas, K. R. Meist, and H. Schneider. Hamburg: Felix Meiner Verlag.

———. 1991. *Elements of the Philosophy of Right*. Translated by H. B. Nisbet. Edited by A. W. Wood. Cambridge: Cambridge University Press.

Houlgate, S. 1992. "Review of *Hegel's Ethical Thought*." *Bulletin of the Hegel Society of Great Britain* 25:1–17.

Kant, Immanuel. 1907. *Gesammelte Schriften*. Edited by the *Königlich Preussischen Akademie der Wissenschaften*. Vol. 6. Berlin: Georg Reimer.

———. 1996. *The Metaphysics of Morals*. In *Practical Philosophy*, translated and edited by M. J. Gregor, 354–603. Cambridge: Cambridge University Press.

Knowles, D. 1983. "Hegel on Property and Personality." *Philosophical Quarterly* 33 (130): 45–62.

Neuhouser, F. 2000. *Foundations of Hegel's Social Theory: Actualizing Freedom*. Cambridge: Harvard University Press.

Patten, A. 2002. *Hegel's Idea of Freedom*. Oxford: Oxford University Press.

Pippen, R. B. 1999. "Dividing and Deriving in Kant's *Rechtslehre*." In *Metaphysische Anfangsgründe der Rechtslehre*, edited by O. Höffe. Berlin: Akademie Verlag, 63–85.

Ripstein, A. 2004. "Authority and Coercion." *Philosophy and Public Affairs* 32 (1):2–35.

———. 2009. *Force and Freedom: Kant's Legal and Political Philosophy*. Cambridge: Harvard University Press.

Teichgraeber, R. 1977. "Hegel on Property and Poverty." *Journal of the History of Ideas* 38 (1): 47–64

Westphal, K. R. 2002. "A Kantian Justification of Possession." In *Kant's Metaphysics of Morals: Interpretative Essays*, edited by M. Timmons, 89–109. Oxford: Oxford University Press.

Wood, A. W. 1990. *Hegel's Ethical Thought*. Cambridge: Cambridge University Press.

7

Capitalism as Deficient Modernity

Hegel against the Modern Economy

MICHAEL J. THOMPSON

Introduction

Do we have duties to modern economic institutions? Are we, as rational agents, required to see the social relations structured by capitalism as legitimate, genuinely modern, and worthy of our obligations? Are we to find a home in a world dominated by those institutions and ways of life? We are accustomed to a negative answer to this family of questions coming from Marxism, not necessarily from Hegel. But I propose a reading of Hegel's social theory and his ethical thought that shows that we do not have obligations to such institutions. I submit that Hegel's political philosophy is intrinsically anti-capitalist in the sense that it outlines a theory of both modern institutions and individual agency that requires as its basic prerequisite the primacy of the universal or the privileging of the common interest. Capitalism, as it has evolved since the death of Hegel, is an economic system that requires the privileging of particular, class interests over the general universal interests of society as a whole. In following other interpreters that view Hegel as a republican, I suggest that the centrality of the universal in Hegel's ethical and political philosophy mitigates against the power of capitalist institutions.[1] By extending the understanding of republicanism to incorporate the concept of human freedom as the insight into the structure of our sociality, Hegel's political theory provides us with an anti-capitalist conception of a republic ordered around the *res publica* conceived as the rational universal. It is this central concept that organizes a Hegelian interpretation and evaluation of capitalism.

Hegel is clear that the nature of social relations that constitute civil society (*bürgerliche Gesellschaft*) are characterized by particular interests and social atomism. When these economic relations come to dominate political life and permeate the logics of other spheres of society, Hegel provides an argument as to why such institutional arrangements are irrational and why we, as rational ethical agents, have no obligations or duties toward them. The essence of modernity is its ability, in contrast to previous sociocultural forms of life, to realize the rational universal in the objective institutions of the political community. My basic thesis is that Hegel's idea of rational obligation implies that rational individuals have obligations only to those social institutions, norms, and practices that realize concrete social freedom—another way of saying the universal, or common interest. Hegel's project is to inform a kind of practical reason that can allow rational individuals to know when they should *affirm* as well as when they should *dissent* from the institutions that shape their social and political world. From this, I construe a Hegelian theory of *nonobligation*, or *dissent*, from deficient forms of modernity caused by the proliferation of capitalist logics and institutions. Hegel can be read as telling us why modern capitalism is a deficient form of modernity and, as a consequence, why we should dissent from such institutions and seek their alteration.

Modern capitalism should be seen not as a system of market exchange coordinated by self-interest, the central idea that characterized modern economic life in Hegel's time. Rather, it needs to be seen as a more comprehensive social formation that is more than an economic phenomenon but also "a system of social relations expressed in characteristic class structures, modes of consciousness, patterns of authority, and relations of power."[2] It is a system that organizes ever larger segments of society around its own logic and imperatives in order to increase profit, or for the benefit of one segment (or class) of society at the expense of others.[3] In this sense, capitalism expands beyond the sphere of civil society or the "external state," as Hegel referred to it, and becomes the dominant logic of our social institutions and social relations.[4] For this kind of economic life to be successful, elites seek to make the interest of a part of the community—that is, those that control capital—the principle determining the whole of society. But if this is the case, then its interests begin to displace the more general, public interests that the universal demands of modern institutions as well as the ends that should guide rational ethical agency. In the process, the core element of Hegel's theory of modern freedom—the ability of individuals rationally to will the good, or what is universal—becomes disabled leading to what I call a *deficient modernity*.

I think this is something that Hegel did not envision because his ideas about economics were trapped within the early-modern, classical liberal understanding of market society rather than the later, industrial and postindustrial forms that characterize the modern period. If one of the core dimensions of modern freedom is our possession of self-determination, both as individuals as well as a social whole, then the more capitalism develops, the more it is able to rob modern institutions and individuals of their self-determining character. Self-determination for Hegel cannot simply be seen as the ability for an individual to determine his own actions (as in liberal theory) but should be seen, in Hegel's sense, to be the individual's ability to determine his interests mediated by the universal, by the essence of man's social interdependence. Our actions and the institutions that shape and form us should be oriented toward this universality if they are to be worthy of our obligations and duties. On my reading, Hegel is able to provide us with an insight into the ends of a more genuinely rational social order, one that is unequivocally critical of modern capitalism because it is a system that does not and, indeed, by its nature *will* not, promote the universal ends that modern freedom requires.

Capitalism as Deficient Modernity

For Hegel the normative validity of modernity lies in its ability to realize what is universal and rational in society. The basic institutions of the modern world—the family, civil society, and the state—are all seen by Hegel to be intrinsically rational and worthy of our obligations, but only to the extent that they promote and support the free individuality and rationality of agents. The basic criterion of this rationality is that we move out of our immediate, arbitrary will (*Willkür*) toward a rational will (*Wille*) that can grasp what is universal in both individual and society as a whole. This means that the essence of modern individuality is grasped by the members of a modern polity as social, interdependent, and part of an intersubjective and solidaristic context within which one's subjective inclinations and will ought to be oriented. The republican project reignited by Rousseau is modified and deepened to emanate from the subjectivity of ethical agents. It is in the rational will that we are to find the source of the modern concept of the good and to ensure the stability of the objective attributes of modern freedom as they manifest themselves in our institutions.

To this end, the institutions of the political community are to be seen as the objectification of the universal within ethical life. It is the institution that must embody the universal interests of the community, of the proper—as opposed to pathological—social relations that will be able to nurture a rational individuality as opposed to the mere understanding of isolated particularity. For the whole to sustain rationality in a modern sense means that it must be realized through the subjective actions, norms, and practices of individual agents. But it equally relies on our recognition of the ontological reality of man's social essence, his interdependence on others. Hegel, not unlike Aristotle, sees that the true end of the individual is the state viewed as the whole structure of social relations that shape and form his life and personality. The Hegelian critique of capitalism that I construct and then defend here therefore begins with the thesis that it is an economic-institutional arrangement that distorts this structure of social relations in specific ways that make the realization of Hegel's own theory of modernity as rational freedom impossible.

Hegel's analysis of civil society and economic modernity does not make room for economic institutions that are able to influence and shape other areas of social and cultural life. The idea that one class of interests should take precedence over others is anathema to the universal interest of the community.[5] The essence of market society, for Hegel, is that it is able to provide three things necessary for modern freedom: (1) the satisfaction of needs; (2) a sphere for the expression of each person's individual self-interests; and (3) to disclose for each individual that he is part of a broader chain of dependence, one that will lead him to the self-consciousness of the universal itself. The division of labor, for instance, has an important role to play in this. From Smith, Hegel was able to derive a justification for the path toward man's self-consciousness of his broader social connections: "By this division, the work of the individual becomes less complex. . . . At the same time, this abstraction on one man's skills and means of production from another's completes and makes necessary everywhere the dependence of men on one another and their reciprocal relation in the satisfaction of their other needs" (PR §198). The pursuit of self-interest and the ability to interact through economic exchange becomes the new coordinating paradigm in a postfeudal world allowing for the emergence of the universal in modern society.[6] Economic activity and the pursuit of self-interest raises the subject to a higher space of ethical reasons once he has recognized that his selfish ends can be attained only through interdependent means: "In the course of the actual attainment of selfish ends—an attainment conditioned in this way by universality—there is formed a system of complete interdependence, wherein the livelihood, happiness, and legal status of one man is interwoven with the livelihood, happiness, and rights of all" (PR §183).

But the limitations of civil society become clear when we realize that it is only able to produce a formal and legalistic conception of human freedom. Restricted to the sphere of exchange and private ownership alone confines us to a deficient concept of freedom, one unaware of the objective and universal nature of (1) our social being as mutual social interdependence, and (2) the way that this relates to us the *content of the good*, the *telos* of our proper actions. There is, then, an *ontological* point of reference for our rational understanding of the good.[7] This is something that needs to take primacy in our understanding of the good since it is the root of our being and part of the concrete universal constituting modern life. Hegel seems to be saying that we cannot simply make anything that we want into the good, even if we construct elaborate reasons to justify it. Rather, there is a specific structure to the ways that humans live their lives together, needs that they possess, potentialities and capacities that can be developed, and personalities to be educated in particular ways for the universal is to become concrete through the wills of individuals. The social nucleus of our individuality simply means that we are dependent on mutual social relations for the satisfaction of our needs; the importance of civil society for Hegel is that individuals come to realize that their individual needs can only be satisfied by their dependence on others. Rational institutions and rational individuals will seek to promote the concept of the common interest as the end of the rational will because this common interest is the very essence of what it means to be human and to be free. When the universal, the common interest, is not placed at the center of our ethical life, we begin to lose one of the core features of modern freedom, that of self-determination.

Herein lies an important point. If we are to see rational freedom as resting on mutual recognition, it is not simply an I-thou relation that is at stake, but a relation that leads me to the realization of a broader social interdependence worthy of my duties and obligations, the " 'I' that is 'We' and 'We' that is 'I' " (*PhG*, 110). This means that if recognitive relations work properly then I should be able to conceptualize my sociality defined as my fundamental interdependence on others, on the complex structure of relations—economic, cultural, and otherwise—within which I am shaped and realized. I begin to form a self-consciousness of myself as a social being, as a member of a structure of social relations, and as constituted by them as well. Now, this means that if we see freedom as the power to have a rational will, then we need also to see that deformed social relations lead to deficient concepts of self, of others, of society, and its institutions. The entire structure of the *Philosophy of Right* pivots, in a certain sense, on the ability of rational agents to conceptualize this social ontology, the totality within which we live and function. Each agent, in order to possess a rational understanding of the world and its institutions, needs to possess an awareness of the objective logic in the ontological structure of his sociality. In this sense, the rational will be at odds with institutions, values, and practices that do not aim at the universal because it is in the universal that the higher good of social and political life is realized. This insight is a deepening and an elaboration of Rousseau's thesis that civic freedom can only find its home in a general will, in the realization that I, as an individual, realize a higher state of freedom and welfare from working toward common interests rather than my own immediate, arbitrary interests.[8] Modern capitalism constitutes such a situation because of its ability to organize society around its own imperatives, reshaping social relations in the process and deforming the recognitive relations that make free, rational agency possible.

Capitalism as a Pathology of Rational Ethical Life

If the rational will is the core element that organizes the modern self and is the very thing that determines the nature of one's personality, then the extent to which the will is shaped and formed by social relations is a crucial element of Hegel's political and social philosophy. Capitalist social relations produce severe pathologies in the shaping of rational agency as Hegel conceives it. Economic institutions are more than merely means of exchange or the satisfaction of needs. In modern societies, capitalism has become the dominant institution because of its constant need to steer and dominate other spheres of social and political life. Modern markets, as they become more global, necessitate the state to involve itself in economic affairs; the nature of education and culture becomes regimented according to both the needs and demands of the broader marketplace and the search for expanded profits; and the practices and norms of everyday life are affected and shaped by the regimented processes of what Max Weber termed "legitimate domination" and "rationalization," where modern habits of work and life become organized around the imperatives of economic efficiency and productivity not to mention rampant consumption. The point I would like to draw attention to here, however, is not historical, but ethical. If Hegel's idea of the rational will is that it relates itself to the good, that is, to what is universal in one's life and social world, then if it can be shown that there exist institutions and forms of social life that inhibit that capacity, or that make the will's relation to the good difficult, impossible, or obscure in certain circumstances, then such institutions do not command my duties. Rational individuals should not commit themselves to those institutions, norms, and practices that actively inhibit their rational freedom.

There are three interrelated pathologies that result from capitalist social relations as they pertain to the nature of the formation of the rational will. First, there is the *pathology of socialization* caused by deficient forms of social structure and social integration that constitute capitalism. Second, and resulting from this, is a *pathology of recognition* (*Anerkennung*), where individuals become unable to recognize in others a generalizable essence that allows them to perceive their greater social interdependence, one of the core elements of Hegel's understanding of the formation of modern, rational selves and social institutions. Lastly, there exists a *pathology of rationality* that results from the above processes where individuals become unable to grasp the core principle of freedom that ought to underwrite their wills as well as the social institutions that constitute their lives. At the end of this, I hope to be able to disclose a more general pathology of ethical life that is caused by capitalist social and economic relations and why rational agents should have no duties to uphold them and, perhaps, even a duty to resist and alter them.[9]

Ethical life is constituted by individuals and their practices, but it is a more objective realm than that of mere "morality," in that it is "imbued with what is inherently right" (*PR* §141). The transition from subjectivity to intersubjectivity is crucial here. The will needs to be related to the good, to that which is universal and which is no longer simply a matter of subjective conscience. But this can only be accomplished in an objective ethical order that can make the abstract convictions of individual conscience concrete as well as give guidance to our ethical commitments. The ethical order needs to possess "a stable content independently necessary and subsistent in exaltation above subjective opinion and caprice. These distinctions are absolutely valid laws and institutions" (*PR* §144). The transition from morality to ethical life consists, then, in the ability of the subjective will to absorb the objective dimensions of what is good; to be free is not simply to possess convictions about an abstract conception of the good, it is rather to belong to an objective ethical order where both the particular inclinations of the agent as well as the broader fabric of institutions and norms are unified and given actuality.[10] Such an individual reaches out of his abstract particularity into a broader space of reasons, into the realm of what is universal, in him as well as in society. "The right of individuals to be subjectively destined to freedom is fulfilled when they belong to an actual ethical order, because their conviction of their freedom finds its truth in such an objective order, and it is in an ethical order that they are actually in possession of their own essence or their inner universality" (*PR* §153).

The mechanism for the transition from "morality" (*Moralität*) to "ethical life" (*Sittlichkeit*) therefore lies in the nature of *socialization* that channels and structures the process of *recognition*. The kernel of this process is a modern republican understanding of virtue, one that is able to capture both modern subjectivity and objective social norms that can secure common, that is, universal, formulations of the good and lead to a genuine, modern free life.[11] Recognition is central here because it provides the means for the subject to leave abstract *Moralität* and begin to grasp his own essence as an interdependent member of a broader community.[12] This intersubjective universality constitutes a crucial element of socialization: the phenomenological means by which we come to grasp the rational, socio-ontological element of our individuality. This is also a process that is delicate and potentially corruptible. Social relations can therefore, if they are not properly constructed and structured, lead to deficient forms of recognition thereby distorting the ability of individual agents to apprehend the universal rationally, if at all. The danger is that such distorted forms of socialization and recognition can lead to what we see in the Master-Slave dialectic in the *Phenomenology* as well as in the *Philosophy of Mind*. In both instances, participants fail to grasp their respective universality and each become imprisoned in identities that are deficient to their potential as free agents.

Within the context of distorted forms of socialization the transition from abstract subjectivity and *Willkür* remains incomplete. The pathology of ethical life can result from this problem: the inability of ethical life to embody the objective good, to be able to instill within the structure of the will of a society's members the proper orientation toward the universal, the rational common interest that is needed to uphold modern freedom. Hegel's thesis about the normative validity of the rational nature of modern freedom rests on the ability of modern ethical life to objectify the universal and for modern subjects to cultivate, absorb, and express those values as norms, practices, and so on.[13] If social relations are constituted in such a way as to distort such a process of socialization, then we must ask about the extent to which deficient social relations are worthy of our duties to uphold them. I come to this point in the last part of this chapter.

Capitalism manifests a *pathology of socialization* when its effects on the totality of social institutions are significant enough to disable ethical life's capacity to be ambient with the rational reasons for the universal in all forms of social life. Ethical life ceases to embody universality and no longer communicates it to social members. Indeed, since, as Hegel claims, ethical life is the objective ethical order to which individuals belong and from which individuals learn or cultivate their ethical personality, if it is unable to instill rational norms and practices, it constitutes a pathological form of socialization. Capitalism therefore shifts emphasis away from a concern with the res publica moving society as a whole toward the arbitrariness of its imperatives. As a comprehensive process of social organization and structuration, it therefore has constitutive power over individual subjects. It is centrally a system that achieves its goals through subordinating other noneconomic spheres of life to its own logic and imperatives. Schooling, culture, the nature of public finance, public space, the family—all become infected by the logic of exchange relations. We become socialized by exploitive social relations, commodification, and values of hedonic self-interest. In a society permeated by corporate capitalism, the central process of recognition in ethical life becomes frustrated and even disabled by the existence of instrumentalized relations between individuals. Hierarchical structures of power, of unequal social relations determined by class relations, vertical relations of interaction resulting from bureaucratic forms of institutional organization, and so on, all can be seen as structural patterns of organization that lead to socialization pathologies. When I interact with an other in such contexts, I do not interact with him as an equal. I see him through partial, instrumental interests and needs, thereby frustrating the recognitive process inherent in a fuller intersubjectivity.

Hegel points to places where such pathologies, or perhaps deficiencies, exist in his own time. England's social and economic development he sees as problematic because civil society has developed at the expense of the rational state, the ultimate embodiment of the universal in Hegel's system.[14] But he also sees the modern forms of production and factory labor as demeaning to human beings, prefiguring in many ways the writings of the young Marx.[15] The problem of socialization, or of social integration, becomes central once we see that the corruption of the mechanism of recognition is the result. The *pathology of recognition* occurs when the pathology of socialization and social integration begins to affect and shape the ways that I conceive of others and, in turn, myself. "I cannot be aware of me as myself in an other so long as I see in that other an other and an immediate existence; and I am consequently bent upon the suppression of this immediacy of his. In the same way, I cannot be recognized as immediate except so far as I overcome the mere immediacy on my own part and thus give existence to my freedom" (*EPG* §431).

A *pathology of rationality* can now be seen to express itself in the sense that the previous processes of socialization and recognition have been deformed. The universal, as I have been using it here, refers to the totality of social life, needs, relations, and potentialities that humans possess. Hegel's reference in the *Philosophy of History* to Aristotle's claim in the *Politics* that the true essence of the individual is the *polis* comes back in a new way after the thorough treatment of the processes needed for modern subjectivity. Rational beings who have been shaped by recognitive relations will come to see this universal as the necessary context within which individual and social freedom exist. Lacking this, they will be caught in the subordinate, deficient understanding of freedom; they will be caught in the partial understanding of the world and their commitments to it. The ability of individuals not only to grasp, that is, conceptualize, the universal as the proper space within which one's reasons and obligations find reference and ground therefore has a deep impact on ethical agency. Both subjective and collective ethical substance begins to deform, and we begin to see a slide away from the kind of modernity that Hegel saw worthy of our commitments and duties. This brings me to the final question I would like to consider in this chapter: Do we have obligations and duties, as members of such a social world, to capitalist institutions, values, and norms?

Do We Have Obligations to Capitalist Institutions?

Only by taking full account of modern subjectivity could a society grounded on the principle of rational freedom make that concept concrete because rational social institutions need to be held in the thoughts of its participants and guide their wills. Each individual needs to have the universal as the ground of his rational will (*Wille*).[16] In this sense, Hegel understands the concepts of "obligation" (*Verpflichtung*) and "duty" (*Pflicht*) as related features of the rational will. "Duty is primarily a relation to something which from my point of view is substantive, absolutely universal" (*PR* §261). I have obligations and duties not simply to what I may arbitrarily think or believe to be right or correct but rather to that which is "good" (*Gut*) or what relates to the universal, to what is in the common interest because that is also in my best interest—my rational freedom cannot be obtained outside of this context.[17] "The particular subject is related to the good as to the essence of his will, and hence his will's obligation arises directly in this relation" (*PR* §133). Any rational subject therefore needs to be able to have the good, what is universal, rooted in his conscience (*Gewissen*): "[t]rue conscience is the disposition to will what is absolutely good" (*PR* §137).

Hegel is clear that an ethical agent is one who "is related to the good as to the essence of his will, and hence his will's obligation arises directly in this relation" (*PR* §133). We have duties only to those things that we can rationally grasp as worthy of what is good, and this means what is beneficial not only for me and my particular welfare (*Wohl*) but what is beneficial to the social totality as a whole of which I am a part. What is "good"—defined as the unity of the concept of the will with the particular will—is seen by Hegel as the determining *telos* of all rational duty and obligation.[18] And this only makes sense because it is by following the dictates of reason that we are able to commit ourselves to what is universal, shared by all, and thereby to relate my subjectivity with the rationality inherent in the objective reality of what it means to live a free, human, social life. The will's movement from mere "particular will" (*Willkür*) to that of "individual will" means that I am aware that the principles that guide my actions are not simply mine, but that I am committed to them because of their universal applicability.

Here we come to a crucial point in my argument. I believe Hegel is telling us that we possess no rational duties or obligations to follow the dictates of capitalist institutions because those institutions do not promote a rational universal. Although market institutions can be seen as moving us toward a universal, and the need for self-interest has a legitimate place in his social philosophy, it cannot justify the ways in which the particular interests of economic elites have been able to transform the nature of work, of education, of politics, of the other core institutions, practices, and values of (a deficiently) modern life. Hegel is arguing that a more genuine modernity will be one in which our rational wills are related to the universal concerns of society as a whole; that we have an obligation to those institutions and norms that enhance and protect our freedom, the essence of what it means to be human. It is not simply those that are not served by the economic system—that is, the poor, the rabble (*Pöbel*)—that ought to dissent from these institutions and practices, but anyone who can grasp that they live in a world where only their particularity and the particularity of others is given primacy and where the institutions and practices of the community are prevented from realizing the universal, the common interests of the community.[19] This is the purpose, the essence of modernity, and modern capitalism is able to distort the aims of the political community to such an extent that social relations do not allow for the permeation of the universal throughout our institutions.

This kind of modernity, deficient modernity, should be seen in a more Weberian light: we confuse obligations and duties, in Hegel's sense, with the dictates of rational domination (*Herrschaft*) where norms and institutions are organized around instrumental and, in the case of capitalist institutions, arbitrary, particular ends of profit maximization and wealth defense not to mention a functionalist promotion of narrow values of consumption, taste, self-interest over public interest, and so on. Capitalist institutions such as the nature of production and consumption, the reorienting of the state to protect capital and the norms that give consumption and working life, and so on, all should be seen as undeserving of our rational obligations. Indeed, because of them, we no longer have the rational universal in mind, the "good" in Hegel's sense, when we follow these dictates; rather, they have become the logic of our second nature. The interests of economic benefit, of profit and surplus, become our values, even when we do not share in the benefits for which we labor. In this sense, posing Hegel's concept of duty and obligation puts us in a critical space against these systemic imperatives. Indeed, I believe from this that we can construct a Hegelian concept of dissent from the excesses of capitalism, from the way it is able to posit a false universal in place of the rational, true universal.

Undergirding the structure of rational obligation is the nature of modern freedom. As Hegel sees it, practical reason needs to be seen as a means for any rational agent to be able to view the social institutions and practices around him as realizing universal ends. This requires that the moral subjectivity of any agent view the world from the point of view of the universal, to judge it from that standpoint. Why should I have duties to institutions, to laws, norms, values, and practices that do not maintain the universal? If I can perceive in the systemic logic of our economic system, pathological consequences for the ethical life of modern society, should I have obligations to those institutions? I believe we do not, and even more, I believe that we even have a duty to *resist* those institutions and values that seek to make not freedom, but class interests the organizing, defining principle of our social world. As I have sought to show earlier, capitalism can produce specific pathologies that deactivate and deform the capacity of rational agents from grasping the rational universal that guides their actions toward rational freedom.

Conclusion

As I have sought to demonstrate in this chapter, I believe that modern capitalism constitutes a deficient modernity when viewed from the vantage point of Hegel's social philosophy. At the core of this problem is the fact that capitalist institutions actively erode and distort the social context and structure of social relations that enable and shape modern, free, rational subjectivity. Any social institution, any practice, that fails to provide me with the recognitive relations necessary to develop my will and rational agency, *therefore violates my freedom* as well as the freedom of the others on whom I depend in manifold ways for the development and maintenance of that freedom. Because the core of Hegel's project is the elevation of the subjectivity of the individual to the sphere of the universal, we must ask ourselves about the extent to which our actions should be directed by the values, institutions, and practices rooted in capitalist imperatives.

If we accept the thesis that modern capitalism is a distortion of Hegel's own conception of the rational structure of modernity, then I believe we are also forced to accept the thesis that modern, rational agents have a duty to resist and to seek to transform capitalist social relations. As I see it, Hegel's thought is clear that there are specific normative elements to modern institutions that make them worthy of our obligations and duties; capitalist economic life distorts these institutions and structures making them unworthy of our duties and our subjective investment. At the same time, this critique also helps us think about alternative ways of shaping social institutions and norms so that they can approximate the universal and objectify social freedom. If my thesis is correct, then we can see Hegel not only as having an anti-capitalist edge, but also of providing us with a crucial framework within which we can begin to create a set of values that can redirect the orientation of modern subjectivity away from a Weberian form of "obedience" toward that which is rational, socially aware, capable of realizing our freedom and worthy of our allegiance. This can go far in combating modern forms of exaggerated subjectivity and alienation, as well as the unjust nature of the modern social order.

Notes

1. Although my approach is distinct, others who put forth a republican interpretation of Hegel's political thought include: Ilting 1971, Buchwalter 1993, Patten 2002, Allen 2006, and Bohman 2010.

2. Sklar 1988, 6, and passim. Sklar goes on to argue that the modern form of corporate-administered capitalism "involves a system of authority inextricably interwoven with the legal and political order as well as with the broader system of legitimacy, the prevailing norms of emulative morality and behavior, and the hierarchy of power" (7). This is crucially distinct from the previous, early-nineteenth-century organization of proprietary-competitive market stage of capitalism that would have predominated Hegel's time.

3. In this sense, capitalism should be seen as a "dominant sphere" over other spheres of social goods in the sense suggested by Walzer 1983, 3–30.

4. As Joachim Ritter has observed with respect to the *Philosophy of Right*, "concealed in it lies the danger that society can come to make its labor- and class-system the sole determination of man" (Ritter 1982, 81).

5. "And no interests of the one class may be exalted at the expense of those of another class" (*LNR* §120).

6. This applies specifically to individuals acting in economic activity: "Individuals in their capacity as burghers (*Bürger*) in this state are private persons whose end is their own interest. This end is mediated through the universal which thus appears as a means to its realization. Consequently, individuals can attain their ends only in so far as they themselves determine their knowing, willing, and acting in a universal way and make themselves links in this chain of social connections [*zu einem* Gliede *der Kette dieses* Zusammenhangs *machen*]" (*PR* §187).

7. I think this goes against the emphasis placed on subjective rationality in Hegel's practical philosophy by Pippin 2008, 2010.

8. See Ripstein 1994 and Baum 2004.

9. As Hegel points out in the *Enzyklopädia*: "the purposive action of this will is to realize its concept, freedom, in these externally objective aspects, making the latter a world shaped by the former, which in it is thus at home with itself, locked together with it: the concept accordingly perfected to the Idea" (*EPG* §484).

10. As Leslie Mulholland has argued, "[f]or Hegel, individual autonomy is not grasped immediately. Rather the objective order historically produced the condition in which its members are in position to opt for it autonomously. That is, individual's recognition of autonomy depends on the historical conditions that teach him about his autonomy. In the process whereby the individual adopts the objective order, we have what Hegel identifies as substance becoming subject" (Mullholland 1989, 65).

11. See *PR* §§147–150 and Buchwalter 1992.

12. See Williams 1997: 77ff.

13. See *PR* §187 as well as the relevant *Zusatz* in addition to Neuhouser 2000, 148ff.

14. Cf. MacGregor 1996, 12–51.

15. This is a theme that Hegel seems to come back to again and again, from the early writings through his later lectures on the *Rechtsphilosophie*. "This is why factory workers become deadened (*stumpf*) and tied to their factory and dependent on it, since with this single aptitude they cannot earn a living anywhere else. A factory presents a sad picture of the deadening (*Abstumpfung*) of human beings, which is also why on Sundays factory workers lose no time in spending and squandering their entire weekly wages" (*LNR* §101). Also see *JR* 331–335; *LNR* §§104, 117, 121; and *VPhR* §198. The comparison with Marx's early manuscripts here is superficial, but still worthy of note.

16. The relevant passage in the *Philosophy of Right* is: "The state is the actuality of concrete freedom. But concrete freedom consists in this, that personal individuality and its particular interests not only achieve their complete development and gain explicit recognition for their right (as they do in the sphere of the family and civil society) but, for one thing, they also pass over of their own accord into the interest of the universal, and, for another thing, they know and will the universal; they even recognize it as their end and aim and are active in its pursuit" (*PR* §260).

17. As Neuhouser correctly emphasizes: "one aspect of the objective freedom embodied by rational social institutions consists in their securing the necessary conditions for the possibility of the *subjective component* of social freedom" (Neuhouser 2000, 146).

18. "In this unity," that is, between the concept of the will and the particular will, Hegel writes, "abstract right, welfare, the subjectivity of knowing and the contingency of external fact, have their independent self-subsistence superseded, though at the same time they are still contained and retained within it in their essence. The good is thus freedom realized, the absolute end and aim of the world" (*PR* §129). The good is thus the supersession of "welfare" (*Wohl*) or the satisfaction of "needs, inclinations, passions, opinions, fancies, etc." (*PR* §123).

19. Mark Tunick claims that it is Hegel's thesis that the poor are morally justified in not obeying: "Hegel recognizes the possibility of justified disobedience and acknowledges that the inequalities of civil society in his day call into question the validity of obligations for a large class of poor people" (Tunick 1998, 530). But it is my argument that, by extension, the implicit thesis nested in the discussion of modernity and the nature of the good and obligation is that no rational person would or should make capitalist institutions and practices the object of their obedience.

Works Cited

Abbreviations for Works by G.W.F. Hegel

EPG   *Enzyklopädie der Philosophischen Wissenschaften III: Die Philosophie des Geistes.* Frankfurt: Suhrkamp, 1986.

JR   *Jenaer Realphilosophie 1803–04* in G.W.F. Hegel, *Frühe politische Systeme.* Edited by Gerhard Göhler. Frankfurt: Ullstein, 1974.

LNR   *Lectures on Natural Right and Political Science.* Translated by J. M. Stewart and P. C. Hodgson. Berkeley. University of California Press, 1995.

PhG   *Phänomenologie des Geistes.* Frankfurt: Suhrkamp, 1970.

PR   *Grundlinien der Philosophie des Rechts.* Stuttgart: Reclam, 1970.

VPhR   *Die Philosophie des Rechts: Vorlesung von 1821/1822.* Edited by Hansgeorg Hoppe. Frankfurt: Suhrkamp, 2005.

Allen, M. P. 2006. "Hegel between Non-Domination and Expressive Freedom: Capabilities, Perspectives, Democracy," *Philosophy and Social Criticism* 32 (4): 493–512.

Bohman, J. 2010. "Is Hegel a Republican? Pippin, Recognition, and Domination in the *Philosophy of Right.*" *Inquiry* 53 (5): 435–449.

Buchwalter, A. 1992. "Hegel's Concept of Virtue." *Political Theory* 20 (4): 548–583.

———. 1993. "Hegel, Modernity, and Civic Republicanism." *Public Affairs Quarterly* 7 (1): 1–12.

Ilting, K.-H. 1971. "Hegel's Concept of the State and Marx's Early Critique." In *The State and Civil Society*, edited by Z. A. Pelczynski. Cambridge: Cambridge University Press.

MacGregor, D. 1996. *Hegel, Marx, and the English State.* Toronto: University of Toronto Press.

Mullholland, L. A. 1989. "Hegel and Marx on the Human Individual." In *Hegel and His Critics: Philosophy in the Aftermath of Hegel*, edited by W. Desmond. Albany: State University of New York Press.

Neuhouser, F. 2000. *Foundations of Hegel's Social Theory.* Cambridge, MA: Harvard University Press.

Patten, A. 2002. *Hegel's Idea of Freedom.* Oxford: Oxford University Press.

Pippin, R. 2008. *Hegel's Practical Philosophy: Rational Agency as Ethical Life*. New York: Cambridge University Press.

———. 2010. "Hegel on Political Philosophy and Political Actuality." *Inquiry* 53 (5): 401–416.

Ripstein, A. 1994. "Universal and General Wills: Hegel and Rousseau." *Political Theory* 22 (3): 444–467.

Ritter, J. 1982. *Hegel and the French Revolution*. Translated by R. Winfield. Cambridge, MA: MIT Press.

Sklar, M. 1988. *The Corporate Reconstruction of American Capitalism, 1890–1916*. New York: Cambridge University Press.

Tunick, M. 1998. "Hegel on Justified Disobedience." *Political Theory* 26 (4): 514–535.

Walzer, M. 1983. *Spheres of Justice: A Defense of Pluralism and Equality*. New York: Basic Books.

Williams, R. 1997. *Hegel's Ethics of Recognition*. Berkeley: University of California Press.

8

Economy and Ethical Community

One of the most pathbreaking achievements of Hegel's *Philosophy of Right* is its conception of the economy as a system of needs belonging to civil society, which is one of three spheres of ethical community, intermediary between the family and the state. Nonetheless, Hegel's identification of the economy as an element of ethical community has been pervasively ignored or misinterpreted, leading Hegel to be commonly placed among the many who question the ethical standing of economic relations and thereby place modernity under suspicion.

To some degree this suspicion derives from a fundamental misunderstanding of the foundation-free character of ethics in general, which Hegel's *Philosophy of Right* seeks to realize without compromise. Hegel is the first to recognize that ethics can neither be a science of a highest good or a procedural construction because what is normative cannot derive its legitimacy from any foundation, be it a privileged given content or a privileged determiner. If what is ethical has its normativity conferred upon it by something other than itself, the ground conferring validity upon it cannot have validity of its own unless it grounds itself. In that case, however, the foundation of normativity ceases to be a ground of something other than itself. This eliminates the ground/grounded distinction on which foundational justification rests and supplants it with self-determination as the one and only possible bearer of normativity. For this reason, ethics must be a philosophy of the reality of self-determination, that is, a philosophy of right.

Moreover, ethics as a philosophy of right will simply specify the structures of self-determination in their totality, without offering any derivation of these structures from any antecedently given end or procedure of construction. The absence of any such mainstays of foundational justification has misled many readers of Hegel's *Philosophy of Right* to doubt its status as an ethics at all. Hegel, however, recognizes that the only "derivation" of the concept of right can consist in the conceptualization of nature and the psychology of the psyche, consciousness, and intelligence, which together provide the enabling, normatively neutral conditions for engagement in self-determination.[1] These cannot determine what conduct is legitimate because they make equally possible all action, right or wrong.

The Persisting Doubts of the Economy's Ethical Standing

Once this fundamental confusion is overcome by understanding why the philosophy of right has no juridical foundations, there still remain two seeming grounds for doubting the ethical standing of the economy.

The first lies in a persisting suspicion regarding the ethical standing of civil society. This suspicion is fueled by Hegel's own remarks that civil society can be regarded as the *appearance* of ethical community insofar as individuals therein pursue their individual self-interest.[2] To many, this suggests that civil society is a field of the war of all against all, leading back to the starting point of social contract theory, which privileges the liberty of choice as if it could serve as a principle of ethical construction.

Needless to say, treating the individual will as a foundation of normativity contradicts the whole framework of ethical community. Ethical community comprises that reality of freedom in which agents determine themselves in function of performing roles that can only be engaged in by acting within the existing normative association that these roles animate and sustain.

Ethical community has been misappropriated by communitarians who regard the contextual character of its agency as the only feasible vehicle for providing nonsubjective norms of conduct. Hegel conceives ethical community as a conceptually determinate association with a priori rights and duties. By contrast, communitarians treat ethical community as a formal framework, whose rights and duties are contingently given, but which still allows individuals to pursue ends that have an intersubjective validity insofar as they can only be pursued by participating in a community in which membership involves acting in recognition of commonly accepted norms. Communitarianism cannot overcome nihilism because the contingency of the content of every ethical community leaves its members subject to an order that is just an accident of history that might as well be overthrown and replaced with another just as arbitrary.

Hegel recognizes that ethical community cannot have any binding authority unless it is a system of associations concretely realizing self-determination, in which normativity resides. Whether civil society in general and the economy in particular are constitutive elements of ethical community must therefore be conceptually determined in terms of the Idea of freedom and not just supported by historical illustration.

In this connection, it is important to take seriously what Hegel argues concerning how civil society can be regarded as the "appearance" of ethical community. Indeed, civil society is the appearance of ethical community because its members act on the basis of ends of their own individual choosing. Nonetheless, in so doing, they realize an underlying ethical bond, whose existence as a specific framework of interaction is the precondition of each member of civil society being in a position of acting in relation to others in function of self-selected particular ends.[3] This underlying ethical bond is not itself the end each member of civil society consciously pursues. Rather, they each aim to realize particular ends of their own choosing, but under the general condition of pursuing ends that can only be realized by enabling others to realize self-selected particular ends of their own in return. This can only be achieved under a very specific social condition, where individuals are already recognized to be persons, moral subjects, and autonomous family members, free to pursue their own particular interest as a right, that is, as an exercise of choice to which all members of civil society are entitled and which all members have a duty to respect. Indeed, the specific modality of civil freedom is one in which individuals can determine themselves in a civil way only by recognizing the civil freedom of others and enjoying their recognition in turn. For this reason, the all-sided pursuit of self-interest in civil society is not a war of all against all, but rather an exercise of freedom in which each individual's efforts to realize particular ends are intrinsically connected to the like realizations of others. Far from representing an obstacle to one's own pursuit of interest, the pursuit of interest by others is precisely what makes it possible for one's own interest to be realized. That is why civil society is a structure of ethical community, enabling a freedom to be realized that can only operate on the basis of an existing framework of interdependence, which makes possible exercising the right of pursuing particular interests, whose exercise animates and sustains that very framework. The interests in question are not equivalent to the ends of choice, of doing as one pleases. They rather are interests that are mediated by the civil freedom of others, which is to say that they have a content allowing them to be realized without conflicting with the civil interests of others.

If this allows civil society to qualify as a genuine sphere of ethical community, the ethical standing of the economy is still held in suspicion insofar as, secondly, it is commonly doubted whether economic relations are compatible with proper civil association. Whether the economy can qualify as a duly ethical civil association has been widely questioned on the basis of none other than Hegel's own analysis of the system of needs.

Hegel, after all, does not accept Adam Smith's sanguine view that the market is a self-regulating mechanism that ensures the welfare of all. Hegel instead maintains that the conditions of market participation can never be counted on to enable individuals to satisfy their needs for the commodities of others and that poverty always haunts the operations of the market so long as it is left to its own devices.[4] Poverty is a wrong for it consists in a violation of the right of members of civil society to realize particular interests of their own choosing in reciprocity with others. Poverty here consists not in the deprivation of just the necessities of life, to which personhood entitles individuals, nor of the resources required for parents to care for their children and spouses to care for one another. Poverty violates social right as well insofar as it deprives individuals of the specifically economic resources they need to enjoy the equal opportunity to earn a conventional living in the market.

If the economy is incapable of freeing itself from the scourge of this socially specific poverty, does the economy not forfeit its standing as a compatible element of civil society? Moreover, if, as Hegel himself maintains, the economy finds itself compelled to engage in colonial and imperialist expansion to obtain the additional market demand and raw materials and cheap labor it needs,[5] does this not further highlight its subversion of the relations of right? In addition, does not the production of an unemployed and underemployed rabble at home and abroad,[6] alienated from the institutions in which it has no viable stake, jeopardize ethical community, not only in society, but in the family and the state, rendering the economy a threat to the entire system of freedom presided over by self-government?

Finally, does not the insecurity of economic welfare engendered by the market put family and political rights in direct jeopardy? The lack of economic equal opportunity threatens the welfare of the family and the ability of spouses to duly care for one another and for parents to duly care for their children. Just as poverty impairs the ability of citizens to participate in the political process on a par with others, so the concentration of wealth threatens to translate economic privilege into political privilege, undermining equal political opportunity by enabling the power of money to condition the political process.

Each of these violations of economic right, of equal economic opportunity, and their associated threats to family and political freedom, would call the ethical standing of the economy into question only if they could not be remedied without eliminating all exercise of economic self-determination. In that case alone would they signify that economic freedom is inherently contradictory and incapable of any abiding realization. If, instead, these violations can each be remedied by additional engagements in freedom, then the endemic possibility of violations of economic right is no different than the endemic possibility of violations of every other right. After all, because engagement in self-determination involves individuals who have a choosing will, individuals can always opt to ignore their duty to respect the rights of others and take malicious actions that intentionally overstep the lawful boundaries of the prerogatives to which they are entitled as self-determining persons, moral subjects, family member, civilians, and citizens. Wherever these possible violations occur, they ought to be countered. Although moral duty obliges individuals personally to take an initiative to right these wrongs, public measures will be required to ensure that all the rights of individuals are upheld in an authoritative and lawful manner. Moreover, to the extent that the exercise of right involves personal initiatives that may be interpreted differently by others, every sphere of right allows for the possibility of nonmalicious wrongs, where individuals act in respect of right but still conflict with the exercise of right of others. Property rights exhibit these dual forms of violations in their most basic form. Persons can always maliciously violate the property of others or enter into nonmalicious property disputes[7] and the private efforts of persons to right these wrongs may always be interpreted by others as a new wrong.[8] Accordingly, property rights cannot be upheld in and through their own exercise or with the supplement of personal moral intervention. Instead, their realization depends on a public administration of justice, which itself ultimately depends on constitutional self-government for its final authority and empowerment.

The situation need not be any different with economic right. The workings of the market may leave commodity owners with no guarantee of enjoying equal economic opportunity and escaping the scourges of poverty, unsafe and unhealthy employment, environmental degradation, and conditions of work that prevent them from exercising their family and political freedoms on a par with others. Nonetheless, other exercises of freedom can forestall these social injustices and Hegel outlines the basic parameters for this righting of social wrong in describing the tasks that social interest groups ("corporations") and the public administration of welfare ("police") should address.[9]

Moreover, although the concentration of wealth and economic power may threaten equal political opportunity, public intervention to protect self-government from domination by economic privilege can seek to

prevent the economy from undermining not only civil freedom and family welfare, but the sovereign autonomy of political freedom. So long as
these private and public efforts are not completely futile, the injustice of
an unbridled market does not rob the economy of its ethical standing
any more than the abiding possibility of theft and murder robs property
rights of normative validity.

The Common Denials of
Any Normativity to the Economy

These remedies will be irrelevant, however, if economic relations are themselves deprived of the very character that would allow them to figure as
normative activities in the first place. Contrary to Hegel, many, if not most
theorists, both ancient and modern, have conceived economic activity in
two ways that each render the economy a normatively neutral domain
beyond good and evil.

On the one hand, the economy has been construed as a sphere of
technique, of instrumental action, where a single agency imposes some
preconceived form on some given material, enabling it to serve some end.
This technical framework applies to any action of a subject upon objects,
with indifference to what end is imposed. Accordingly, it has nothing specifically economic about it and can just as well be employed in other
domains of action wherever technical considerations come into play.[10]
Provided ends, agents, and materials are given, questions of the efficient
application of technique can be addressed. Yet because technical concerns
take for granted the ends for whose realization the application of technique supplies the means, technique is in and of itself normatively neutral.
Although family, society, and state all involve activities that can include
applications of technique, it is one thing to recognize the employment of
technology in their affairs and it is another to reduce their associations
to engagements in technique. The latter amounts to ignoring the role of
interaction in ethical community and treating its associations as if they
comprised monological relations of a single agency manipulating things
or manipulating other individuals as if they were things.

Such reduction of association to instrumental action has been applied
to the economy by viewing both the production and distribution of goods
as instrumental functions of a single agency. On the one hand, the production of commodities gets construed as if it were merely a monological
engagement of an artificer who imposes form upon materials using tools.
On the other hand, the distribution of goods is specified as if it were a
technical allocation determined by a single distributer. These reductions

have their counterpart in the psychological treatment of price formation, according to which the prices of commodities are determined by estimations of the individual's evaluation of the marginal utility of scarce goods. If economic relations were determined in this technical manner, they would all amount to relations of an agency to things, a relation lacking both the dialogical dimension in which rights and duties can enter and any consideration for what ends can be unconditionally valid.

A similar elimination of any ethical standing to the economy results from the alternative approach of treating the economy as if it were a sphere of natural metabolism, wherein human beings engage in the activities needed to satisfy their physiological survival needs. On these terms, to paraphrase Marx, the economy is a sphere of necessity, mandated by our species being, and only beyond which the realm of freedom can begin. Instead of being a sphere of rights and duties, the economy is governed by natural necessity. Any thought of making the economy what it ought to be ignores that economic matters comprise a given fate of the human condition whose basic parameters are defined by nature and cannot be otherwise.

The Economy as an Institution of Right

Hegel challenges both of these reductions by showing how the economy is a system of needs that consists in a specific interaction of right, wherein individuals interrelate by determining themselves in pursuit of self-selected particular ends that can only be realized in reciprocity with others doing the same. Insofar as economic relations comprise such an intersubjective convention of freedom, they can be given neither by nature nor as a function of the single agent. Instead, the economy can only come into being in history as a normative institution with its own specific rights and duties.

Economic relations are relations of right because they are all rooted in the basic situation of commodity exchange, where, as Hegel shows,[11] individuals act on a socially specific need for the commodities of others that can only be juridically satisfied by offering them in return some commodity that they need. This context becomes the general framework for production and consumption only as a result of specific historical transformations. First, individuals must no longer be able to satisfy a significant portion of their needs by dealing directly with nature or through the autarchy of their own household and its possessions. This entails that a principal range of the objects of need satisfaction must have come to fall under the legitimate control of others. This includes both goods to be consumed and goods required to produce objects of consumption. Second, individuals must all have been liberated from traditions and authorities requiring them to engage in occupations and consumptions determined independently of their will. Third, individuals must have achieved recognition as property owners so that they can freely dispose of alienable factors that can be brought to market as commodities that their owners can exchange.[12]

These conditions do indicate that the universal realization of property relations comprises a necessary condition for the economy to emerge as an independent sphere in which all individuals participate. Nonetheless, it is fundamentally mistaken to conflate economic rights with property rights. This has been the common mistake of traditional social contract theorists and their contemporary followers, who generally treat right as limited to the enforcement of property entitlements, predicating political authority upon contract and restricting government to an administration of civil law. On this basis, any entitlements to equal economic opportunity become swept aside by the claim that any redistributions of property or restrictions on its use violate right if they go beyond protecting the person and property of individuals.

This is symptomatic of how the social contract argument, which treats the choosing will as a foundational principle of ethical construction, cannot comprehend ethical community of any sort. The family gets treated as some peculiar amalgam of property relations,[13] even though marriage comprises an agreement that establishes a union within which contractual relations no longer properly apply and where parental duties go beyond mere respect for person and property. The state gets reduced to an adjudicator and enforcer of property rights, with no recognition of how political freedom involves a form of self-determination that cannot be exercised apart from participation in institutions of self-government and that involves universal ends of an entirely different character from those at stake in dispositions over property.

Economic right may contain recognition of property, but it cannot be reduced to property right precisely because the economy is an ethical community, with rights and duties specific to the freedoms at play in market participation. Whenever individuals engage in economic activity, they do something more than merely dispose of property and enter into a relation of contract.

The difference does not involve engaging in an interaction with other agents as opposed to a unilateral action. As Hegel emphasizes, the two forms of self-determination that do not involve ethical community, namely property right and morality, both consist in interrelations of agents. One cannot determine oneself as an owner without having the presence of one's will in a factor recognized by others who are equally recognized to have embodied their will in other factors.[14] Property ownership can only occur as a mutual engagement, which is why no one can have property in complete isolation from other owners. This reciprocity of property is emblematic of the intersubjective character of right in general. Right is not a privilege but a universal entitlement insofar as exercising a right involves being respected by others whose similar prerogative one equally respects. The self-determination of right always thus involves relating to others whose self-determination is a condition for the realization of one's own freedom. This is true of morality as well, for exercising moral responsibility always comprises acting in respect to the right and moral accountability of other conscientious subjects.[15] What distinguishes the interaction of property right and moral accountability from ethical community is that individuals determine themselves as owners and as moral subjects irrespective of being members of an association that already realizes the ends they pursue. Individuals determine themselves as owners simply by recognizing one another as disposing exclusively over their own bodies and then over factors in which they recognizably lay their wills. Similarly, individuals act with moral accountability not in and through membership in a community already embodying the moral good, but precisely by seeking to realize a good that is *not yet* at hand and whose content and fulfillment must both be personally determined by the moral individual.

Economic Self-Determination as a Form of Ethical Community

Economic self-determination is a form of ethical community because one can only engage in commodity relations by participating in an existing market in whose interdependent nexus of self-seeking individuals find themselves already embroiled. Unless the pursuit of interdependent self-selected particular ends is already realized in an ongoing production and circulation of commodities, individuals have nowhere to exercise their economic freedom. Supply and demand must already be available and this requires the context of a sphere of interaction in which individuals relate to one another solely in terms of chosen needs for what others have on the condition of supplying them in turn with something they have chosen to need.

This context does require that its participating individuals recognize one another as property owners and as conscientious individuals who are capable of being held accountable for what they do on purpose and for consequences of their actions that they intend. To engage in economic activity, however, property owners and moral subjects must further act in pursuit of self-selected particular ends whose satisfaction takes on the form of right. Each participant employs alienable property to this end, bringing something to market in order to obtain means of satisfying his or her own need for what others have and are willing to exchange in return. In this context of reciprocated need and alienation of property, the pursuit of particular interest becomes an entitled exercise of freedom insofar as it proceeds such that it can only be realized through facilitating the realization of the same sort of pursuit by others. On these terms, each market participant recognizes the legitimacy of the self-seeking of others while having his or her self-seeking respected as well.

As Hegel points out, because self-seeking here takes on a lawful, universalized character, the needs and objects of satisfaction at play are set free from any natural or traditional limitations and can permissibly include any factor that does not violate the property, moral, household or economic rights of individuals.[16] Individuals may satisfy their biological and psychological needs through economic activity, provided the objects meeting those needs are offered for exchange. They can, however, just as well seek any objects they choose to need so long as other economic agents have chosen to produce and market such goods on affordable terms without violating the rights of others. Within the ethical community of the market economy of the system of needs, need and commodities both obtain a universal character, standing as they do in interrelation to the needs for commodities and to the commodity ownerships of all participants in market interaction. Market need, commodities, and the activities providing for the production and marketing of commodities are thereby subject to a discrimination and multiplication conditioned not by natural necessity or psychological calculation, but the entitled scope of choice within the interdependent economic self-determination of market agents.[17] In this nexus of interdependent self-seeking, individuals are able to exercise not just their property rights, but the rights to satisfy self-selected needs in reciprocity with others and to engage in earning activities of their choosing in reciprocity with others. The ethical community of the market provides individuals with the continually reproduced context within which they can engage in the socially specific roles by which they can exercise the *right* to realize particular ends of their own choosing. Neither property rights, nor morality, nor household, nor political association can realize this specific form of self-determination.

Like all other rights, these economic rights comprise a specific type of equal opportunity. In this case, the equal opportunity can only be enjoyed if individuals have access to market participation on a par with others. As Hegel well knows, although every exercise of economic opportunity requires engagement in the reciprocal relations of commodity exchange, the working of the market guarantees neither that all individuals can find

others willing to purchase what they have to offer or to sell what they want
to buy on affordable terms, nor that the outcome of market transactions
will not generate new imbalances of commodity ownerships that leave the
less fortunate with greater impediments to participating in market activity.[18]
Only because the system of needs is an ethical community with economic
rights and duties extending beyond those of property relations, moral
accountability, and family association, can there be a legitimate claim to
equal economic opportunity. This claim mandates both private and public
correctives to the specifically economic injustices perennially generated by
the self-regulation of the market.

The Challenge of Fulfilling the
Ethical Imperatives of Economic Opportunity

These imperatives include, as Hegel duly recognizes, a civil administration
of law that can uphold the property entitlements on which market activity
depends.[19] This undertaking is not just a matter of upholding property
rights in the manner of the administration of law to which social contract theory restricts public institutions. Civil legality is itself a relationship
of ethical community within civil society, serving the exercise of social
freedom. This is because one cannot exercise one's rights as a legal subject without belonging to an existing legal framework in which civil laws
as well as the authority of civil courts and penal institutions are already
recognized. That standing institutional recognition is crucial to the very
existence of legality, which is why desuetude undermines law.

Moreover, civil legality has no field of social application unless it proceeds within an ethical community in which market relations have already
established an ongoing network of interdependent activity operating with
the universality and reciprocity commensurate with legalization. This is
why Hegel, in the *Philosophy of Right*, introduces civil legality after the
system of needs.[20] He properly recognizes that unless a market system
has emerged, the material activities of individuals will remain caught in
particular conventions that lack the universalization of conduct compatible
with legalization. Precisely because the system of needs is a prerequisite for
the emergence of civil legality, markets can emerge before an administration of civil law has been fully established. Nonetheless, until civil legality
has been established, market relations remain hobbled by the insecurity
of property relations. Without an ongoing civil formalization and enforcement of property entitlements, property cannot be fully mobilized as an
instrument of market activity. As Hernando de Soto has powerfully argued
in *The Mystery of Capital*,[21] one of the greatest obstacles to fostering equal

economic opportunity in "developing" countries is the lack of an effective civil legality to certify property relations, leaving economic resources with an uncertain ownership, preventing their optimal utilization in the market.

Civil legality, however, is only the beginning of the civil enforcement of equal economic opportunity. The members of civil society have the right to join together in common pursuit of shared particular interests, so long as they do so without violating the economic opportunity of others. Hegel misconstrues this private intervention in the market by conceiving it in terms of corporations, whose vestiges of feudal and guild traditions restrict the very exercise of economic freedom that private intervention should be trying to make truly accessible to all.[22] If he had more properly identified social interest groups as trade unions, consumer groups, tenant associations, business associations, and the like, the limitations of private remedies to economic injustice would be more easily apparent. Although such groups may succeed in advancing the particular interest of their members in the marketplace, their dependence on other economic agents always leaves their efforts subject to failure. It also always leaves open the possibility that the success of one interest group will diminish the economic fortunes of other groups or lead all to bankruptcy. Moreover, because social interest groups unite civilians in pursuit of shared, but particular, aims, they do not serve to mediate between the particularity of social freedom and the universality of political self-determination, which always wills to order the whole body politic on behalf of the entire citizenry. Hegel pretends that corporations can bridge the alleged gap between civil society and the state, but his claims rest upon subverting political freedom by allowing corporations to have special political privileges in an estate assembly.[23] This imposes a feudal subjection of rule to social divisions based at least in part on natural differences of birth. Instead, the exercise of political freedom mediates itself with all subsidiary forms of freedom by upholding them in conformity with equal political opportunity. In the case of economic freedom, this involves a distinctly political regulation of the economy, ensuring that citizens have equal access to the resources to run for office and to support political campaigns, while preventing concentrations of economic power from becoming sources of privileged political influence.

What social interest groups cannot achieve on behalf of equal economic opportunity calls for further public interventions to enforce economic justice. Hegel's identification of the system of needs as a form of ethical community is of key importance in deflecting the criticisms of such public intervention that social contract theorists commonly make by invoking the exclusive sanctity of property rights. The failure to acknowledge that markets involve any more than contractual entitlements underlies

Hayek's critique of the welfare state in *The Constitution of Liberty*,[24] which fuels conservative objections to social security, publicly guaranteed access to health care, graduated income taxes, public works employment, and public protections of labor organization. As a structure of ethical community, markets involve not just property rights, but economic rights that can only be exercised in and through commodity relations. These economic rights involve the genuine right to work. This is not a right to escape paying union dues after a majority of employees have voted for unionization. The true right to work rather consists in the publicly guaranteed entitlement to employment at a wage sufficient and at hours so limited as to enable individuals to exercise all their rights without prejudice. As Hegel points out, putting the under- or unemployed on the public dole does not remedy the real injustice of poverty, which consists in depriving individuals of the opportunity to exercise their economic freedoms of occupation and need in the market.[25] What does remedy the injustice is providing real job opportunities, enabling those able to work to support themselves through exercising their own social autonomy. Because the market can never be counted on to provide universal employment, public authority must step in with sufficient public works to rescue all able and willing individuals from the injustice of under- and unemployment. The funding for such public works employment can be obtained in harmony with equal economic opportunity by highly graduated income and wealth taxes that put the financial burden on those most able to pay. This is no more a violation of property rights than any other taxation that takes a portion of private wealth for the sake of upholding the freedom of all. Insofar as the institutions of freedom form a system, where nonpolitical freedoms depend on the state to uphold their exercise, while political freedom must incorporate them under certain limitations to maintain equal political opportunity, the partial restrictions on property rights are enabling conditions for the freedom of owners, rather than violations of it.

Hegel may not have conceived what the economy should be and how it should be regulated in complete or entirely consistent detail, but his fundamental identification of the system of needs as a form of ethical community anchors the challenge to remake "capitalism with a human face."

Notes

1. Hegel 1991, §2, 26.
2. Ibid., §184, 221.
3. Ibid., §183, 221.
4. Ibid., §241, 265.

5. Ibid., §246, 267–268; §248, 269.
6. Ibid., §244, 266.
7. Ibid., §84–96, 117–123.
8. Ibid., §102, 130.
9. Ibid., §230–256, 259–274.
10. David P. Levine characterizes this approach to economics as that of "economic calculation," and succinctly outlines these ramifications. As Levine points out, this approach has been extended to characterize modernity as a whole by Max Weber, who sees the general prevalence of economic calculation and instrumental rationality as "the hallmark of the modern age" (Caporaso and Levine 1992, 21–24). The Weberian view has been embraced by Heidegger and his students, including Hannah Arendt, Leo Strauss, and Herbert Marcuse, as well as by Theodor Adorno, Max Horkheimer, Michael Oakeshott, and Jürgen Habermas.
11. Hegel 1991, §189, 227.
12. Marx describes the historical process of expropriation and liberations from serfdom and guild controls providing for these conditions in his account of "The Secret of Primitive Accumulation" (Marx 1906, 784–787).
13. See, for example, Kant's account of family relations under the strained rubric of "On Rights to Persons Akin to Rights to Things" in Section III, paragraphs 22–30 of *The Metaphysics of Morals*. Kant 1996, 426–432.
14. Hegel 1991, §51, 81.
15. Ibid., §113, 140.
16. Ibid., §190–191, 228–229.
17. Ibid.
18. Ibid., §200, 233; §207, p. 239; §241, 265.
19. Ibid., §208, 239.
20. Ibid., §209, p. 240.
21. de Soto 2000.
22. Hegel 1991, §250–256, 270–274.
23. Ibid., §255, 272–273; §300–311, 339–351.
24. Hayek 1960, 253–323.
25. Hegel 1991, §245, 267.

Works Cited

Caporaso, J. A., and D. P. Levine. 1992. *Theories of Political Economy*. Cambridge: Cambridge University Press.
de Soto, H. 2000. *The Mystery of Capital: Why Capitalism Triumphs in the West and Fails Everywhere Else*. New York: Basic Books.
Hayek, F. A. 1960. *The Constitution of Liberty*. Chicago: University of Chicago Press.
Hegel, G.W.F. 1991. *Elements of the Philosophy of Right*. Translated by H. B. Nisbet. Cambridge: Cambridge University Press.
Kant, I. 1996. *Practical Philosophy*. Translated and edited by M. J. Gregor. New York: Cambridge University Press.
Marx, K. 1906. *Capital: A Critique of Political Economy*, vol. I. Translated by S. Moore and E. Aveling. New York: Random House.

9

Two Ways of "Taming" the Market

Why Hegel Needs the Police and *the Corporations*

LISA HERZOG

Introduction

The recent financial turmoil has also had its repercussions among Hegel scholars: there has been increasing interest in how Hegel's writings deal with economic issues. Can one find inspiration in them for understanding the problems of today's economy? But to what degree is Hegel an economist at all? How much did he know about economics, how seriously did he take the economic views of his time, and how did he react to them? Hegel is usually seen as a thinker of the state—how does his account of the modern, "rational" state deal with the problems of a nascent capitalism?

In this chapter I discuss some aspects of the economic thought of the mature Hegel, as found in his account of "civil society" in the 1820/21 *Philosophy of Right*. For Hegel, civil society is the realm in which modern society grants subjective freedom to its citizens: "particularity" is here "indulging itself in all directions as it satisfies its needs, contingent arbitrariness, and subjective caprice."[1] Individuals encounter one another in instrumental relationships, with "their own interests as their end."[2] Within the framework of positive law, every individual is free to do whatever he or she likes, which is why this is an "apparently scattered and thoughtless activity"[3] in a sphere full of "contingent circumstances."[4] The economic realm is "teeming with caprice," as Hegel formulates in one lecture;[5] it is a space in which "all waves of fortune and misfortune and of all passions pour out," as he says in another.[6]

As such, the free market is potentially destabilizing and socially disruptive. It "affords a spectacle of extravagance and misery" that provides some individuals with immense riches, and throws others into dire poverty; the result being the "physical and ethical corruption common to both" extravagance and misery.[7] This is one of the reasons why for Hegel the market needs to be tamed and "sublated" by other institutions, in particular the political state. Not only in the state, however, but also in civil society itself there are institutions that are meant to prevent the worst excesses of the market and to stabilize civil society: the police and the corporations. Hegel calls them the *"external state, the state of necessity and of the understanding."*[8]

In what follows, I focus on the police and the corporations as the two institutions that, in Hegel's account, tame the unpredictable and chaotic realm of the free market and insert some "universality" into it.[9] The main focus is on these two models of bringing order into a chaotic sphere in which individuals have subjective freedom, and on the different views of human nature that can be associated with them. For the sake of simplicity and clarity, I call these the economic and the sociological view of human nature, the core question that distinguishes them being how constant or pliable human preferences and human identity are taken to be. I argue that, although Hegel claims to have taken up economic insights of his day, he does not think that a purely economic consideration of the economic realm, and its control in terms of a purely economic approach, are sufficient. Rather, his account of the corporations can be understood as the nucleus of a theory of how preferences and identities are shaped in social groups and classes, and of why this matters for bringing some order into the economic realm. In the conclusion I show that these two models are still present in modern approaches to economic ethics, and that they offer a fruitful way of understanding different approaches for bringing order into today's economic world.

The Laws of the Market

Hegel's account of the "system of needs," the free market, starts from a sense of wonder and amazement: How can a sphere in which individuals are left completely free to do whatever they want, as "particulars," exhibit any orderly structure at all? He calls it "at first sight incredible"[10] that one can find any laws in it, comparing the science of economics to astronomy, which finds regularities in the "irregular movements" that the planets "present [. . .] to the eye."[11] The "manifestation [*Scheinen*] of rationality"[12] in the economic realm is explored by economics, which is a distinctively modern science:

> *Political economy* is the science which begins with the above viewpoints but must go on to explain mass relationships and mass movements in their qualitative and quantitative determinacy and complexity.—This is one of the sciences which have originated in the modern age as their element [*Boden*]. The development of science is of interest in showing how *thought* extracts from the endless multitude of details with which it is initially confronted the simple principles of the thing [*Sache*], the understanding which works within it and controls it (see Smith, Say, and Ricardo).[13]

Hegel had developed an active interest in economic questions early in his intellectual career, at least since his time in Bern.[14] But if one takes a closer look at the theoretical accounts available in his time, it seems that his reception of economic literature was nevertheless not very profound, and remains at the level of buzzwords and general arguments.

From Adam Smith (1723–1790), who is often cited as the founder of economics as an academic discipline, Hegel adopts the idea that markets can coordinate human behavior: in them, "*subjective selfishness* turns into a *contribution towards the satisfaction of the needs of everyone else.*"[15] Hegel also shares the idea that the division of labor increases productivity, as exemplified by the pin factory,[16] and, in some lectures, raises some of Smith's worries about its harmful effects on the workers' minds.[17] But Hegel does not show any interest in the free play of market prices as the mechanism in which this "dialectical movement"[18]—Smith's "invisible hand"—actually works. In the Griesheim lectures he notes that in England all taxation of groceries is abolished and the setting of prices is left to "the bakers, brewers, etc."—apparently an allusion to Smith's famous quote—in the hope that competition will on average lead to a low price. Hegel is skeptical about this argument; he argues that it is costly and complicated for customers to examine the quality of groceries; therefore market surveillance is needed.[19] Hegel does not argue for a flexible labor market either, but for its regulation through the corporations[20]—he had no faith in Smith's argument that a flexible labor market leads to an optimal allocation of labor, but rather thought that individuals, who are usually equipped with very specialized human capital, fall into unemployment if they are dismissed from their jobs.[21] Whereas Smith distinguished different social classes *analytically*, according to their source of income, Hegel's division of classes into agricultural, business and universal class remains within a traditional framework.[22]

Maybe the most important difference is that Hegel does not expect the free market to solve the problem of poverty in a peaceful, gradual process of economic growth; nor does he discuss the role of capital accumulation for such growth.[23] When Hegel speaks of the "infinitely varied means and their equally infinite and intertwined movements of reciprocal production and exchange,"[24] it becomes clear that his vision of the market is not that of the benevolent, self-adjusting social mechanism that Smith has in mind. It is much closer to Steuart's picture of a watch that is "continually going wrong;"[25] he even uses the Hobbesian metaphor of a "field of conflict"[26] and speaks of the "remnants of the state of nature."[27] Although Hegel thus shares some of Smith's central insights, he omits crucial elements of the latter's systemic perspective on economic processes as well as his optimism about the market's ability to solve social problems.[28]

There are no signs that Hegel incorporated central insights of Jean-Baptiste Say (1767–1832) or David Ricardo (1772–1823), either. For none of them there is any evidence that he read them in the original;[29] he maybe knew about them from newspapers or review journals.[30] One argument in his discussion of measures against poverty stands in clear contradiction to Say's famous law. Hegel argues that if one tried to create artificial opportunities of employment for the unemployed, this would lead to overproduction, intensifying the problem of poverty.[31] According to Say's law, however, supply creates its own demand. For this to hold, all income must be used for consumption rather than hoarding.[32] Hegel might have found the idea that the use of money creates imbalances between global supply and demand possible in James Steuart (1713–1780), whose *An Inquiry into the Principles of Political Economy* (1767) he had studied in detail early in his life,[33] and either did not know, or did not believe in, Say's law. As to Ricardo, there are no traces of a detailed discussion of any of the contents of the notoriously difficult to read *Principles of Political Economy and Taxation* (1817): no hint of his labor theory of value, little on the accumulation of capital, and nothing on the theory of land rents and the effects of different kinds of taxation, maybe Ricardo's most important contributions. Marx's judgment that Hegel was at the height of the economic theorizing of his time thus needs to be taken with some caution.[34]

The universality that enters into the chaotic appearances of economic life through "economic laws" thus does not seem to be at the center of Hegel's attention. His interest in economic theorizing seems to be lukewarm, at best. As I argue in the remainder of this chapter, however, there are systematic reasons for this, reasons worth taking seriously today as much as in Hegel's time.

Hegel calls the science of economics a theory of the "Understanding." Without going into a detailed discussion here, one important feature of

Understanding in contrast to Reason should be recalled: Understanding tends to take things as given; holding fixed what Reason recognizes as contingent and open to challenge. The thing that economists hold fixed when they derive economic "laws" are people's preferences, and, more generally speaking, all features of the individuals' identity and character. For Smith, the "desire of bettering our condition"[35] is constant enough to allow for generalizations about people's behavior; for John Stuart Mill economics focuses on the "consequence of the pursuit of wealth," the "aversion to labor" and the "desire of the present enjoyment of costly indulgences."[36] The modern methodology of rational choice by and large also works with such an assumption of fixed preferences, which are reduced to very few dimensions, for example, income and labor time. Without this methodological move, which assimilates the structure of human agency to that of material particles on which a small number of forces work, economists could not arrive at the quasi-mathematical characterizations of equilibriums or the processes that lead to them. The laws of economics become visible because economists abstract from a large number of factors, and aggregate others at a general level, so that the logical relations between them can be derived. Hegel recognizes this move in *PR* §192, when he speaks of "isolated and abstract needs, means and modes of satisfaction" (which, however, become "*concrete, i.e. social* ones," a remark that becomes clear later).

Economists have been eager to emphasize that this assumption of theirs is nothing but a methodological device—sometimes justifying it by pointing to the universal medium of money that makes possible the reduction of many different wants and desires to the desire for money—and that it should not be understood as a characterization of human nature. Be this as it may, this methodology implies a certain way of "taming" the market when it has undesirable side effects. With the individuals' preferences being held constant, what needs to be analyzed are incentive structures. When it turns out, for example, that there is an undersupply of public goods, because no one has an incentive to supply a good that can be used by everyone without access being controllable, this good needs to be supplied in some other way, for example, by forced contributions or directly by the state. Somehow, the framework needs to be changed, for example, by making some options more expensive and others less costly, so that individuals whose preferences are the same as before will behave differently. This is the way in which economists since the time of Adam Smith have responded to market failures, and structurally, this is also how one of Hegel's institutions in civil society, namely the police, proceeds.[37]

Hegel describes the police as "the universal which acts with regard to civil society."[38] Its two tasks are, firstly, to remove "*contingencies* which interfere with this or that end" and to attain "*undisturbed security* of *persons and property*," and secondly, to realize the right of individuals to "livelihood and welfare," that is, to fight poverty.[39] The measures for this include market surveillance through "means and arrangements which may be of use to the community,"[40] the arbitration of disputes caused by the "differing interests of producers and consumers,"[41] the oversight of "the large branches of industries" that are especially vulnerable to "external circumstances and remote combinations" and, in extraordinary circumstances, the fixing of prices for "the commonest necessities of life."[42] These measures certainly go further than what most economists would typically recommend, at least economists who work within a mainstream framework that assumes full information and perfect competition. Methodologically, however, they remain within the orbit of economic thinking: they are external measures—Hegel explicitly calls the police an "external order" in *PR* §231—and do not touch the inner lives of individuals. As far as the police is concerned, Hegel may show a greater concern for people's well-being than the cliché of a liberal economist would, but, like the latter, he takes their preferences and identities as given and asks how the external framework of incentives and rules should be changed.

Hegel's Sociological Perspective

But this model is not the only way in which Hegel sees the universal as a principle that is active in civil society. The second instrument for overcoming the particularity of civil society are the corporations, the professional associations of those who work in the same craft or in the same branch of some other business.[43] They are discussed at a key moment in the architecture of the *Philosophy of Right*, namely at the end of the section on "Civil Society," immediately before the transition into "The State." The introduction of these social institutions in Hegel's theory of civil society, however, raises a number of questions. The first puzzle is that it remains somewhat vague what kind of associations Hegel actually means. As Schmidt am Busch points out, Hegel does not seem to have in mind any concrete historical institution that existed in his time.[44] His wording is not consistent, and in the lectures he also suggests that local communities or church parishes might belong into this category.[45] Commentators have seen their historical origins in Roman law[46] or in medieval constitutionalism,[47] but this does not help much for clarifying what these institutions should look like in Hegel's time. The second puzzle is that Hegel does not discuss how these institutions, which regulate the labor market rather heavily, can coexist with a free market for goods and services—he does not ask, for example, what happens if a nonmember of a corporation enters a market and offers products at a competitive price, crowding out the products offered by the corporations.[48]

I do not claim to resolve these puzzles in the course of this chapter, nor do I want to answer the question of whether, as questions of textual exegesis, they can be resolved at all, or whether there remain tensions. I take them, however, to indicate that Hegel was interested not so much in the concrete historical form the corporations assumed, but rather in their function within civil society. I take it that his theory of the corporations, together with his theory of the different classes,[49] is the nucleus of an answer to a question left open by the economic approach: Where do people's preferences actually come from, and how are their identities as market participants shaped?

Hegel emphasizes that biological necessities, which would have some fixedness, do not play a central role in commercial society.[50] Human "contingent arbitrariness, and subjective caprice"[51] stand in stark contrast to the unrefined and undifferentiated needs of animals. This is, for Hegel, a liberating moment in human history.[52] But it also means that human desires become extremely variable. Human beings, however, are social animals, and so the opinions that shape their desires are not only their own opinions, but also "universal" opinion, that is, the opinions of others.[53] Imitation, the wish to be similar to others, is a major determinant of people's preferences.[54] Hegel also observes—without criticizing—that the imitation of others often has practical reasons, as it is often easiest to follow conventions: "in the manner of dress and times of meals, there are certain conventions which one must accept, for in such matters, it is not worth the trouble to seek to display one's own insight, and it is wiser to act as others do."[55]

Hegel, who was very much aware of the social character of human nature, could not have left undertheorized the question of where the preferences that underlie the processes of civil society come from. Preferences are expressions of people's identities, a topic untouched by most economic theories. If one turns to the notorious line that economics is the science of how people choose, and sociology is about why they have no choice, but are formed by their social contexts, then one can say that Hegel is a sociologist as much as an economist (while using the insights from these disciplines into what is, in the end, a philosophical account). He shows a clear sense of the degree to which individuals are influenced by their social background, arguing that the different social classes all have a specific character. The members of the agricultural class, although not untouched by modern developments such as the introduction of civil law, are shaped by their "mode of subsistence" and develop the "substantial disposition [. . .] of an immediate ethical life based on the family relationship and on trust."[56] The business class is equally shaped by its activities: it "relies for its livelihood on its *work,* on *reflection* and the understanding,"[57] whereas the class of civil servants reflects the "universality" of its activity for the state.[58]

It is not surprising that the classes and the corporations are so important for the formation of individuals' preferences and identities. Hegel puts great emphasis on the "Bildung" that the individuals receive in civil society through their work; it is, for him, not something external and instrumental, but something that shapes the individuals through and through.[59] The social space within which this work takes place, however, are the classes and the corporations. This underlines their role in shaping the individuals' character. The corporations are also the place where individuals find recognition in the particularity of their different professions; here, they are seen by others and by themselves as members of a particular group[60] and have "*[their] honour in [their] estate.*"[61] The relation between the individuals and the corporations is quite affectionate: they are their "second famil[ies],"[62] and also offer an insurance against existential risks, as members who fall into poverty can receive help that does not have the "humiliating character" that other forms of support for the poor often take on.[63]

All these factors contribute to making the corporations crucial for the formation of the individuals' preferences. They are the social spaces in which individuals develop a professional *identity*—they "are" brewers, butchers, or bakers, rather than just "having" these jobs as something external to them.[64] There might also be a national, or even regional or local, dimension to it, if individuals do not produce just *any* version of a good, but rather the version that has traditionally been produced in this geographical area, and while such traditions are open to be changed by individuals, they can reinforce the individuals' identification with their corporation and with practices in which they jointly engage.

The individuals' habits, including their consumption patterns, are shaped by these social contexts. In fact, Hegel is highly critical of the consumption patterns of those *without* a membership:

> If the individual [*der Einzelne*] is not a member of a legally recognized [*berechtigten*] corporation [. . .], he is without the *honour of belonging to an estate*, his isolation reduces him to the selfish aspect of his trade, and his livelihood and satisfaction lack *stability*. He will accordingly try to gain *recognition* through the external

manifestations of success in his trade, and these are without limit [*unbegrenzt*].[65]

As Schmidt am Busch notes, this endless desire is a misplaced desire for recognition, which the members of a corporation receive from their colleagues for their professional achievements.[66] Without such membership, individuals have, in Muller's words, no "sense of an appropriate level of consumption" and can fall into a "continual, irritable search for more and more."[67] If one is recognized by the members of one's corporation, in contrast, one does not have to strive for recognition by luxury consumption, but can adopt an established way of life.[68]

This is a very different process of how general patterns of behavior are brought into the market than the ones observed by economists. It does not arise as a consequence of how people's static preferences interact, but concerns the formation of these very preferences: these become standardized, and, as the corporations are ethical communities, also "ethicized." What Hegel does in the theory of corporations is to turn the social institutions in which the individuals' preferences and identities are formed into an explicit object of theorizing. In the ideal corporation, people develop an ethos that brings order into civil society. Consumption becomes less excessive, because recognition is sought for good work, not for the ostensive show of luxury. This makes the overall consumption patterns in civil society less unstable, as people are less inclined to follow the ups and downs of fashion. Importantly, however, the ethos of the corporations also includes interests that go beyond people's immediate desires. The care for members who have fallen into distress teaches them to pay attention to the needs of others and to develop a sense of solidarity.[69] Individuals become engaged in the running of the corporation and its internal politics.[70] They learn to pursue collective interests rather than merely their narrow self-interest, and to represent these in the political realm.[71] Although the ethos of the corporations is not yet the full ethos of the political citizenship, but limited to a smaller group, it is, for Hegel, an important step in the development of the latter.

The individuals' preferences and identities are thus shaped in ways that prepare the ethos of the citizen—the citoyen, not the bourgeois—that Hegel describes as mark of the state.[72] The very place in which people's preferences for a certain way of life and certain patterns of consumption are formed in civil society is also the place where they already learn to partly transgress their own interests, and to think in terms of a universality, however limited it may be. Whereas the measures taken by the Hegelian police act on the individuals in a purely external way, the corporations are the "second" "*ethical* root of the state," the one "based in civil society,"[73] and as such, they shape individuals in a thoroughgoing way.

Conclusion

I have discussed the two institutions that, for Hegel, create universality in the sphere of civil society, where individuals are free to pursue their own interests within the framework of positive laws. I have argued that the way in which the police functions corresponds to the economic approach: taking people's preferences as given, it changes the external framework within which they operate. The approach suggested by Hegel's theory of the corporations, in contrast, looks at the world from a sociological perspective: it asks where people's preferences come from, how their identities are shaped by their social context, and what these contexts must look like in order to develop an ethos that prepares the individuals for the ethos of the political state.

Today, the need to "tame" the market and to curb its negative side effects seems to be greater than ever. Although some problems, for example, the risk of old-age poverty, have partly been curbed in Western countries by institutions such as the welfare state, other problems have become even greater, from the stability of the international financial system to exploitative labor contracts and environmental issues. The question of how to tame the markets is a topic of ongoing research in economic ethics, business ethics, and political philosophy. Interestingly, Hegel's two models correspond quite closely to two ways in which questions of economic ethics have been discussed in the last few years.[74] The debate in the 1990s between Karl Homann and Peter Ulrich turned on the question of whether making the market more moral is a question of changing the institutional framework, or of changing people's attitudes and preferences. Building on James Buchanan's institutionalist approach, Homann argues that it is crucial to create a framework that sets the right incentives, because companies and individuals cannot be moral on their own in situations in which they might be out-competed by less moral competitors. This approach takes their preferences as given, and endorses the striving for profit by arguing that it leads to efficient market outcomes.[75] Ulrich, in contrast, uses a "republican" approach, arguing that companies must take into account the legitimate concerns of all stakeholders.[76] This approach wants to "transform" the logic of economic thinking and integrate moral concerns into it. Both approaches contain a true core, and there may be situations in which one or the other is more appropriate. It is likely that we cannot rely on only one of them, and forego the other, if we want to address the problems of today's economy, especially in its global dimension.

In the Hegelian conception, it is the "rational" state that supersedes the sphere of civil society. The police is supervised by the executive branch of the government,[77] and the corporations equally need to stand under the "higher supervision of the state," otherwise they might "become ossified and set in [their] ways, and decline into a miserable guild system."[78] Today, with a globalized economy and political structures that are still largely national, this structure has become precarious. This implies that the power relations between markets and states have undergone a major shift, making it even more questionable whether taming the market by means of institutional controls can be sufficient. We also have to ask what I have called the "sociological" question: What ethos dominates the working sphere in different industries? Where do people's professional identities and ensuing consumption patterns come from? Do they prepare the ground for—or rather undermine—an ethos of responsible citizenship? These questions are particularly relevant with regard to the sector that stands in the center of the recent turmoil: the global financial industry. But they are also relevant for other sectors, such as agriculture, which have traditionally been seen as spaces in which a strong identification of individuals with their roles was made possible, but which seem to be dominated more and more by global patterns of supply and demand.

An important point to be considered, when reflecting on this question, is that there has been an asymmetry in the way in which the two models that correspond to Hegel's police and corporations have been received. Especially since the "Chicago school" has become dominant in economics, the idea of man as "utility maximizer" has become more and more pervasive and socially acceptable, and the footnote that this might be nothing but a methodological device has often gone by the board. The question as to whether it is descriptively adequate and normatively desirable to look at all forms of human behavior, from family life to voting decisions, through the lens of utility maximization has often been neglected. But the reasons that Hegel had for *not* considering the economic approach sufficient still hold today: we need to ask not only what happens when people try to follow their interests, but also what these interests are, where they come from, and what social influences are instrumental in shaping the identities on which they are based. Ironically, today this must include the question about the performative effects of that kind of economic theorizing that precisely neglected asking these questions. It seems difficult to deny that it has changed the way in which individuals, especially those trained in mainstream economics, look at their own behavior and that of others.[79] All the social mechanisms that Hegel describes with regard to the corporations—imitation, the development of habits, and mutual recognition—may, for some people, have contributed to considering as normal a character that is really quite close the *homo oeconomicus* of their textbooks. This maybe contributes to making it more difficult to reform the current economic system.

All this is not to deny the importance of good frameworks and the right incentives, and the need for reform in this area. But at least as much thought and discussion should be directed to the approach suggested by Hegel's theory of the corporation: How do human beings become who they are, what influences the formation of their preferences—and how might the social spaces in which these preferences and identities are formed be transformed such as to contribute to the good of the social whole? Hegel does not give us the key for reinventing such institutions today, but he gives us good reasons not to neglect this way of looking at economic problems.[80]

Notes

1. *PR* (= Hegel 1991), §185.
2. Ibid., §183, §187.
3. Ibid., §189Z.
4. Ibid., §200.
5. Griesheim (= Ilting 1974a), 487. All translations are my own.
6. Hotho (= Ilting 1974b), 567. All translations are my own.
7. *PR* §185.
8. Ibid., §183.
9. Hegel also discusses the "administration of justice" in the context of civil society, but it less interesting for my topic, because hardly any theorist, apart from a few anarcho-libertarians, denies the necessity of a basic framework of laws (especially for securing property rights) and of courts of justice for the existence of markets. The interesting differences lie in what other measures are seen as necessary for, and capable of, "taming" the market. These measures (or at least some of them) might also take on the form of positive law, or positive regulations of some kind, and be enforced through courts of justice (see, e.g., *PR* §253 for the need of corporations to be publicly authorized). In this sense, the administration of justice is the precondition for the further regulation of the market through the police *and* the corporations.
10. *PR* §189Z, cf. also Hotho, 587.
11. *PR* §189Z.
12. *PR* §189.
13. Ibid.
14. On the development of his economic thought see, for example, Neschen 2008, chapter I–III.

15. *PR* §199. For a discussion see, for example, Henderson and Davies 1991.

16. Cf. Waszek 1985 on how Hegel first took up Smith's pin factory example in 1803/04. As Waszek shows, Hegel did not always reread Smith in the subsequent years of lecturing on this topic, sometimes using different figures.

17. Cf. in particular Waszek 1988, chapter IV, for a discussion of the similarities between Smith's and Hegel's accounts of the division of labor.

18. *PR* §199.

19. Griesheim, 597.

20. Cf. also Priddat 1990, especially 189ff. More on the corporation follows later.

21. Hotho, 610, 698f., cf. similarly Griesheim, 600. In addition, Hegel mentions age and habituation as factors that make it difficult or impossible for individuals to change into another industry (Griesheim, 625).

22. As Waszek shows, he is here much closer to Steuart than to Smith, and might also have drawn on Prussian law and the situation in Germany in his time (1988, 171ff.). Waszek characterizes Hegel's theory of social classes as "much more hesitant and traditional" than Smith's (ibid., 176, cf. also Winfield 1987, 53ff.).

23. Cf. Priddat 1990, 26, 52, 152. Hegel does speak of the growth of "universal and permanent resources" in *PR* §199, but his remarks stay at a general level, without discussing, for example, whose capital is amassed and how the value created by it is distributed in society. For his views on poverty, the news about mass pauperization in London, which he received through newspapers and magazines, might have played a role. See Waszek 1988, 215ff., on the newspapers and magazines Hegel read.

24. *PR* §201.

25. Steuart 1966, II.XIII, 217.

26. *PR* §289.

27. Ibid., §200.

28. Smith's and Hegel's account of market society are compared in detail in Herzog 2013.

29. Cf. Stedman Jones 2001, 116.

30. Waszek 1988, 116.

31. *PR* §245.

32. For a discussion see, for example, Blaug 1996, chapter IV.

33. Cf. Chamley 1965, 254.

34. Cf. also Priddat 1990, 9ff.

35. Smith 1976, book II, chapter III, para. 28.

36. Mill 1949, book VI, chapter 9, sect. 3.

37. This is not to imply that Hegel's approach is identical to Smith's with regard to the police. For a discussion see, for example, Neocleous 1998, who emphasizes the influences of cameralist doctrines and of Steuart (who might in turn have been influenced by cameralist thought) on Hegel's conception of the police.

38. Hotho, 587. For a detailed discussion see Priddat 1990, 88ff. On the intellectual traditions behind the concept of "police" in the German-speaking context, see also Schmidt am Busch 2011, 228ff.

39. *PR* §230.

40. Ibid., §235.

41. Ibid., §236. This includes, for example, quality controls for groceries and drugs, cf. Griesheim 597ff.

42. *PR* §236. For a discussion see, for example, Waszek 1988, 198ff.

43. Ibid., §202ff., 250ff.

44. Schmidt am Busch 2011, 233.

45. Ibid.

46. Heiman 1971.

47. Lee 2008. Lee argues that Hegel did not want to keep the "Zünfte" in their concrete historical forms (as is indicated by the fact that he does *not* use the term "Zunft," cf. ibid. 630), but in their function of preventing an atomization of individuals, a position that would sit between the reactionary and the progressive views of his time. Lee thus also suggests a functional reading of the corporations, although one that focuses on a different (but compatible) function to the one I focus on.

48. For a discussion see Schmidt am Busch 2002, 139ff. See also Priddat 1990, 189ff.

49. Hegel holds that the agricultural and the universal class (the civil servants) do not need corporations (*PR* §250). With regard to some functions of the corporations—for example, the support of members who fall into poverty—it is not clear how the other classes fulfill this responsibility. With regard to other functions—for example, the political representation—it is clear why the first and third class do not need corporations. For the aspect I discuss in the following, classes and corporations can be considered as playing a parallel role, which is why I treat them together.

50. *PR* §194.

51. Ibid., §185.

52. Ibid.

53. Ibid., §194.

54. Ibid., §193.

55. Ibid., §192Z.

56. Ibid., §203.

57. Ibid., §204.

58. Ibid., §205.

59. Ibid., §187.

60. Cf. *PR* §207.

61. *PR* §253.

62. Ibid., §252.

63. Ibid., §255.

64. This is explored in more detail, and in a direct comparison with Adam Smith, in Herzog 2013, chapter IV.

65. *PR* §253.

66. Schmidt am Busch 2011, chapter 5.

67. Muller 2002, 158f.

68. *PR* §253, cf. also Grisheim 617ff.

69. Ibid., §253.

70. Ibid., §252.

71. These activities include choosing new members, protecting each other against "particular contingencies," and educating others to become members (*PR* §252). Cf. also *PR* §289 on the politics of the corporation, which Hegel describes

rather critically, but holds that this sphere belongs to "the moment of *formal freedom*" and "provides an arena in which personal cognition and personal decisions and their execution, as well as petty passions and imaginings, may indulge themselves." But this behavior is nonetheless "acceptable" from the point of view of the state, because of its "triviality" and "relative unimportance" (ibid.). On the political role of the corporations see *PR* §299.

72. *PR* §267ff.

73. Ibid., §255.

74. I here mainly refer to the debate in the German-speaking countries. There are some parallels in the Anglophone world, but the focus there has been more on "business ethics," understood as the ethics of individual companies, and on "professional ethics" for individuals in different professions. To my knowledge, there has not been a comparable debate about the systematic place and role of ethics in the economy. Choosing Homann and Ulrich as two points of reference is also justified because they come from the two "schools" of Hegelian philosophy in post–WWII Germany: Homann studied under Joachim Ritter in Münster, whereas Ulrich is influenced by Habermas and the Frankfurt School.

75. See, for example, Homann and Suchanek 2000.

76. See, for example, Ulrich 1997. For a discussion of these and other approaches to economic ethics and a comparison with Hegel's account see also Neschen 2008, chapter IV. The distinctions drawn in this chapter, however, are not discussed by Neschen.

77. *PR* §287.

78. Ibid., §255Z.

79. Cf., for example, Frank et al. 1993. For obvious reasons, however, research into the performative effects of economic teaching are controversial.

80. I would like to thank the audiences at the University of Warsaw's seminar in German Idealism and at the conference of the Hegel Society of America, and in particular Jakub Kloc-Konkolowicz, Andrew Buchwalter, and Karin de Boer, for helpful comments and suggestions.

Works Cited

Abbreviations for Works by G.W.F. Hegel

Griesheim   *G.W.F. Hegel, Vorlesungen über Rechtsphilosophie 1818–1831. Vierter Band.* Stuttgart-Bad Cannstatt: Frommann-Holzboog, 1974. This volume includes the lecture notes by K. G. v. Griesheim 1824/25.

Hotho   *G.W.F. Hegel, Vorlesungen über Rechtsphilosophie 1818–1831. Dritter Band. Nach der Vorlesungsmitschrift von H. G. Hotho 1822/23.* Stuttgart-Bad Cannstatt: Frommann-Holzboog, 1974.

PR   *Elements of the Philosophy of Right.* Edited by A. W. Wood, translated by H. B. Nisbet. Cambridge: Cambridge University Press, 1991 [1820/21]. Cited by paragraph. Z marks quotations from the "Zusätze" added by Eduard Gans.

Blaug, M. 1996. *Economic Theory in Retrospect*. 5th ed. Cambridge: Cambridge University Press.

Chamley, P. 1965. "Les origines de la pensée économique de Hegel." *Hegel-Studien* 3: 225–261.

Frank, R., H. T. Gilovich, and D. T. Regan. 1993. "Does Studying Economics Inhibit Cooperation?" *Journal of Economic Perspectives* 7 (2): 159–171.

Heiman, G. 1971. "The Sources and Significance of Hegel's Corporate Doctrine." In *Hegel's Political Philosophy: Problems and Perspectives*, edited by Z. A. Pelczynski, 111–135. Cambridge: Cambridge University Press.

Henderson, J. P., and J. B. Davies. 1991, "Adam Smith's Influence on Hegel's Philosophical Writings." *Journal of the History of Economic Thought* 13 (2): 184–204.

Herzog, L. 2013. *Inventing the Market. Smith, Hegel, and Political Theory*. Oxford: Oxford University Press.

Homann, K., and A. Suchanek. 2000. *Ökonomik. Eine Einführung*, Tübingen: Mohr Siebeck.

Lee, D. 2008. "The Legacy of Medieval Constitutionalism in the Philosophy of Right: Hegel and the Prussian Reform Movement." *History of Political Thought* 29: 601–634.

Mill, J. S. 1949 [1843]. *A System of Logic*. London: Longmans, Green.

Muller, J. Z. 2002. *The Mind and the Market. Capitalism in Western Thought*. New York: Anchor Books.

Neocleous, M. 1998. "Policing the System of Needs: Hegel, Political Economy, and the Police of the Market." *History of European Ideas* 24 (1): 43–58.

Neschen, A. 2008. *Ethik und Ökonomie in Hegels Philosophie und in modernen wirtschaftsethischen Entwürfen*. Hamburg: Meiner.

Priddat, B. 1900. *Hegel als Ökonom*. Berlin: Duncker & Humblot.

Schmidt am Busch, H.-Ch. 2002. *Hegels Begriff der Arbeit*. Berlin: Akademie-Verlag.

———. 2011. *'Anerkennung' als Prinzip der kritischen Theorie*. Berlin, Boston: De Gruyter.

Smith, A. 1976 [1776]. *An Inquiry into the Nature and Causes of the Wealth of Nations*. 2 vols. Edited by R. H. Campbell and A. S. Skinner; textual editor W. B. Todd. Oxford: Clarendon Press.

Stedman Jones, G. 2001. "Hegel and the Economics of Civil Society." In *Civil Society: History and Possibilities*, edited by S. Kaviraj and S. Khilnani, 105–131. Cambridge: Cambridge University Press.

Steuart, J. 1966 [1767]. *An Inquiry into the Principles of Political Economy*. Edinburgh, London: Oliver & Boyd.

Ulrich, P. 1997. *Integrative Wirtschaftsethik. Grundlagen der lebensdienlichen Ökonomie*. Bern: Haupt.

Waszek, N. 1985. "Miscellanea: Adam Smith and Hegel on the Pin Factory." *Owl of Minerva* 16, 229–233.

———. 1988. *The Scottish Enlightenment and Hegel's Account of "Civil Society."* Dordrecht, Boston, London: Kluwer.

Winfield, R. D. 1987. "Hegel's Challenge to the Modern Economy." In *Hegel on Economics and Freedom*, edited by W. Maker. Macon, GA: Mercer University Press, 32–64.

10

Hegel's Logical Critique of Capitalism

The Paradox of Dependence and the Model of Reciprocal Mediation

Nathan Ross

Is capitalism an ethical form of society? It is my argument that the philosophy of Hegel gives us resources to answer this question in a powerful and insightful way that veers between two better known approaches: Kantian ethics allows us to critique the subjective disposition of the person who treats others merely as means (and thus offers an implicit ethical limit to many forms of economic behavior), while Marx offers a highly detailed objective analysis of how capitalism works to reproduce itself and how it runs into inherent contradictions that lead to its demise. Hegel offers an approach that differs from both of these by asking whether capitalism is a part of ethical life or, to put it another way, whether it makes up a *rational whole* in which true self-determination is possible. In asking this kind of question, Hegel asks not merely about the validity of the ethical disposition of the capitalist, nor merely about the limits to the smooth economic functioning of the economy in distributing wealth, but about the *logic* of how the subject finds itself in its objectified needs, works, and institutions.

According to his method, Hegel offers a determinate negation of capitalism, which is treated most explicitly in the Civil Society section from the *Philosophy of Right*.[1] He sees in the actions of investors, consumers, and workers each pursuing their self-interested motivations a "system of needs" that results in overproduction, poverty, and general disintegration of segments of society into what he terms a rabble.[2] However, the true power of his approach rests not in any specific forecasts or prognostications that he makes about the functioning of capitalist economies, but in his logical and ethical approach to understanding economics as an aspect of ethical life. Although he offers a trenchant critique of *unmediated capitalism*, he does not merely offer a defense of state intervention or mediated capitalism, but seeks to develop a model of *reciprocal mediation*, in which economic activity plays an important role in forming individuals for civic engagement, while the state plays an important role in protecting individuals against the dangers of the dangers of the market place. This paper is dedicated to proving that the logic of reciprocal mediation, which Hegel develops in the syllogism and mechanism sections of the *Science of Logic*, offers the key to understanding how he thought of the limits of capitalism and the relation between market and state in ethical life.

I argue that the basic logic of capitalism is mechanistic in its way of treating the relation of individual to society. In his *Science of Logic*, Hegel describes mechanism as the most basic and immediate form of objectivity, in which objects are self-sufficiently isolated and aggregated by external forces, rather than any internal principle.[3] Such a logic seems to match the central paradox that Hegel finds in the system of needs: that as our pursuit of self-interest becomes more isolated and unmediated by other ethical concerns, we become increasingly dependent on market forces that are beyond our control.[4] This leads in capitalism to a form of dependence that is always accidental, and potentially destructive, because it is not yet posited as a moment in ethical life. Although true autonomy consists in being with oneself in otherness, Hegel is critical of economic structures in which we are dependent on mere market forces, which are not a result of any willing. In a logical context, Hegel argues that a merely mechanistic understanding of objects involves a stubborn contradiction between the *absolute independence* (*Selbständigkeit*) of objects and their *absolute dependence* (*Unselbstständigkeit*) on the forces that aggregate them.[5] They are unable to make their relations to each other a matter of self-determination, and so their autonomy is neither self-sustaining nor transparent. In economics, Hegel means to show that the very system that allows for the unlimited pursuit of wealth is itself responsible for the production of an ethically intolerable poverty: false independence begets spurious dependence. My thesis is that Hegel's insight into the contradiction at the heart of the *mere mechanism* explains the ethical untenability of unmediated capitalism, while the doctrine of reciprocal mediation in *absolute mechanism* provides the path to understanding the role of economic life within ethical life.

Certainly any discussion of capitalism must take up not only the relation of market actors, but also the implicit role of political institutions in making economic behavior possible in the first place. One of the most difficult challenges in interpreting Hegel's *Philosophy of Right* as a cohesive social theory consists in understanding how the separate moments relate to one another, and this applies particularly to the way that he understands the relation of civil society and the state. To say that the state is the *sublation* of civil society leaves it unclear to what degree the problematic structures of economic life are still allowed to exist, forgiven and forgotten by the state.[6] In order to give a deeper understanding of how Hegel performs a determinate negation of capitalism in his treatment of civil society and the state in the *Philosophy of Right*, I look away from its text to a text from the *Science of Logic* that gives a distinct and interesting formulation of how civil society relates to the state: the passage on the syllogism of syllogisms from the absolute mechanism section of the doctrine of the concept.[7] Hegel's demand to think of civil society and the state in terms of patterns of reciprocal mediation represents not so much a logical argument for the sustaining of capitalism through state support, as a critique of any conception of economic or political behavior that does not take seriously the ethical needs of human beings within the system that produces them.

Hegel gives us ample reason to consider the chapter on mechanism in relation to social philosophy. Mechanism is not merely a way of understanding the organization of natural bodies, but also describes any form of practical activity that is "devoid of spirit,"[8] and he ends the section on mechanism by arguing that the absolute mechanism allows us to understand the interaction of economy and state as a rational whole by virtue of its model of reciprocal mediation. What is vital in this figure of absolute mechanism is that it allows us to think the co-existence, mutual implication, and interpenetration of different forms of mediation within a unified sphere. Not only are citizens mediated with the state to the degree that the state helps them realize their private interests, but also the citizens relate to their own needs and wants through the form of universality that state life gives them. But the state can only relate to the particular needs and wants of the individuals through the participation of the citizens. (Hence three syllogisms: Singular-Particular-Universal, Singular-Universal-Particular, and Universal-Singular-Particular.)[9]

If this figure of absolute mechanism from the logic is to be truly fruitful in offering a theory of capitalism, then it cannot simply be a matter of mapping the schema of the syllogisms onto the schema of the institutions that Hegel describes (a project that Henrich tentatively undertakes). Instead, it must be possible to consider the logic of mechanism and absolute mechanism as offering a set of partial mediations (to borrow a term from John McCumber)[10] that serve first to critique mere capitalism and then to explain how economic life can function according to the notion of ethical life.

The Critique of Mere Mechanism in the System of Needs

In the *Science of Logic*, Hegel defines mechanism as a form of objectivity in which the objects only relate to each other as complete, self-sufficient entities. Because these objects are defined not by their mutual dependence, any relation that coordinates them is not part of their essence. "This makes up the character of mechanism, that whatsoever relationship exists between the things connected, this relationship is foreign to them, which does not affect their nature; even if they have the appearance of a unity, it is nothing other than a setting together, mixing, piling."[11] Hegel goes on to stipulate that such a mechanistic form of objectivity can be found not only in the natural world, but in the realm of human praxis: he gives the example of a mechanical memory, as when one learns words in a dead language, or a mechanical practice of religion. However, there are a rich variety of texts in which Hegel considers much of human economic activity as mechanistic in the same sense that is described here. While human economic activity is driven by the underlying teleology of need, in which one being seeks to complete itself and see itself as essential through the negation of another object, such teleology is essentially repressed as the division of labor develops and each person works not to negate the object or stamp it with ones essence, but rather works to modify the object in some way as to make it exchangeable.[12]

The division of labor, which undergoes an enormous intensification when capital owns and revolutionizes the means of production, makes the work process increasingly mechanistic. There are descriptions in Adam Smith, the young Hegel, and the early writings of Karl Marx,[13] which describe the increasingly repetitive, specialized, and dehumanizing nature of work in a capitalist factory. However, not only the work process takes on the quality that Hegel attributes to the mechanistic object in the *Science of Logic*: exchange, consumption, and investment can each be described as following a similar pattern, as money stands in for exchange value, consumer needs become a matter for commercial manipulation, and the process of capital investment is controlled by purely quantitative calculations. Indeed, the notion of mechanism seems to apply not only to the actual objective behaviors of workers, consumers, and investors in capitalism, but also to the form of subjectivity that it engenders (what later theory would call the *ideology of capitalism*). A form of consciousness emerges relative to commerce in which each person defines freedom as a central value in economic life, and freedom is understood in just the way that the mechanistic object understands itself: one is free to the degree that one can pursue ones self-interest in an unmediated way, through a marketplace in which one exchanges ones labor for that of others. (This neoliberal definition of freedom naturally does not accord very well with Hegel's definition of freedom as the autonomy of the self-determining concept.)

In his logical treatment of mechanism, Hegel diagnoses a central contradiction in the mechanistic object: the very feature that makes it completely free also makes it completely dependent. The false and spurious way in which the object defines independence leads to a bad form of dependence that is destructive in nature.[14] Because it is unable to make its relation to other objects a part of its own nature, it must constantly find itself outside of itself in relations that are foreign to it. The very way in which it defines its freedom as absence of relation makes it sure to be heteronymous. In a logical context, this leads to the destruction of the mechanistic object, and the positing of the mechanistic process as the real truth of the mechanism. I believe that this contradiction at the heart of the mechanistic object, whereby independence begets dependence, represents a key insight into the volatile and self-contradictory nature of capitalist society, an insight that Hegel only partially conveys in his treatment of the System of Needs in the *Philosophy of Right.*

Hegel's treatment of the System of Needs is his most direct, sustained discussion of capitalist society. The section has three primary concerns: to explain the emergence of civil society as a "system of atomism" out of the unity of the family; to describe the ethically positive value of work in civil society as a form of education in which the subject embraces the nature of objects and becomes accountable to other subjects; and to warn of the severely volatile and violent features of a capitalist labor market in producing inequality, poverty, mass unemployment, and a *rabble* that does not belong to the culture of ethical life. In my argument, the first and third features demonstrate the applicability of the logic of mechanism to Hegel's understanding of capitalism (the second, positive feature of the system of needs can only be saved by integrating it as a syllogism into the notion of ethical life).

For the moment I look away from the aspects of civil society that Hegel regards as ethically positive, because these are salvaged later in my discussion of a more logically nuanced notion of absolute mechanism. Instead, I note how Hegel's fears about the development of unmediated capitalism demonstrate a mechanistic logic: in a capitalist society, we are all dependent on the labor of others, and yet our ability to partake of the "fortune" (*Vermögen*) of society depends primarily on our share of capital.[15] In economic life we are driven primarily by the pursuit of our needs, not merely naturally given, animal needs, but socially produced desires, which are multiplied and increase our dependence on one another. Hegel thus notes that although the economy as a whole produces greater luxury, it also produces greater inequality in the ability to partake in this bounty, an insight largely shared by political economy. However, Hegel's ethical judgment of the story told by political economy reaches a climax in §243–244 of the *Philosophy of Right,* in which he claims that the growing inequality of capitalist economies produces a segment of society that is excluded from the benefits of economic growth to such a degree that it represents an "injury to the freedom" and "loss of the feeling of right."[16] Hegel does not argue that the injury to right here consists in the mere deprivation of material goods (as if there were universal human rights to food, shelter, etc.), but rather in the growing connection between the *dependency* of all and *exclusion* of some from the fortune of society. Dependency is a basic fact of economic life, and yet the form dependency takes here is spurious because it is not produced in a way that allows the members of society to posit it as an ethical relation between their own activity and the comprehensive activity of society.

Although far more attention could be devoted to Hegel's insight into the connection between dependence and independence in unjust socioeconomic structures,[17] the core insight of this chapter requires a shift to understanding dependence in its ethically rich form. The central contradiction of mechanism, that absolute independence begets absolute dependence, leads Hegel to the argument that we can only grasp a rational whole in which true freedom is possible by means of a *syllogism of syllogisms.* This figure of a syllogism of syllogisms allows Hegel to think of a form of economic life that is mediated by political representation, as well as a form of politics that is mediated by economic life.

"Everything Rational Is a Syllogism"

First it must be clarified what Hegel means with his overall notion of syllogistic mediation. In treating the syllogisms in the logic he writes: "Everything rational is a syllogism."[18] The form of the syllogism applies not in the first order to a set of propositions tied together to reach a conclusion, but to a conceptual structure in which the three moments of the concept (the universal, the particular, and the singular) relate to each other, two terms being extremes and the other mediating between them. He argues that the syllogism is the *form* of the rational, but in so doing he means form in a different sense than in a traditional conception of formal logic. For Hegel the form of the rational is not rational in abstraction from a rational content, for the rational form is the form that determines and penetrates its content. "It must be the case that logical reason, when it is taken in its formal capacity, can also be recognized in that reason that has to do with content; indeed, all content can only be rational through a rational form."[19]

For Hegel the discussion of the syllogisms provides a key to understanding the difference between finite content and truly rational content. The judgment (*Urteil*) provides the logical form for *finite things*, for in finite things the singular and the universal co-exist in a manner that is indeterminate and separable. "Socrates is a man" tells me what universal concept corresponds to Socrates, but it does not express what in Socrates allows him to be described in this way. Judgment holds the moments of the concept apart while identifying them through a medium that is not itself conceptual. The body and the soul co-exist but do not imply one another. But the syllogism relates two moments of the concept not through the mere copula, but through a further conceptual moment. In so doing it expresses, for example, the truth that the individual only becomes universal through particularity. The moments of the concept only relate to each other through the medium of each other.

> Everything is concept, and its determinate being is the difference of the moments of the concept, so that its universal nature gives itself external reality through particularity, and by way of this reflection-in-itself makes itself singular. Or on the other hand, the real is a singular that through particularity raises itself up to universality and makes itself identical with itself.[20]

The syllogism contains the form in which we must think individual things so as to make their individuality into a moment in a rational understanding of the real.

For Hegel what is rational in the syllogism is not just the fact of mediation, that is, that one moment in the concept mediates between the two others, but the necessity in seeing each form of mediation as implying the others. In Hegel's logical account of the syllogisms, each of the syllogism forms is immanently related to the others, that is, the basic form of the syllogism (S-P-U) generates the others. The syllogism really only explains its own act of mediation when the *middle term* is so concrete that it includes the whole concept within it: for example, the true *singular* is one that can posit its distinguishing *particularity* in a way such that it relates itself to the entire sphere of action that gives it this particularity, whereas only the abstract singular is not yet marked by any distinguishing particularity. Thus the *concrete singular*, as opposed to the abstract singular, is one that already contains the moments of particularity and universality in it. Only this concrete singular can then act as a mediating term in the syllogism "particular-singular-universal." But the singular is only thought as concrete in this way because it has already undergone mediation in the other two syllogisms: S-U-P and S-P-U. Singularity goes from being an extreme (i.e., an isolated conceptual determination) to a mediating concept through the positing of the other two syllogisms in which it is an extreme. "It belongs among the most important logical insights that a determinate moment that, when taken in opposition, is an extreme, ceases to be such and becomes an organic moment in that it is taken as a middle term."[21] Hegel's argument here is that the middle term always has to be thought of as a result of prior mediation in another syllogism, and that only through this concretion can it serve to make the other moments concrete. Thus it is only able to act as a real mediating term if it is thought not in isolation from the other syllogisms, but as the result of them. The same applies to the moments of particularity and universality. In approaching any syllogism that Hegel lays out it is important to understand that the middle term has a distinct logical status from the two extremes: the extremes are taken as forms of abstract conceptual moments, while the middle term is thought as having passed through the two other syllogisms. Thus the term "S" in S-P-U is a singular thing that is not yet defined in its relation to a whole through its particular nature (indeed, this is what is to be accomplished through this syllogism, as its result); but in the syllogism, U-S-P, the term "S" is thought of as a singular thing that has recognized or posited its relation to the entirety of things by means of particularity.

This notion of three syllogisms, each acting in order to explain and make good on the conceptual demands of the other, is for Hegel a key insight into the nature of the concept. It gives Hegel a pattern for thinking real, systematic wholes throughout the rest of his philosophy. "It is only through the nature of syllogizing (*die Natur des Zusammenschliessens*), through this triplicity of syllogisms of the same terminorum, that an entirety is truly grasped in its organization."[22] It is at first important to understand this structure as a definition of what makes something rationally self-determining within objectivity according to Hegel. A finite thing is one that is not able to posit its middle term, for example, between its individual existence and its universal nature. But this finite thing takes on a new meaning when it belongs to a structure of activity in which it can explain or posit from its own activity the relation between its existence and its universal nature through its relations to the sphere around it. Through this mode of explanation, the originally finite thing is no longer simply a given nature, but it is one that posits its own nature through its relating to the systematic context of its activity.

This distinction between finite existence and rational self-determination has vital implications for Hegel's social philosophy. Here Hegel is concerned with demonstrating that human freedom is only made possible through participation in the right kinds of social and political institutions. The question of human freedom or self-determination thus becomes developed by raising the question: What social institutions allow us to be "with ourselves"? Which institutions make the volitional activity by which we give content to our will a real relation to self that does not get lost in meaningless indeterminacy or become dependent on an externality that is altogether foreign? The project of describing human freedom through an account of the economic structures thus finds its logical justification for Hegel in his model of how syllogisms relate to form an objective whole. But this basic point about the nature of self-determination within rational systems will get fleshed out much more thoroughly in looking at how Hegel relates this structure of absolute mechanism to the state.

The Absolute Mechanism:
The State and Society as a Syllogism of Syllogisms

From early in his philosophical career Hegel was fascinated with planetary mechanics. In his *Logic*, he describes the "absolute mechanism" as a kind of objective system in which there are three distinct kinds of objects: the center point, the dependent objects, and the non-self-sufficient objects (i.e., satellites). This system of objects makes up a form of mechanism that is absolute to the degree that each of these kinds of objects mediates between the other kinds of objects and the objective entirety. Thus the coherence of motion in such a system is explicable purely through the conceptual logic of how the different kinds of objects relate. But how can this conception of an absolute mechanism serve to describe an ethical economy? It must first be made clear that the three kinds of objects in this system do not correspond to three kinds of workers or citizens (for this would lead to a rather antiquated and hierarchical conception of the state as a solar system). Rather they correspond to three distinct aspects of social existence to which every member of society is exposed: first there is the relation between the individual and his or her socially produced needs; then there is the relation of the state as a form of political administration to these needs; finally there is the relation of the individual to the state administration. I argue that for Hegel, the task of social theory is to demonstrate how each of these spheres of our modern social-political existence serves to mitigate the one-sidedness of each of the other spheres. Each of these spheres of social activity is both incomplete and instrumental to each of the others, but together they form an account of economic and political life in which the individual is free in relation to these institutions. Only a state that really manages to capture this set of syllogistic relations can reconcile us with those aspects of economic experience that are inherent in modern society. On the other hand, a state that attempts to posit one of these relations without taking it as a product of the others will lead to an institution with a kind of social-political finitude that leaves the individual unable to reconcile his or needs with the actual conditions of modern social life.

In the passage on absolute mechanism from the *Logic*, Hegel gives the following formulation of the application of this syllogistic structure to the state:

> Thus the government, the individual citizens and the needs or the external life of the individuals are three terms, of which each is the mediating term for the other two. The government is the absolute center, in which the extreme of the individual is mediated with its external existence; equally, the individuals are a middle term, which activate that universal individual [i.e., the government] to external existence and translate its ethical essence into the extreme of reality. The third syllogism is the formal one, the syllogism of appearance, that the individuals are joined to this universal absolute individuality by their needs,—a syllogism, which since it is merely subjective passes over into the others and has its truth in them.[23]

Thus we have three syllogisms out of which Hegel tries to grasp the rational structure of the state:

1. S-U-P. This syllogism describes the fact that individuals only attain to the satisfaction of their particular desires as family members and civic individuals through the activity of the government. Thus it describes the role of those state institutions that act to resolve the inherent deficiencies of the market, namely the public authority and the corporations, as well as the administration of justice. Hegel's notion is that even our basic identity as workers and consumers assumes a system of justice and mechanisms of market regulation. Thus, though the state comes last in Hegel's exposition, it had to be there all along to make possible his account of the family and civil society. One of the most challenging aspects of Hegel's social philosophy is his notion that in civil society we have a "right to have our particularity satisfied." This is to say that all citizens have a right not only to private property, but also to attain to a level of material comfort and security that is consistent with the immense wealth of modern industry. For Hegel this right is, however, not fully realized in capitalist economies, such as England, because the right political structures are not in place. Hegel argues for political intervention in the economy on two different levels, through what he calls the public authority and what he calls the corporations. In discussing state intervention of the economy, Hegel demonstrates an acute awareness of the dilemma inherent in such regulation of the economy, namely that it robs individuals of the formation through their own activity that is particular to civil society. But the crux of his argument seems to be that such regulation can only really work to restore the right of the individual to have its particularity satisfied if it is grounded in a political structure that is truly representative. But this points to the next syllogism.

   2. *U-S-P.* This syllogism describes the fact that the government can only act correctly on the sphere of market factors if it acts in a way that is *representative* of the interests of the members of the state. The middle term of singularity is the factor of political representation in Hegel's conception of the internal constitution. Hegel rejects the notion of representation through direct voting on laws or elected officials, and believes that the individual only gains a real substantial voice in the state through organizations that represent one's economic identity within the whole. Thus the singular that Hegel has in mind here is the *concrete singular,* one that has a differentiated functional identity within a social whole. Thus, for Hegel the key to a representative government consists in the activity of the corporations, those industry-specific professional organizations that regulate the production and employment within an industry and also serve to elect legislators to the lower house of parliament. Why does Hegel think such a structure, rather than direct democracy or election of legislators, better serves the interests of political representation? He argues that in a modern industrial society, individuals relate to the rest of society through the specific identity that they acquire in the division of labor. But in parliamentary democracy, individuals are atomized, taken out of the context in which they actually relate to the rest of society, and hence are not able to deliberate on their concrete interests.[24] The corporations on the other hand, like labor unions, allow members of the industrial working class to organize in such a way that they can deliberate on the basis of their class interests. In turn, only if the state is informed through such a concrete act of deliberation can it serve to regulate the economy in such a way that it does not rob individuals of the aspect of political formation that occurs through the division of labor.

3. S-P-U. This syllogism stands for the formative aspect (*Bildung*) of work in civil society. The needs of the individual are not mere natural or individual needs, but social needs, such as the need for recognition, for work that is rewarding, and for stability. It describes the manner in which the individual comes to relate to the universal through the pursuit of its needs, that is, its economic self-interest. In the modern state, individuals feel that the state is an extension of their selves only because it serves to promote their vital interests as family members and workers and consumers. Civil society's function within a rational conception of the state is that it serves to form our desires and sensuous natures in accordance with social standards, and in so doing, it serves as a precondition for the formation of a general will in political bodies.

Conclusion

It might be asked in closing what has really been gained in the interpretation of Hegel's social and political thought by reading it in terms of the structure of absolute mechanism. Did this structure merely give us an organizational device for structuring what is already clear in the text of the *Grundlinien*, or does it have deeper philosophical implications in understanding the foundations of Hegel's practical philosophy? I believe this question can best be answered by returning to the question posed in the introduction, whether Hegel's absolute idealism can offer any real distinctive basis for a social theory that is critical of capitalism.

The young Marx rejects Hegel's absolute idealism as a method for social critique because he believes that the sublation, by which Hegel overcomes the negativity in economic life and posits the state, merely leaves all of the negativity in civil society intact. The state represents a mere appearance of a higher form of ethical life, while it is in a material sense determined by the economic life that has not really been altered. This critique then serves as the basis for preferring the method of dialectical materialism, which looks at the concrete structures of economic reproduction in order to understand how they produce the superstructure of intellectual and political life.

It is my argument that the figure of reciprocal mediation that Hegel develops in the *Science of Logic* offers a far more robust version of idealism than that critiqued by the young Marx. It shows that the relation between economic and political institutions is not merely causal in nature: the state is not merely a force that seeks to act on the economy, or an appearance that is conditioned by the force of economic interests. While the logical categories of substance, causality, and appearance can indeed be insightful in understanding the insufficient forms that political life can take in modern capitalism, Hegel's idealism demands that we also think of structures in which reality is self-determining according to patterns in which the moments of the concept mediate between each other. Such patterns of reciprocal mediation are *more real*, not in the sense of being more descriptive of social reality, but in the sense of offering an ethical norm that is better able to sustain motivation and stand up to scrutiny than the merely capitalist forms of economic life. Instead of the notions of substructure and superstructure, reality and its intellectual reflection, such a social theory allows us to consider how forms of labor represent an education of subjectivity, and how forms of politics give more or less adequate representation of economic interests. Rather than merely describing modern institutions, Hegel grasps the points in them that could be taken up as part of an ethical social and political life. Such a social theory is idealistic, not in the sense of ignoring the realities of the productive sphere that condition the mind, but in the sense of grasping the system of production as mediated by structures of thought (labor begets a form of subjectivity, S-P-U), while these structures of thought are also mediated by the system of production (political representation must engage with economic the economic identities of workers, U-S-P).

Another common critique of Hegel as a social theorist comes from the liberal viewpoint: both critics and proponents of Hegel's political views have argued that Hegel rejects the notion of individual liberty, and instead has a notion of freedom, which constructs the sovereignty of political institutions at the expense of the liberty of individuals who live within them. The strongest support for this view (that does not completely ignore Hegel's own thinking) is worked out by Karl-Heinz Ilting, who supports his view with reference to a famous passage in which Hegel describes the state as an "ethical substance" and the individuals as mere accidents within this substance.[25]

In my view, the distinct advantage of reading the Hegelian notion of the state in terms of the theme of absolute mechanism is that it provides us with an ontological concept that is more insightful and less misleading than that of substance for thinking through the notion of self-determination in Hegel's social philosophy. If we interpret the state as a substance and the individuals who live in it as accidents, then we run the danger of simply turning liberalism on its head, and reducing the happiness and liberty of individuals to a matter of nonimportance in Hegel's philosophy.[26] The model of absolute mechanism, as laid out in the set of syllogisms above, provides a more effective model, in that it conceives of self-determination as resting neither in the submission of the individual to the universal, nor in the mere freedom of the individual from constraint. Rather this model demonstrates that each social institution only makes freedom possible in that it serves as a point at which each part of the social fabric relates to each other part. This logical figure thus gives a rich schema for thinking through the meaning of Hegel's famous definition of freedom as the will's "being with itself in otherness." What this notion of absolute mechanism demonstrates is that if we want to think the will as "with itself" in a set of social and political institutions, then these institutions must be constituted with the notion that each institution act as a moment of concrete conceptual mediation: each of the as yet abstract or unmediated aspects of human willing must be tied together with each other through patterns of mediation that are themselves the result of human social activity.

Notes

1. The notion of capitalism, as a system of production owned by private capital, is not very well developed by Hegel in the *Grundlinien*, precisely because such a system in its pure form would not be a recognizable part of what he calls *Sittlichkeit* (ethical life). He uses the word *capital* just once, in §200 of the *Grundlinien*, to lament the tendency of the riches of economic growth to be unevenly distributed. However, we can extrapolate from this and other passages that Hegel foresaw the spread of capitalist systems and saw the need to offer a critique of them.

2. SW 7 §§243–244, 389.

3. SW 6, 409.

4. Hegel writes in introducing the concept of civil society: "The selfish aim in its realization, conditioned by universality, founds a system of dependency on all sides. . . . One can regard this system first as the *external state, state of need*, and *of the understanding* (*Not- und Verstandesstaat*)" SW 7, 340.

5. The German terms *Selbständigkeit* and *Unselbstständigkeit* are hard to translate into English; something is lost with "independence" and "dependence," because the former is actually a positive, while the latter is a privative in German. These terms must be distinguished from the German *Abhängigkeit*, which describes a necessary and potentially positive form of dependence.

6. The early Marx in particular seizes on this critique of Hegel in his 1843 "Contribution to the Critique of Hegel's *Philosophy of Right*." As I argue, the Marxist critique of Hegel can best be answered by deepening our understanding of the relation of civil society and the state so as to include the moment of reciprocal mediation. Indeed, the ontology of reciprocal mediation represents an alternative to the dichotomy of idealism and materialism that Marx's critique establishes: rather than a theory of causality or of essence, in which the *real* determines the *ideal*, Hegel gives us tools in the doctrine of the concept to think of a rational whole as one in which there are multiple patterns of integration between the different moments of the concept.

7. SW 6, 425. This brief text plays a remarkable role in Hegel's social philosophy, not just because it is virtually the only systematically important formula-

tion of political ideas that Hegel completed in the formative years between the *Phenomenology* (1807) and the *Encyclopedia* (1817), but also because it is one of the few texts where Hegel discusses the economy and the state as an integral whole, moments that he treats separately from one another in the *Philosophy of Right*. Cf. Denis 1987, chapter vi. He writes of the absolute mechanism in the *Science of Logic*: "*Ce passage est isolé dans l'ouvrage, mais il est d'une imprtance capitale pour nous puisqu'on y voit réappairaître la thèse selon laquelle la vie sociale doit être étudiée comme d'une organisme dont les moments sont l'individu, la communauté économique et le gouvernement* (101)." ("This passage is isolated in Hegel's work, but of great importance for us, because in it we see once again the thesis reflected that social life has to be studied as an organism consisting of the individual, the economic community and the government.")

    8. SW 6, 410.

    9. Dieter Henrich argues that this particular figure of the syllogism of syllogisms makes up the characteristically speculative aspect of Hegel's thought, for it involves a totality governed by the principle of mutual implication and co-existence between diverse structures of mediation within a rational whole. One form of mediation does not cause the other, but each contains, implies the other, even though they are distinct and even paradoxical from the perspective of the understanding (Henrich 1982).

    10. This term is used by John McCumber to describe how specific dialectic arguments from Hegel's *Science of Logic* come to bear on areas of history of social theory of which Hegel himself might have had no grasp. See McCumber 2009. Although I have found it useful to compare moments in the logic to Hegel's stated social theory, I have also found it liberating to consider the moments in the logic in their own right rather as tools to understand social processes.

    11. SW 6, 409.

    12. This mechanization of labor is developed prominently by Hegel in two places: in his 1802 text *The System of Ethical Life*, he writes of two different "potencies" of labor, the primitive one being teleological in nature, while the social form of labor is mechanistic because an increasing division of labor robs it of its direct purpose. In the *Phenomenology of Spirit*, I believe that the notion of labor in the master-slave dialectic undergoes a similar development. The slave learns to work not according to desire, but according to the nature of physical things, and so learns to respect the objective truth of things as independent realities. In both of these texts, the mechanization of work is both dehumanizing and, paradoxically, an education (*Bildung*) that enriches the subject.

    13. See Waszek, 205–229. Waszek demonstrates that Smith's conception of the division of labor had a profound impact on Hegel. Smith had a profound sense of not only the productive potential latent in the division of labor, but also its dehumanizing impact on the worker.

    14. The key terms in Hegel's argument on the mechanistic object are *Unselbständigkeit* and *Selbstständigkeit*, which he shows to be mutually implicated in their spurious form. In the *Encyclopedia* of 1830 he writes: "The objects remain in their relationship and their lack of independence (*Unselbständigkeit*) at the same time independent (*selbstständig*), offering resistance, external to one another. . . . The

lack of independence, by which the object suffers violence, pertain to it only insofar as it is independent" SW 8 §§195–196.

15. Curiously, Hegel uses the term *capital* only once in the *Philosophy of Right* in an economic sense (and never speaks of capitalism), in the context of a passage that speaks of the unequal and arbitrary share of producers in the fortune of society (SW 7, 353).

16. SW 7, 389.

17. I have provided only a very brief analysis of the notions of dependence and independence in the System of Needs from the *Philosophy of Right* in order to show parallels to the logic of mechanism. I believe that a consequential treatment of the role of these concepts in Hegel's ethical and social philosophy would have to begin in the master-slave dialectic from the *Phenomenology*, which shows that the apparent independence of the master represents not only an injury to the right of the slave, but also begets a pattern of mutual dependence that is (1) ruinous in the case of the master and (2) ethically progressive in the case of the slave. A similar pattern is at work in Hegel's account of civil society, for he both laments the arbitrary nature of capitalist labor markets and praises the education that work provides. What is at work here is the notion that a richer form of ethical dependence must be developed out of the consciousness of the slave or the education of work.

18. SW 6, 352.

19. Ibid.

20. SW 8 [1827] §181.

21. SW 7 §302, 472.

22. SW 8 [1827], §198.

23. SW 6, 425.

24. "For some time past . . . the lower classes, the lower classes, the mass of the population have been left more or less unorganized. And yet it is of the utmost importance that the masses should be organized, because only so do they become mighty and powerful. Otherwise they are nothing but a heap, an aggregation of atomic units. Only when the particular associations are organized members of the state are they possessed of legitimate power" (Hegel 1986b §290 Zusatz).

25. Ilting 1978, 219–239. The problem of substance as a metaphor for the state is also discussed by Avineri 1972, 28.

26. This danger could perhaps be prevented by giving a critical conception of the meaning of the concept of substance in Hegel's *Logic*, pointing out that for Hegel the concepts of substance and accident are mutually constitutive concepts that ground one another. But the deeper problem then looms that this logical operation from the doctrine of essence does not seem really sufficient to describe a logic of freedom in such a full sense as a moment from the doctrine of the concept, for it reduces the elements within a relation to a complete dependence on the relation as that which posits them. The logic of the concept, on the other hand, makes the relational elements into points at which the entire self-mediation of the relation occurs, and so it does not run the same danger of instrumentalizing the individual for the sake of the collective.

Works Cited

Abbreviations for Works by G.W.F. Hegel

SW   *Werke in zwanzig Bänden.* Edited by E. Moldenhauer and K. M. Michel. Frankfurt: Suhrkamp, 1986. Unless otherwise noted, all citations of Hegel are translated by the author from the Suhrkamp edition (SW) and cited as follows: SW 6: *Wissenschaft der Logik II*, SW, Bd. 6; SW 7: *Grundlinien der Philosophie des Rechts*, SW, Bd. 7; SW 8: *Enzyklopädie der philosophischen Wissenschaften I*, SW, Bd. 8.

Avineri, S. 1972. *Hegel's Theory of the Modern State.* Cambridge: Cambridge University Press.
Denis, H. 1987. *Hegel Penseur Politique.* Paris: Editions l'Age d'Homme.
Henrich, D. 1982. "Logische Form und reale Totalität." In *Hegels Philosophie des Rechts: Die Theorie der Rechtsformen und ihre Logik*, edited by D. Henrich and R.-P. Horstmann. Stuttgart: Klett-Cotta.
Ilting, K.-H. 1978. *Aufsätze über Hegel.* Jena: Klett-Cotta.
McCumber, J. 2009. "Hegel and the Logics of History." In *Hegel and History*, edited by W. Dudley. Albany: State University of New York Press.
Waszek, N. 1988. *The Scottish Enlightenment and Hegel's Account of Civil Society.* Dordrecht: Kluwer.

11

Hegel and Capitalism

Marxian Perspectives

TONY SMITH

Marx never renounced his early vehement and unequivocal condemnation of Hegel's philosophy. Nonetheless, as he composed the first extended draft of his critique of political economy Marx wrote that Hegel's *Logic* "was of great use to me."[1] Marx's project was to reconstruct in thought the essential determinations of the capitalist mode of production, beginning with the simplest and most abstract social forms and proceeding step-by-step to progressively more complex and concrete determinations. The term for this sort of project is *systematic dialectics*, and Hegel's *Logic* provided an example Marx could creatively adapt.[2] The main theme of this chapter is a second way in which Hegel's work proved to be "of great use" to Marx: he came to believe that "capital" can only be comprehended adequately with the aid of Hegelian categories. I argue that Marx was correct, but not quite in the manner he thought.

Hegel and Generalized Commodity Production

In the *Philosophy of Right* Hegel argues that generalized commodity production and exchange[3] must be taken as an essential moment of any rational and normatively acceptable modern sociopolitical order. Following the classical political economists, he emphasizes the mutual benefits obtainable through trade. If something I own meets your wants and needs better than mine, while you possess something I value more than you do, a trade could obviously benefit both of us. If only one of us possesses what the other desires, however, there will be no trade. This shows that the generalization of commodity exchange requires a *generalized* means of exchange, money, for which any commodity can in principle be exchanged, and with which any commodity can in principle be obtained.[4] Then if the wants of potential trading parties do not coincide in the right way, one agent can sell a commodity (C) to the other for money (M), which can then be used to purchase another commodity (C) that is desired from a third party. The use of goods and services to meet our wants and needs is an important component of human flourishing. Insofar as money makes the process of acquiring goods and services more efficient and convenient, money too can be categorized as a means to further human flourishing.

In Hegel's framework generalized commodity production is conceptualized primarily as a system of C–M–C circuits. There are also innumerable M–C–M' circuits, in which social agents invest money (M) in the production and circulation of commodities (C), with the goal of obtaining a monetary return exceeding the initial investment (M'). But for Hegel, as for the classical political economists, money is at most merely a *proximate* end, sought because it can be used as a means for obtaining goods and services at some future point.

Hegel's account of generalized commodity production and exchange makes two major contributions to social theory. First, he provides a precise categorial analysis of its crucial social forms as understood in mainstream economic theory from his day to ours.[5] Second, Hegel develops perhaps the strongest normative defense of generalized commodity production ever given. In Hegel's account this "system of needs":

- Is a sphere of *freedom*, in which individuals forge their own life plans and decide for themselves how to carry them out.

- Institutionalizes a *mutual recognition* of self and "other" as *equally* free, a major normative advance over slavery and serfdom.

- Coordinates individual behavior within a *higher-order unity-in-difference*, a higher order web of connections, than that instituted in families.

- Leads to an unprecedented development of new productive capacities and new wants and needs, thereby liberating humanity from the constraints on human development and well-being found in premodern societies.

For generalized commodity production to be normatively acceptable, however, a coercive state apparatus (the "Administration of Justice," in Hegel's terminology) must enforce rights of property and contract, and resolve disputes about the interpretation of these rights in particular cases. Hegel also acknowledges that the general tendency in market societies for freedom and well-being to be conjoined does not necessarily hold in every individual case. The free decisions of consumers and producers, for example, may result in some individuals suffering involuntary unemployment (as it does in "overproduction," when free choices result in productive capacity expanding at a faster rate than markets can absorb the increase in output). Hegel also recognizes a systematic tendency for markets to fail to provide the necessary preconditions of their own effective operation (e.g., infrastructure) adequately. Another shortcoming is the manner the systematic interconnection of individuals is experienced as an alien force ("market laws") externally imposed on them "behind their backs."

Hegel concludes that "the state in civil society" cannot be limited to establishing and maintaining the "rule of law." It must also provide public goods like infrastructure. And it must ensure that the well-being of all individuals is addressed to the greatest extent compatible with individual autonomy.[6] Even then, however, mutual recognition achievable in civil society remains restricted, motivating Hegel's systematic transition from "the state in civil society" to the "the state proper." Although the former is experienced as a mere instrument to help attain private ends, the latter provides a space in which agents can develop a self-conscious awareness of the extent their very identity as individuals depends on membership in a political community. This explicit mutual recognition of a shared substantive unity with fellow citizens can be expressed in a variety of ways, from the emotional trust of patriotism to the reflective grasp of the rationality of the state developed in Hegel's own work.

Marx accepts a great deal of Hegel's assessment of generalized commodity production. He too regards it as a normative advance over previous social formations with respect to both personal freedom and the provision of the material preconditions for human flourishing. Marx also understood that a market society requires a state to resolve rights disputes, provide adequate infrastructure, and so on. And he grants that state interventions in markets can institute significant reforms in the name of the common good (for example, laws limiting the length of the working day and abolishing child labor).

Needless to say, however, Marx's position is not identical to what he took to be Hegel's. The point where his views most diverge from his picture of Hegel is precisely the point where Marx finds Hegel's most profound contribution to the comprehension of capitalism.

Marx's Homology Thesis

As we have seen, Hegel conceptualizes money as essentially a means to further human ends. The heart of Marx's critique of political economy is a critique of this standard view.

Marx begins by noting that commodity production is privately undertaken production. The only way to establish its social necessity is through successful sale of the produced commodities for money. Further, at the completion of any given period money is required to obtain inputs for the next period. In a system of generalized commodity production, then, units of production must necessarily tend to make the appropriation of money their end. They must, in fact, necessarily tend to seek as high a level of monetary returns as possible, given the threat of finding themselves at a competitive disadvantage vis-à-vis their competitors in the next cycle of production and exchange. For them,

> [U]se-values must never be treated as the immediate aim. . . . [The] aim is rather the unceasing movement of profit-making . . . [t]he ceaseless augmentation of value.[7]

Units that do not systematically direct their endeavors to "valorization" in M–C–M' circuits, that is, to the appropriation of monetary returns (M') exceeding initial investment (M), tend to be pushed to the margins of social life, when not forced out of existence altogether.

Most individual agents, in contrast, do *not* make the acquisition of money their preeminent goal, seeking money as a means for obtaining goods and services to address their wants and needs. But this does not make money simply a tool for making exchange more convenient. In generalized commodity production individuals are *compelled* to obtain monetary resources in order to purchase the commodities they require. The primary way to obtain access to monetary resources is through the sale of labor power for a wage, and labor power will generally be purchased if and only if its use is foreseen to contribute to the transformation of M into M'.[8] Most individuals may operate within C–M–C circuits (labor power–wages–commodities), but these are systematically subordinated under M–C–M' circuits.

The next step in the argument requires a consideration of the Marxian theory of value. When sales occur in generalized commodity exchange, commodities obtains a new property, "value," which can be defined as the property "produced by private labor that has proven to be socially necessary." This property can also be defined as "(indirect) general exchangeability," because the money for which the commodity is exchanged can be used to obtain any other commodity in principle. Money, in contrast, has the property "(direct) general exchangeability" (to lose this property is to lose the ontological status of being money). M–C–M' circuits can therefore be seen as processes in which value takes on a series of different forms in turn, proceeding from the initial monetary value invested, to the production of commodities (which have first an imputed and then a realized value), and concluding with a representation of the commodity's realized value in a monetary value exceeding the initial investment.

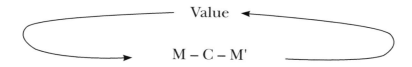

A central thesis of Marx's critique of political economy is that if we wish to comprehend the historical specificity of modern capitalism we cannot define capital simply as a physical thing used in production or an embodied skill; examples of both go back to prehominid eras. We must instead begin with an understanding of capital as value-in-process (Marx terms this the "general formula of capital"), a unity-in-difference taking on the form of money and commodities in turn. In generalized commodity production the key notion of capital is *capital-in-general*, with capital understood as the underlying unity-in-difference of a valorization process on the level of society as a whole, commencing with the initial money invested in the society in a given period, moving to the aggregate set of commodities produced and distributed in the course of that period, and culminating with the total sum of monetary returns appropriated from sales of those commodities. The account can be made yet more complex and concrete by noting that the initial money capital (M) is invested in two sorts of commodity-inputs (C), means of production (raw materials, machinery, plants, and so on) and labor power, enabling a production-process (P) in which labor-power is set to work on the means of production, and resulting in the output of a new set of commodities (C') to be sold for profit (M'):

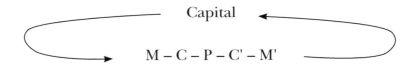

$$M - C - P - C' - M'$$

From Marx's standpoint Hegel's most significant contribution to the understanding of modern society is not found in his own discussion of civil society and the state. His notions of value and money are formulated in use-value terms that hold for *any* society that uses things to meet human needs (see note 5). They thereby do not capture what is historically specific to generalized commodity production. Similarly, his notion of capital refers to stored wealth, a concept as applicable to the temples of ancient Mesopotamia as it is to modern economies. The descriptive inadequacy of Hegel's categorial analysis of modern society is inseparably conjoined with a normative failure: Hegel, like the political economists whose work he appropriated, failed to comprehend the fundamental inversion of means and ends instituted in modern capitalism.

In generalized commodity production money is not merely a means that serves human ends (or at least would do so if appropriate political regulations were in place). Human ends are instead systematically subordinated to the *valorization imperative*, the accumulation of money capital as an end in itself. In everyday experience this subordination is often invisible. Capital exists and is reproduced through the pursuit of ends by individuals and groups in a radically open-ended process. An indefinite range of human actions can in principle further valorization, and new forms of human activity are constantly required for new sites of accumulation to emerge. For the fortunate, the fulfillment of their individual ends will more or less coincide with the fulfillment of capital's end, while the less fortunate can blame their fate on mistaken choices, bad luck, or contingent injustices that could be overcome with the proper public policies. But the systematic sacrifice of human ends for the sake of capital's end, of human good for the sake of the good of capital, of human flourishing for the sake of the flourishing of capital, is all around us. Examples range from the manner in which radical economic insecurity and debilitating stress at the workplace is increased, rather than lessened, by technological change in capitalism, to the threat to humanity posed by the environmental costs of accumulating as much capital as possible, as fast as possible, even as wastes are generated at a faster rate than ecosystems can absorb, and resources are depleted at a faster rate than they can be replenished. The recurrent sacrifice of well-being due to overproduction crises and financial crises on a scale far beyond anything anticipated in the *Philosophy of Right* can be mentioned as well.[9]

Despite Hegel's profound shortcomings, in Marx's view he nonetheless provided an indispensable (if completely unintended) framework for the comprehension of capitalism, as Marx's summary of the "general formula of capital" suggests:

> (B)oth the money and the commodity function only as different modes of existence of value itself . . . [Value] is constantly changing from one form into the other, without becoming lost in this movement; it thus becomes transformed into an automatic subject. . . . [V]alue is here the subject of a process in which, while constantly assuming the form in turn of money and commodities, it changes its own magnitude, throws off surplus-value from itself considered as original value, and thus valorizes itself independently. For the movement in the course of which it adds surplus-value is its own movement, its valorization is therefore self-valorization. . . . [V]alue suddenly presents itself as a self-moving substance which passes through a process of its own, and for which commodities and money are both mere forms.[10]

The notion of a nonhuman "subject" that is somehow a "self-moving substance" both identical to and yet different from the particular forms it assumes as it "passes through a process of its own" is clearly meant to echo Hegel. Marx condemned the perverse metaphysics of what he took to be Hegel's Absolute Idealism. But for Marx the very perversity of Hegel's framework makes his work indispensable for understanding the perverse social order that is capitalism. *In Marx's view there is a precise homology between the structure of Hegel's Absolute and the structure of capital.* Capital is in fact the subject of the bizarre process of self-externalization and return Marx termed "the self-valorization of value." From capital's standpoint the moments of this process are of no interest apart from their contribution to capital's self-valorization. Human agents, their activities, and their creations are of interest only insofar as they are incorporated into capital circuits and subordinated to the totalizing end of capital accumulation. To comprehend capital adequately, in brief, is to grasp that it is an "Absolute Subject" in what Marx took to be the Hegelian sense of the term.

Prominent interpreters of Marx who have thought seriously about Hegel's contribution to understanding capitalism have accepted this view. For example:

> Marx does not simply invert Hegel's concepts in a "material-
> ist" fashion. . . . Marx suggests that a historical Subject in the
> Hegelian sense does indeed exist in capitalism. . . . His analysis
> suggests that the social relations that characterized capitalism are
> of a very peculiar sort—they possess the attributes that Hegel
> accorded to *Geist* ["Spirit"].[11]

More specifically, "the *Geist* constitutes objective reality by means of a process of externalisation or self-objectification, and, in the process, reflexively
constitutes itself" in a manner precisely isomorphic to capital's reign as a
subject and self-moving substance.[12]

Marx's interpretation of Hegel unquestionably helped him formulate
his view of capital. There are, however, good reasons to think that his
reading is very questionable.

A Critical Assessment of Marx's Homology Thesis

Textual support for the standard Marxian interpretation of Hegel is easy
enough to find. Nonetheless, there are good reasons to think it may not
be the best "all things considered" view. For one thing, it does not suf-
ficiently take on board the extent to which Hegel defines crucial terms in
very idiosyncratic ways. We may deplore Hegel's verbal peculiarities. But if
we wish to understand him properly, they need to be noted.

It is natural enough for Marx to have assumed that when Hegel speaks
of "Absolute Thought" he is referring to some sort of transcendent thinking Being above human agents, and therefore isomorphic to capital, understood as an alien Subject greedily subsuming human beings under its alien
ends. When we read the culminating section of the *Logic* devoted to "the
absolute," however, we do not find hymns of praise to a Grand Puppet
Master. This section is devoted instead to a discussion of the methodological framework underlying the book as a whole:

> One can, to be sure, vacuously spout on end about the absolute
> idea; the true content, meanwhile, is nothing but the entire sys-
> tem, the development of which we have considered upon to this
> point.[13]

Hegel tells us further that, "thinking is true in terms of content only
if it is immersed in the *basic matter* at hand," undistorted by quirks of
the subject doing the thinking.[14] This suggests that *anyone's* thought is
"absolute" in so far as it "cognize[s] the immanent soul of [the] material

and . . . concede[s] to it its right to its own proper life." This last passage
expresses Marx's commitment to exactly the same theoretical standard.[15]
To put the point provocatively: to the extent that Marx's systematic reconstruction in thought of the essential determinations of capitalism truly
captures the "immanent soul" and "proper life" of the capitalist mode
of production, his own thinking exemplifies absolute thought in Hegel's
sense of the term!

Hegel unpacks the extremely odd sounding idea of a content of
thought that is "active on its own and productive" along the same lines.
He means by this phrase a "content that is determinate in and for itself,"
that is, a content that is objectively determined by the essential features
of the matter itself.[16] This, once again, is identical in all relevant respects
to Marx's requirement that cognition concedes to the material "its right
to its own proper life."

Similarly, it is natural to assume that Hegel's talk of a "universal" that
"acts upon itself" treats an abstraction as if it were an entity somehow capable of action. This was Marx's reading, who took it as a bizarre metaphysical
reification that (unintentionally) provided the most accurate way to think
about the bizarre (but all too real) reification that is "the self-valorization
of value." But here, too, what Hegel means turns out to be different from
what Marx assumed. The idea of a universal that acts on itself is Hegel's
(inexcusably) idiosyncratic way of describing the relationship between our
thinking as an activity and the thoughts that are its products:

> [Thinking's] *product* . . . is the *universal*, the abstract in general.
> *Thinking* as an *activity* is thus the *active* universal, and, more pre-
> cisely, the universal that acts upon *itself* in so far as its accomplish-
> ment, i.e. what it produces, is the universal.[17]

To take a final example, "infinite thought" is another of Hegel's
strange terms. When we attend carefully to his usage, however, we discover a meaning that isn't so strange. Infinite thought is simply Hegel's
very unusual way of distinguishing the relationship between thinkers and
their thoughts from relationships among objects in the world:

> [The] finite . . . ceases where it is connected to its other and is
> thus limited by the latter. . . . In having a thought as my object,
> I am with myself. I, the thinking, is accordingly infinite because
> in thinking it relates itself to an object that it is itself.[18]

Even by the admittedly odd standards of philosophy it is exceedingly
odd to talk about an absolute idea, a content of thought that is "active"

and "productive," a universal that "acts upon itself," or a thought that is "infinite." But when we look closely at what Hegel means by these terms we do not find anything odd in the way capital understood as an "automatic subject" and "self-moving substance" is odd. The relationship between these themes of Hegelian philosophy and capital is by no means as intimate as Marx supposed.

Another compelling reason to question Marx's homology thesis emerges when we consider Hegel's own account of the connection between his deepest philosophical commitments and his normative theory of institutions. In Hegel's (unsurprisingly idiosyncratic) sense of the term, the "rationality" of any ontological region is constituted by the mediation of universality, particularity, and singularity in that region. This objective rationality can be established theoretically through successful reconstruction of the fundamental determinations of the given region in a system of syllogisms, with each moment serving in turn as the mediating middle term. The appropriate form of intermediation differs in different regions. In the sphere of socio-political institutions and practices ("Objective Spirit") rationality requires more than a set of intermediations constituting an "organic" system capable of reproducing itself over time. It must have in addition a strong normative dimension based on instituting the freedom and well-being of individuals and communities.

Hegel believed that the complex mediations in modern political society connecting *individual* persons (nurtured within families), a civil society incorporating generalized commodity production (*particularity*), and the modern constitutional state (*universality*) could be successfully reconstructed in terms of a system of syllogisms establishing its objective normativity:

> [T]he state . . . is, in the practical sphere, a system of three syllogisms. (1) The *individual* (the person), joins itself through its *particularity* (physical and spiritual needs, what becomes the civil society, once they have been further developed for themselves) with the *universal* (the society, justice, law, government). (2) The will, the activity of individuals is mediating factor which satisfies for these needs in relation to society, the law, and so forth, just as it fulfils and realizes the society, the law, and so forth. (3) But the universal (state, government, law) is the substantial middle [term] in which the individuals and their satisfaction have and acquire their fulfilled reality, mediation, and subsistence.[19]

The *Philosophy of Right* should be read as Hegel's most comprehensive attempt to establish the strong normative justification of the modern social world in this manner.

Hegel's argument for the rationality of a social order incorporating generalized commodity production cannot be accepted, in my view. His account lacks an adequate notion of capital, and that, as they say, is like *Hamlet* without the prince. The question here, however, is not whether Hegel's own social and political theory is satisfactory. It is whether Hegel profoundly (if unintentionally) contributed to the understanding of capitalism by developing a philosophy whose culminating categories are homologous with capital. This would be the case if it were possible to reconstruct a social order incorporating generalized commodity production as a rational system mediating universality, particularity, and singularity in the requisite manner *after* capital has been made visible. I do not believe this is possible. A social world subjected to the valorization imperative is one in which legitimate and fundamental human ends are at best furthered in a profoundly partial and precarious way. At worst they are systematically sacrificed when they conflict with the end of capital. It cannot be said of individuals subjected to capital as an end in itself that "their certainty of their freedom finds its truth in such an objective order."[20] Capital is therefore *not* homologous with the deepest principles of Hegel's philosophy, whatever Marx and subsequent generations of Marxists have thought.

The "Essence Logic" of Capital

The fact that Marx's homology thesis cannot be accepted does not imply that he was mistaken in thinking that Hegelian categories profoundly contribute to comprehending the social ontology of capitalism. Before considering how this is the case a brief digression on Hegel's *Logic* is in order.

Hegel defines the project of the *Logic* as follows: "The business of logic can be expressed by saying that in it thought-determinations are considered in terms of their ability to capture what is true."[21] The first part of the *Logic*, the Doctrine of Being, considers explanatory frameworks ("thought-determinations") in which truths regarding the qualitative, quantitative, and measured aspects of a "something" can be articulated. Hegel establishes the inadequacy of this level by showing that the thought forms supposedly referring to a something logically require a *transition* to its "other." This is not to deny that the categories of Quality, Quantity, and Measure have a "capacity to hold truth"; there are theoretical and practical contexts in which these categories are completely adequate. Hegel's point is simply that there are more concrete and complex ontological structures (or, better, structured processes) the truths about which cannot be adequately formulated with these relatively abstract and simple thought determinations.

In a sense, Marx's theory begins where the Doctrine of Being ends. Hegel starts with the pure simplicity and utter emptiness of a category enabling a mere affirmation of being; Marx begins with the complexity of generalized commodity production, including the massive gulf separating the (nonetheless inseparably conjoined) dimensions of use-value and exchange-value in commodities. Hegel goes on to consider attempts to categorize a supposedly separate something in terms of what it is in itself, apart from its relationship to its other, with the ultimate incoherence of all such attempts a *result*. Marx, in contrast, *begins* his critique of political economy with a social world in which no separate commodity can be adequately comprehended apart from its relations to other commodities, and in which no separate act of production can be adequately comprehended apart from its relations to the social division of labor as a whole.

In Hegel's *Logic* the Doctrine of Essence follows the Doctrine of Being. The categories considered in the former have a greater "ability to capture what is true" than those of the latter, that is, they enable more concrete and complex truths to be articulated. The determinations of the Doctrine of Essence come in pairs, neither of which can be considered apart from the other. In Hegelian jargon, each is *reflected* in the other, as an essence is reflected in its appearances, a cause in its effects, or a substance in its accidents (and vice-versa in all these cases). Marx's account of the relationship between value and money is a paradigmatic instance of an essence/appearance relation.[22] Value is only an actual (as opposed to merely imputed) property of commodities through sale for money; money is the socially objective form in which value is realized. Each is "reflected" in the other, with the value of commodities the "essence" that necessarily must appear in money. Further, the underlying truth of this essence, value, is adequately manifested in its form of appearance, money. Value is an abstract, homogeneous, and quantitative property of commodities ("[indirect] general exchangeability") that is adequately represented in the abstract, homogeneous, and quantitative units of money that possess (direct) general exchangeability.

As Marx shows, however, matters are more complicated than this. The commodity form and the money form possess a "content" that must be explicitly taken into account: human sociality, as organized within generalized commodity production. This sociality has two key historically specific features. It is more extensive than the sociality of previous epochs; social connections of unprecedented scale and scope are established as commodity producers respond to the wants and needs of geographically dispersed agents. And it is a *dissociated* sociality in that producers have no ex ante assurance that their endeavors will contribute to social reproduction. If their privately undertaken production isn't socially validated ex post through monetary exchange, their efforts have been wasted.

Value is the property commodities acquire when privately undertaken production proves to have been socially necessary through successful sale for money. Neither value nor money, then, can be adequately comprehended in abstraction from dissociated sociality. In other words, there is a sense in which value and money together are the *explanadum*, while the *explanans* is sociality in the historically specific shape it takes in generalized commodity production. From this perspective sociality is the essence of the situation. This essence, however, is *not* manifested in a form adequately expressing its truth. Social power, for example, now appears in the form of an apparently independent thing, money. (When Marx writes that "each individual . . . carries his social power, as also his connection with society, in his pocket" we are to take this assertion quite literally.[23]) Despite this fetishism, the form of sociality dominating in our epoch remains the essential matter:

> In proportion as the producers become dependent upon exchange [that is, in proportion as sociality takes the form of dissociated sociality, T.S.], exchange appears to become independent of them. . . . Money does not create this opposition and this contradiction; on the contrary, their development creates the apparently transcendental power of money.[24]

Marx reveals the social ontology of generalized commodity production to be more complex, and more bizarre, than anything found in Hegelian social theory. Nonetheless, its adequate comprehension requires the use of categories from Hegel's *Logic: the social ontology of generalized commodity production is defined by two incommensurable essence logics in Hegel's sense of the term.* On the one hand, value is the essence commodities must possess to play a role in social reproduction, an essence adequately appearing in the form of money. But the value of commodities, and the money representing that value, are themselves manifestations of human sociality in our epoch, fetishized appearances of a quite different sort of essence, dissociated sociality.

In stark contrast to Hegel's affirmative systematic dialectic, in which later theoretical levels overcome the fundamental contradictions and shortcomings of earlier determinations, in Marx's critical systematic dialectic more complex and concrete theoretical levels reproduce and deepen the initial contradictions and shortcomings. More specifically, the peculiar essence logic just examined is not overcome after it has been made explicit that generalized commodity production is *capitalist* commodity production; Marx's concept of capital is a more concrete and complex form of the same social ontology:

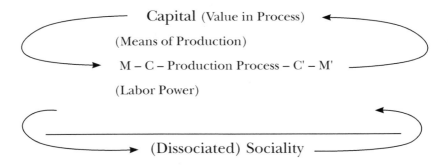

From one point of view (captured in the "general formula of capital") capital is an all-powerful essence, uniting its various moments in a dynamic structured process of self-valorization. But from another point of view (in which the content underlying the general formula is made explicit) this power rests entirely on the peculiar organization of social relations in our historical period. Nonetheless, categories from Hegel's *Logic* are required to conceptualize capitalism properly: *the social ontology of capital is defined by two incommensurable essence logics in Hegel's sense of the term.*

In all social divisions of labor human wants and needs are met by mobilizing the creative powers of social agents (and the powers of nature, scientific and technological knowledge, tools or machinery, the cultural achievements of previous eras, and so on, that social agents mobilize in the course of acting). In previous epochs these powers were exercised within structures where most persons were subjected to the personal domination of others. In generalized commodity production today, in contrast, agents are (in principle) freed from personal domination. But unlike previous epochs—in which access to the objective preconditions of social reproduction (the means of production and subsistence) was generally guaranteed—for most people today these objective preconditions take the form of commodities owned by others. Due to this historically unprecedented separation from their objective conditions, individuals are generally forced to put their creative powers at capital's disposal, making them in effect capital's powers.[25] From this perspective capital's "activity," the self-valorization of value is nothing but the mobilization of creative powers of living labor (along with the powers of nature, science, machinery, other cultural achievements, and so on, that living labor mobilizes).[26] So long as the social forms of "dissociated sociality" remain in place, everything functions *as if* capital were an Absolute Subject with transcendent powers standing over the social world, subsuming all other powers under its valorization imperative. But if this historically specific form of sociality were to be replaced, the supposedly absolute powers of capital would dissipate at once:

> The recognition of the product as its [living labor's] own, and its awareness that its separation from the conditions of its realisation is an injustice—*a relationship imposed by force*—is an enormous consciousness, *itself the product* of the capitalist mode of production and just as much the KNELL TO ITS DOOM as the consciousness of the slave that he *could not be the property of another* reduced slavery to an artificial, lingering existence, and made it impossible for it to continue to provide the basis of production.[27]

Hegel did not affirm the rationality of the modern (capitalist) order because his philosophical framework is homologous with capital. Hegel affirmed its rationality because, lacking an adequate concept of capital, he did not recognize how coercion, alienation, and expropriation pervade modern society, ruling out the harmonious reconciliation of universality, particularity, and singularity required for a rational social order. When Hegel discerned institutional orders in previous epochs exhibiting an "essence logic" in which human autonomy and well-being were systematically subordinated to alien ends, he subjected them to critique.[28] *Pace* Marx and most Marxian theorists, Hegel's philosophy provides a categorial framework within which capital can be *critiqued* in the name of a form of sociality in which human freedom and well-being are no longer subordinated to the alien ends of capital.[29]

Notes

1. Marx 1983, 248.

2. See Smith 1990, Smith 2002, and Moseley and Smith 2014.

3. "Generalized commodity exchange" and "generalized commodity production" are two sides of the same coin; whenever one term is used here, the other is implied.

4. Hegel 2008, 90–91 (§80).

5. For our purposes his notion of the value of commodities, and of the money that expresses the value, is of most interest: "[T]he specific need which it [a thing] satisfies is at the same time need in general and thus is comparable on its particular side with other needs, while the thing in virtue of the same considerations is

comparable with things meeting other needs. This, the thing's *universality* . . . is the thing's *value*. . . . Money, as something abstract, merely expresses this value" Hegel 2008, 75 (§62).

6. Hegel believed that state policies of colonization could address unemployment and overproduction problems in the domestic economy only in the short term, before colonized peoples demanded emancipation. Hegel held that expanding foreign trade provides a more attractive employment policy for the long run. State-sanctioned corporations in Hegel's sense of the term—industry associations including workforces—can also help by providing unemployment insurance, training, health care, pensions, and so on. In Hegel's view, however, it is not possible to eliminate completely undeserved harm due to the vagaries of markets while simultaneously respecting the freedom institutionalized in generalized commodity production. This is one reason Hegel regards the level of rationality attainable in the sphere of objective spirit as restricted in comparison to art, religion, and philosophy.

7. Marx 1976, 254.

8. The life chances of the economic dependents of wage laborers are a function of this primary relationship. The same can be said of the income of individual investors and pensioners (and their dependents). Insofar as state revenues are collected from units of capital and individuals connected to them, the income of state officials, state clients, and their dependents, are indirectly connected to capital accumulation as well.

9. These issues are obviously far too large to address here. See Smith 2010 and 2012, which argue that "golden ages" of capitalist development may be a thing of the past, due to the compression of the time in which significant profits can be won from innovation (a result of the proliferation of reasonably effective national innovation systems). This compression encourages accumulation strategies centering on rent-extraction and financial speculation, both of which have pernicious consequences for substantive autonomy and well-being in the world market.

10. Marx 1976, 255–256.

11. Postone 1993, 74–75.

12. Postone 1993, 72.

13. Hegel 2010, 300 (§237). More specifically, we find a sober defense of Hegel's claim that the progression from one category to the next in the *Logic* has been both analytic (each succeeding category is implicit in what has gone before) and synthetic (each determination adds a new content to its predecessor).

14. Hegel 2010, 57 (§23).

15. Marx 1986, 10.

16. Hegel 2010, 188 (§121).

17. Ibid., 51 (§20).

18. Ibid., 69 (§28).

19. Ibid., 273 (§198).

20. Hegel 2008, 160 (§153).

21. Hegel 2010, 62 (§24).

22. See Murray 1993.

23. Marx 1986, 94.

24. Ibid., 84.

25. "In exchange for his labour capacity as a given magnitude [i.e., a wage] he [the worker] surrenders its *creative power*, like Esau who gave up his birthright for a mess of pottage. . . . [T]he creative power of his labour establishes itself as the power of capital and confronts him as an *alien power*" Marx 1986, 233.

26. "The capitalist obtains, in exchange, labour itself, labour as value-positing activity, as productive labour; i.e. he obtains the productive power which maintains and multiplies capital and which therefore becomes the productive power and reproducing power of capital, a power belonging to capital itself" Marx 1986, 204. Note that the central point of Hegel's normative justification of wage labor—the distinction between ownership of another's capacities for a restricted period of time (wage labor) and ownership of another simpliciter (slavery)—does not weaken Marx's point in the least (Hegel 2008, 78–79, §67).

27. Marx 1986, 390–391. This passage shows that Marx does *not* reject what Hegelians rightly take to be "the fundamental principle of modern political life, the principle of the autonomous personality" (Buchwalter 2012, 267). He does insist that this principle cannot be realized adequately when individuals are separated from the "conditions of [their] realization."

28. The tyranny of ancient Egypt, religious communities subjected to the dictates of an alien God the Father, and the Absolute Terror of Robespierre, were all critiqued by Hegel for institutionalizing an essence logic, in which an alien power systematically subordinates human autonomy and well-being to alien ends.

29. There is not space here to consider in detail what a rational set of social forms in Hegel's sense of the term might look like. Schweickart's model of economic democracy is extremely interesting in this regard (Schweickart 1993). It includes consumer and producer markets, thereby institutionalizing the freedom and dynamism central to Hegel's normative defense of the "System of Needs." But labor and capital markets are abolished, and so commodity exchange is not "generalized." Rights to employment and subsistence are constitutionally guaranteed. Enterprises are organized according to the democratic principle that the exercise of authority should be subject to the consent of those over whom the authority is exercised. The level and general direction of new investment is decided by democratically elected bodies operating on a variety of geographical levels. And new investment funds are distributed to regions on a per capita basis and then allocated decentrally by community banks with a mandate to further employment in their region. As a result of these and other features, capital does not reign, subordinating human ends to its alien end on the level of society as a whole. Nothing like the institutional framework of economic democracy exists today. Yet it would still be "actual" in Hegel's sense of the term if (1) it mediates universal, particular, and individual moments in a manner corresponding to "the fundamental principle of modern political life, the principle of the autonomous personality" (Buchwalter 2012, 267), and if (2) deep structural tendencies moving in its direction can be discerned in the present moment of world history. If these conditions were not met, the rational reconciliation with our present historical moment Hegel hoped for would not be possible. See Smith 2000, chapter 7, and Smith 2009, chapter 8, which in effect attempt to substantiate (1) and (2).

Works Cited

Buchwalter, A. 2012. *Dialectics, Politics, and the Contemporary Value of Hegel's Practical Philosophy*. New York: Routledge.

Hegel, G.W.F. 2008. *Outlines of the Philosophy of Right*. New York: Oxford University Press.

———. 2010. *Logic: Encyclopaedia of the Philosophical Sciences in Basic Outline: Part I: Science of Logic*. New York: Cambridge University Press.

Marx, K. 1976. *Capital Volume I*. New York: Penguin Books.

———. 1983. Letter to Engels (January 16, 1858). In *Marx-Engels Collected Works*, vol. 40. New York: International Publishers, 248.

———. 1986. *Outlines of the Critique of Political Economy Rough Draft of 1857–58*. *Marx-Engels Collected Works*, vol. 28. New York: International Publishers.

Moseley, F., and T. Smith, eds. 2014. *Hegel's Logic and Marx's Capital*. Leiden: Brill.

Murray, P. 1993. "The Necessity of Money: How Hegel Helped Marx Surpass Ricardo's Theory of Value." In *Marx's Method in Capital: A Reexamination*, edited by F. Moseley. Trenton, NJ: Humanities Press, 37–62.

Postone, M. 1993. *Time, Labor, and Social Domination*. New York: Cambridge University Press.

Schweickart, D. 1993. *Against Capitalism*. New York: Cambridge University Press.

Smith, T. 1990. *The Logic of Marx's Capital: Replies to Hegelian Criticisms*. Albany: State University of New York Press.

———. 2000. *Technology and Capital in the Age of Lean Production: A Marxian Critique of the "New Economy."* Albany: State University of New York Press.

———. 2002. "Hegel: Mystical Dunce or Important Predecessor: A Reply to Rosenthal." *Historical Materialism* 10 (2): 191–206.

———. 2009. *Globalisation: A Systematic Marxian Account*. Chicago: Haymarket Books.

———. 2010. "Technological Change in Capitalism: Some Marxian Themes." *Cambridge Journal of Economics* 34 (1): 203–212.

———. 2012. "New Technology and the 'New Economy.'" In *The Elgar Companion to Marxist Economics*, edited by B. Fine and A. Saad-Filho, 259–264. Northampton, MA: Elgar.

12

Hegel's Ethic of *Beruf* and the Spirit of Capitalism

Louis Carré

For people who have money and keep to the military highway the world is in good shape.

—Hegel, Letter to His Wife, September 18, 1822

The "Spirit" of Modern Capitalism

The aim of this chapter is to show the affinities between the ethical theory Hegel developed in his *Philosophy of Right* (1820) and Max Weber's famous thesis on the Protestant origins of modern capitalist "spirit" as presented in the essay *The Protestant Ethic and the Spirit of Capitalism* (1904–1905). Showing those affinities may not be a task as obvious as retracing the direct and already much investigated connection between Hegel and Marx on the topic of capitalism.[1] Weber rarely mentions Hegel, and then only in a rather disparaging—or dismissive—way (Weber 2001, 32). Still, it is worthwhile to confront the two authors if we want to grasp the specific kind of spirit that underlies modern capitalism. By this should mean the type of "subjects" modern capitalism demands in order to function properly. Defining the kind of "human being" (*Menschentum*) required by modern capitalism was Weber's aim in his essay.[2] It might also have been Hegel's point, as is suggested by the passage in the *Philosophy of Right* where he associates the anthropological figure of "the citizen as bourgeois" with the modern economy (the "system of needs") (Hegel 2008 §190R, 188).

Searching for the kind of spirit (or "subjectivity") that modern capitalism demands doesn't necessarily lead to undermining the question of its "material" or "objective" structure, as some Marxists have argued against both Hegel and Weber. According to Marx, there are at least three main features that characterize the material structure of modern capitalism as an economic system. First, modern capitalism rests on a material distinction between the sphere of domestic life and the sphere of economical enterprise. As a result, modern capitalism is based on the separation of the workers from their means of production, who are confronted by a class of capitalist entrepreneurs who control the means of production. Second, modern capitalism presupposes the establishment of a market economy mediated by monetary exchange rather than barter or personal services. Third, modern capitalism reproduces itself by the means of "free" labor, formally understood as the ability of an individual to exchange his "productive force" for pay. Many other elements have contributed to the emergence of modern capitalism, such as a centralized bureaucratic state, flourishing of modern cities, and the development of science and technology. Still, the three main features as identified by Marx suffice to characterize modern capitalism as the specific form of economic organization that gradually took shape in Western Europe at the beginning of the sixteenth century.

Hegel and Weber would have largely agreed with Marx on the material structure of capitalism. Weber's conception of modern capitalism was explicitly inspired by Marx's work.[3] Hegel, an assiduous reader of the "economical science"[4] that will later be criticized by Marx, starts with the distinction between the domestic sphere (the "family") and the economic sphere (the system of needs), a distinction that in his view was absent from ancient forms of ethical life (Hegel 2008 §182A). He also provides a capitalist definition of the market, asserting that "separate commodities are exchanged the one for the other, principally through the use of the universal medium of exchange, money" (Hegel 2008 §204, 195). And, finally, he clearly distinguishes the "limited" alienation in time of the modern worker's skills from the "total" alienation of his personhood in antique slavery or feudal serfdom (Hegel 2008 §67A).

In his *Capital*, Marx explains the emergence of modern capitalism through material violence. The "secret of capital's primitive accumulation" lies in the forced separation of the workers from the means of production. Although violence has undoubtedly been a factor in the process of primitive accumulation, material violence alone is not a good policy. To function properly, the economic system of modern capitalism is also in need of "ethical" legitimacy on which it can rest and justify itself.[5] I argue that this is a point that Weber and Hegel, probably better than Marx, can help us stress.

In what follows I first present the Weberian thesis on the Protestant origins of capitalist spirit, concentrating on the notions of "calling" (*Beruf*) and "inner worldly asceticism." I then turn to Hegel's own ethic of *Beruf*. Both Weber and Hegel emphasized the particular role played by Protestantism in shaping the spirit of the modern world. I show, though, that Hegel offered a wholly secularized version of the Protestant ethic of work analyzed by Weber. I conclude with some remarks on the conceptions and the responses both authors provide concerning the "fate" of modern capitalism as it confronts us today.

The Weberian Thesis

The Protestant Ethic and the Spirit of Capitalism begins with a very broad definition of the spirit of modern capitalism. Modern capitalist spirit is "ideal-typified" by Weber as "the particular frame of mind (*Gesinnung*) that strives systematically and rationally *in a calling* (*Beruf*) for legitimate profit" (Weber 2002, 26). As broad as it may first seem, this definition already allows Weber to distinguish the modern capitalist spirit from other frames of mind, such as those entailed by "adventure capitalism" and "traditional economics." In contrast to adventure capitalism, the spirit of modern capitalism is based on an ethos that tends to pursue profit in a systematic and rational way. Its genesis "could be understood in terms of the transformation of the *romanticism of economic adventurism into the economic rationalism of methodical life practices*" (Weber 2001, 119). The spirit of modern capitalism presupposes a rational life-conduct (*Lebensführung*) that cannot be confounded merely with greed. Weber remarks that greed as such has been observed in many other cultures, and so cannot be considered a distinctive feature of modern Western capitalism. In contrast with traditionalism, the disposition to pursue legitimate gain by exercising a calling does not fit with the traditional ways in which people usually meet economic needs. In modern capitalism work, as a way of seeking legitimate profit, should be undertaken for its own sake and not just as a means to meet material needs. The example discussed by Weber speaks for itself. Considering a group of rural workers in late nineteenth-century Germany whose wages depended on piecework production, Weber notes that their "traditional" ethos induced them to work only long enough to meet their basic needs, even after their wages had been increased by their employers. From this particular case he draws the conclusion that,

it is necessary [within modern capitalism] to have a frame of mind
that emancipates the worker, at least *during* the workday, from a
constant question: With a maximum of ease and comfort and a
minimum of productivity, how is the accustomed wage nonetheless
to be maintained? This frame of mind, if it manages to uproot
the worker from his concern, motivates labor as if labor were an
absolute end in itself, or a "calling." Yet such frame of mind is
not inherently given in the nature of the species. Nor can it be
directly called forth by high or low wages. Rather, it is the product
of a long and continuous process of education and socialization.
(Weber 2002, 24)

In his essay Weber wants to show the "elective affinities" (*Wahlverwand-
schaften*) between "the modern economic *ethos*" and "the rational economic
ethic of ascetic Protestantism" (Weber 2002, 161). In the first part, he
considers how the notion of calling "in the sense of a position in one's
life for a demarcated realm of work" (Weber 2002, 39) has emerged within
the Protestant cultural context due to the impact of Luther. In opposition
to official Church doctrine, Luther advanced the view that each human
being, on the basis of his *Beruf,* has a divinely ordained duty he must fulfill.
By promoting the idea of calling both in its material (the profession one
exercises within society) and religious (the task given by God) sense, Luther
directly criticized the ecclesiastic institutions of his time. In Luther's view,
there should no longer be any distinction between those (such as the monks
and priests atop the ecclesiastic hierarchy) who decided to dedicate their
life entirely to God and those who of necessity were condemned to lead
a merely profane life. All human beings are equally recognized as responsible before their Maker, whatever occupation they may have, as long as
they accomplish their calling with duty. However revolutionary this ethical
promotion of the idea of calling might have been at the time, Lutheranism
was still confined—so Weber—to the limits of traditional economics.[6] Like
the traditional Church, Luther condemned any form of "unnatural" profit.
Moreover, in scholastic fashion he presented the division of society into
"estates" (*Stände*) as an emanation of the divine will, so that every believer
should fulfill his duty in conformity with his social status, not "freely" but
in blind obedience to God. In further elaborating his thesis, Weber argued
that, next to the ethical promotion of *Beruf* espoused by Lutheranism, the
origin of the modern capitalist spirit is also found in the more radical religious currents generated by the Reformation, such as Calvinism and other
Protestant movements like Pietism, Methodism, and the Baptists.

In the second part of the essay, Weber begins with a discussion of the
predestination doctrine developed by Calvin. At the center of this doc-

trine lies the idea that the will of God is profoundly unfathomable. In His inscrutable omnipotence God decided from the very beginning which souls would be saved and which damned in the afterlife. The doctrine of predestination distinguished sharply between the life here below and the life hereafter. Accordingly, it entailed a completely "disenchanted" (*entzaubert*) view on the world, leaving no space whatsoever for superstitious or magical beliefs, and placing the believer in a permanent state of existential anxiety concerning his individual salvation. At stake here for Weber is not so much the theological doctrine itself than the indirect practical and psychological impact it had on members of Protestant communities. The major impact of this doctrine was the development of a specific kind of "inner worldly asceticism" (*innerweltliche Askese*). Because he could neither foresee the divine purpose nor hope for salvation either through the ecclesiastic institutions or directly through works and deeds, the isolated believer could reassure himself of his divine eligibility (*certitudo salutis*) only by seeking, in the process of dutifully exercising his calling, "confirmation" (*Bewährung*) from the other members of his religious community. The systematic and rational exercise of a *Beruf* through hard work and honesty appeared as a way to glorify God on earth. Weber speaks of an "inner worldly asceticism" to designate the "methodical rationalization of the life-conduct." Protestant asceticism differed therefore from the "other worldly asceticism" (such as monasticism) that merely rejected the world here below in the name of the hereafter. It assumed that the salvation of the individual's soul can be confirmed through his acting "in" the world without depending "on" the natural world as such. Protestant asceticism as exemplified mostly by Anglo-Saxon Puritanism thus tended to reproduce the ascetic ideal of monkish self-control, but outside the monastery, within the material world: "Christian asceticism [. . .] sought to reorganize practical life into a rational life *in* the world rather than, as earlier, in the monastery. Yet this rational life in the world was *not of* this world or *for* this world" (Weber 2002, 101).

This last point allows Weber to make a final step in demonstrating his thesis. First, "inner worldly asceticism" strongly contrasts with Lutheranism by placing emphasis not so much on blind belonging to a social estate but on the free decision of the individual to become a member of a religious community (*Gemeinde*).[7] Second, it is only with Protestant asceticism that some of the features characterizing capitalist spirit historically arose. On the more negative side of rational life-conduct, the Puritan condemned any form of immediate pleasure, enjoyment, or luxury. The ethical aim behind his actions was not to possess and make immediate use of material goods and commodities, but to seek "confirmation" of his salvation. The condemnation of pleasure and luxury, the last deemed typical of aristocracy, not only helped to establish a middle-class bourgeois ethos, but made visible *"the formation of capital* through *asceticism's compulsive saving"* (Weber 2002, 117), a practice essential for constituting modern capitalism. On the more positive side, the Puritan not only received the permission but even had the moral duty to enrich himself so as to confirm his divine election. At the conclusion of the essay, Weber is able to show how the spirit of modern capitalism, as ideal-typically distinguished from "adventure capitalism" and "traditional economics," has its historical roots in the Protestant work ethic:

> A specifically middle-class vocational ethos (*Berufsethos*) arose. Now the middle-class employer became conscious of himself as standing within the full grace of God and as visibly blessed by Him. If he stayed within the bounds of formal correctness, if his moral conduct remained blameless, and if the use he made of his wealth was not offensive, this person was now allowed to follow his interest in economic gain, and indeed should do so. Moreover, the power of religious asceticism made available to the businessperson dispassionate and conscientious workers. Unusually capable of working, these employees attached themselves to their work, for they understood it as bestowing a purpose on life that was desired by God. (Weber 2002, 120)

The spirit of modern capitalism historically emerged from the shift of the Puritan figure to that of the bourgeois "isolated economic man" (Weber 2002, 119). This could only occur on the basis of an already existing capitalist structure, predicated on a class of entrepreneurs confronting a class of free workers, the accumulation of capital, and a market economy mediated by monetary exchange. Weber never meant that the Protestant ethic of work *alone* produced modern capitalism,[8] but he did claim that it affirmed its ethical legitimacy by forming a specific kind of "human" characterized by methodical and rational life-conduct. With its promotion of *Beruf* and its "inner worldly asceticism," the Protestant work ethic contributed to an "ethical glorification" (Weber 2002, 109) of the "specialized human being" (*Fachmenschentum*) required for the functioning of modern capitalism.

The spirit of modern capitalism as it historically emerged from Protestant asceticism was not confined to the economic sphere.[9] It can be seen as well in other sectors of modern Western societies, including the erotic, juridical, political, artistic, and even scientific spheres. In all of these domains, the same rational ethos based on a calling dutifully performed for its own sake can be seen at work, so that the spirit underlying modern capitalism constitutes one of the most important features of

"Western rationalism" generally.[10] It is well known that Weber was quite pessimistic about the rationalization process subsequently experienced by Western societies. In his view, "the capacity and dispositions of persons to *organize their lives* in a practical-rational manner" (Weber 2002, 160) tends to transform individuals into narrow-minded specialists living in a totally "disenchanted" world dominated by instrumental rationality. In concluding this chapter, I return to Weber's *fin de siècle* pessimism by contrasting it with Hegel's more optimistic view on modernity.

Hegel's Ethic of *Beruf*

In the same vein as Weber, Hegel insists on the role played by the Reformation in shaping the modern world. The importance of Christianity in general and especially the Reformation lies in the way both grasped "the principle of unity of the divine and human nature, the reconciliation of the objective truth and freedom which have appeared within self-consciousness and subjectivity" (Hegel 2008 §358, 322). Hegel understands "reconciliation" (*Versöhnung*) not as a mere identification of the here below and the hereafter, the temporal and the spiritual, the human and the divine, but as their true mediation, one that presupposes rather than negates their difference. In this sense, the theme of reconciliation perfectly fits with Hegel's central thesis as articulated in the Preface to his *Philosophy of Right*, according to which modernity consists in a process whereby what is the rational becomes actual and what is actual becomes rational (Hegel 2008, 14). With regard to the historical process of rationalization characterizing modernity, Hegel considers Protestantism as the purest and truest manifestation of religion. Compared to the traditional Church, the Reformation made a twofold step toward rationalization (Hegel 1990, 94–104). First, it permitted religious belief to detach itself from any sort of superstitious or magical endorsement of the mundane (like the adoration of saints and relics, or the holy sacraments offered by the Church). Second, it contributed to the worldly realization of the principle of subjective freedom by placing, without any interference from the Church and its institutions, the moral conscience of the believer in direct relation to God (*sola fide*). Like Weber, Hegel also underscores, against the praise of poverty that had been part of official Church doctrine, the importance of the Reformation as regards its ethical promotion of worldly work:

> the repudiation of work (*Arbeitslosigkeit*) no longer earned the reputation of sanctity; it was acknowledged to be more commendable

for men to rise from a state of dependence by activity, intelligence, and industry, and make themselves independent. [. . .] Industry, crafts and trades now have their ethical validity recognized, and the obstacles to their prosperity which originated with the Church, have vanished. (Hegel 1956, 423, trans. modified)

If we compare Hegel's conception of the role played by the Reformation in shaping the modern world with Weber's thesis, some important differences remain evident. For Weber, Protestant asceticism, while assuming a strict demarcation between the life here below and the life hereafter, led to a total "disenchantment of the world" and to the emergence of the idea of free individual subjectivity. For Hegel, the reconciliation brought forth by Christianity does not involve a strict separation between the temporal and the spiritual but rather their true mediation. This means that the detachment of religious belief from superstition went hand-in-hand with the introduction of free subjective spirit into the world. In his *Lectures on the History of Philosophy* dealing with the Reformation, Hegel goes so far as to say: "From the hereafter man has been called (*gerufen*) to the presence of the spirit, and the earth and its bodies, human virtues and ethical life, his own heart and his own moral conscience, began to have a value for him" (Hegel 1970, 48, my translation). Compared to Weber, Hegel thus conceives the modernization process effectuated by the Reformation as a "spiritualization" of the world rather than its "disenchantment."[11] The spiritualization of the world, whereby free subjectivity is acknowledged as "the universal effective principle of a new form of world" (Hegel 2008 §124R, 122), characterizes modernity as a whole. Although originating in religion and Christianity, the principle of free subjectivity was progressively extended to all spheres of modern Western society.[12]

The idea of a modern spiritualization of the world appears more clearly if we consider the ethic of *Beruf* that can be found in Hegel. Even if the notion of calling that is so crucial for Weber's definition of capitalist spirit does not emerge as a philosophical concept in the ethical theory Hegel presented in the *Philosophy of Right* (1820), it still can be found in some of his earlier writings. While a professor and director of a Gymnasium in Nuremberg (1808–1816), Hegel gave lessons to his youngest pupils on the "doctrine of duties" where he discusses at length the idea of *Beruf*. It seems that Hegel understood this notion in the broad, not strictly philosophical, sense shared by his audience. He begins his lessons with an anthropological thesis: man possesses the double aspect of singularity and universal essence. He adds that the very "destination" (*Bestimmung*) of every human being is to elevate himself above his natural particularity to attain his true universal and rational essence:

Man is, on the one hand, a natural being. As such he behaves according to caprice and accident as an inconstant, subjective being. He does not distinguish the essential from the unessential. Secondly, he is a spiritual, rational being and as such *he is not* by nature *what he ought to be*. The animal stands in no need of education (*Bildung*), for it is by nature what it ought to be. It is only a natural being. But man has the task of bringing into harmony his two sides, of making his individuality conform to his rational side or making the latter become his guiding principle. (Hegel 1986 §41R, 41)[13]

In the general cultivation process (*Bildung*), whereby human beings achieve their spiritual essence, calling belongs to the duties every rational being has "to himself." More specifically, *Beruf* constitutes part of the practical formation through which every human being must "(a) stand away from and be free from the natural, (b) on the other hand, be *absorbed* in his avocation (*Beruf*), in what is essential and therefore (c) be able to confine his gratification of the natural wants not only within the limits of necessity but also to *sacrifice* the same for higher duties" (Hegel 1986 §43, 43). These passages excerpted from Hegel's early doctrine of duties show some affinities with the "inner worldly asceticism" Weber analyzes in his essay. In both cases, emphasis is placed on the dualistic nature of human beings, their natural and spiritual sides. Those affinities notwithstanding, it seems on the other hand that Hegel proposes a wholly secularized form of *Beruf*. Man has to "reconcile" (and not to oppose) his two sides by exercising his calling in order to achieve his rational essence. Hegel withdraws any reference to a divine will, placing the idea of calling within the very human social world: "The vocation is something universal and necessary, and constitutes a side of the social life of humanity. It is, therefore, *part of the all human work* (*ein Teil des ganzen Menschenwerkes*). When a man has a vocation, he enters into cooperation and participation with the universal. He thereby becomes objective" (Hegel 1986 §45R, 45, trans. modified). The secularization of the idea of calling is most obvious when Hegel speaks of the "calling to a social estate" (*der Beruf zu einem Stande*), by reference to its material (the profession one exercises in society) and not so much to its religious sense (the task given by God). In contrast with Protestant asceticism, the idea of calling appears in Hegel's ethical theory as a way for human beings to attain their rational essence by entering into the "spiritualized" world of human society.

In his later *Philosophy of Right*, Hegel refers to the ethical notions of "rectitude" and "honor of one's estate" as two kinds of "ethical disposition" (*Gesinnung*)[14] enacted in the modern "system of estates":

> In this system of estates, the ethical disposition is that of *rectitude* and the *honour of one's estate*, i.e. the disposition to make oneself a member of one of the moments of civil society by one's own act, through one's energy, industry, and skill, to maintain oneself in this position, and to provide for oneself only through this process of mediating oneself with the universal, while in this way gaining recognition both in one's own eyes and in the eyes of others. (Hegel 2008 §207, 196–197)

In his earlier doctrine of duties, Hegel already mentioned rectitude (*Rechtschaffenheit*) as the most general duty an individual has "toward others."[15] Rectitude means acting in accordance with the duties every human being, as a participant in ethical relations, must fulfill on a daily basis.[16] The ethical notion of rectitude appears as an exact complement to that of *Beruf*, formerly defined by Hegel as a duty the individual has "to himself." If this is so, then the notion of "honor of one's estate" (*Standesehre*) in the later *Philosophy of Right* plays a role very similar to the idea of calling that Hegel earlier linked with occupying a certain social position. It may have been that between the periods of Nuremberg and Berlin Hegel decided to abandon the notion of calling because of its vagueness. Whatever reasons there may have been to replace the notion of *Beruf* with that of social esteem, the ethical disposition characterizing "the citizen as bourgeois" (Hegel 2008 §190R, 188) consists in the rectitude of fulfilling daily duties toward others as well as in the "honor" one acquires through the profession he exercises in civil society. Once again, Hegel seems here to offer a secularized version of the Protestant work ethic: Whereas the Puritan described by Weber sought "confirmation" of signs of salvation through hard work and honesty, the "citizen as bourgeois" acts in order to gain social recognition from the other members of society to whom he has various obligations.

The ethical notion of honor, as it appears in the later *Philosophy of Right* and which seems equivalent to the idea of calling discussed by Hegel in his earlier doctrine of duties, denotes the existence of social estates (*Stände*). Hegel employs this apparently old-fashioned term to describe the division of modern society into "*particular systems* of needs, means, and types of work relative to these needs, modes of satisfaction and of theoretical and practical education (*Bildung*), i.e. into systems, to one or other of which individuals are assigned (*zugeteilt*)" (Hegel 2008 §201, 193). However old-fashioned the late medieval notion of *Stand* might have sounded at the beginning of the nineteenth century, Hegel nevertheless combines the existence of social estates with the modern principle of free subjectivity. Assigning individuals to social estates is effected neither through the sovereign decisions of rulers (as in Plato's *Republic*) nor on the basis of natural birth (as in the Indian caste system), but "by the mediation of the arbitrary will" (Hegel 2008 §206, 196). For Hegel every modern "citizen as bourgeois" has the right to freely choose his own profession. Against Lutheranism and Puritanism, Hegel apparently rejects the idea that social estates exist by the will of God and the restriction of society to small religious communities,[17] because the division of modern society is mediated *at large* by the free subjective will of the individuals as spiritual beings (and *not by God*). This means that their decisions in adopting a profession are made on universal and objective grounds: "when subjective particularity is upheld by the objective order in conformity with it and is at the same time allowed in its rights, then it becomes the animating principle of the entire civil society, of the development alike of thoughtful activity, merit, and dignity" (Hegel 2008 §206R, 196).

This last point echoes Hegel's thesis on the modern spiritualization of the world as well as the idea of the *Bildung* process he linked in his earlier doctrine of duties with calling. Free to choose and to exercise a profession in society, the "citizen as bourgeois" gets the chance to elevate himself above his mere particularity to his true universal essence. The individual is recognized as "somebody" (Hegel 2008 §207A, 197) as long as, through his particular work, he contributes to and collaborates in the "animation" of the universal system of estates. Hegel insists both on the objective side of the universal system of estates and on the subjective side of the particular right of every "citizen as bourgeois" to freely choose his profession. These are the two sides that modern individuals must "reconcile" during their cultivation process; this "limits" their natural wants and needs, while at the same time assuring social recognition of the spiritual skills and talents they acquired in the course of their professional lives. As Hegel said in his earlier doctrine of duties: "If a man is *to become something he must know how to limit himself*, that is, make some speciality his vocation. Then this work ceases to be an irksome restraint to him. He then comes to be at unity with himself, with his externality, with his sphere. He is a universal, a whole" (Hegel 1986 §45R, 45).

Hegel's sociology of the modern estates reveals to some extent the capitalist spirit already at work in his time. He compares the "agricultural" and the "business estate" in a way that recalls the ideal type of the modern capitalist spirit defined by Weber. The ethical disposition that characterizes members of the agricultural estate consists in "the simple attitude of mind not directed towards the acquisition of riches": "What comes to [the member of this estate] suffices him; once it is consumed, more comes again" (Hegel 2008 §203A, 194). By contrast, the business estate "for its means of livelihood is thrown back on its own work, on reflection and understanding

[. . .]. For what this estate produces and enjoys, it has mainly *itself,* its own activity, to thank" (Hegel 2008 §204, 195). This peculiar kind of ethical disposition is clearly that of the bourgeois self-made man who distinguishes himself from the traditional ethos of the "substantial estate." But Hegel also opposes the member of an estate to the isolated individual who willingly refuses to be part of any special one and therefore "has to try to gain recognition for himself by giving external proofs of success in his business, and to these proofs no limits can be set" (Hegel 2008 §253 R, 226). The egoistic businessman fails to undergo the formation process enabling his elevation from mere particularity to true universal essence. He is condemned to live in a so-called bad infinity and to seek recognition endlessly. In contrast to the "traditional" idea of self-sufficiency and the nonsystematic life of the "adventurous capitalist," Hegel seems thus to have grasped perfectly the specific kind of capitalist spirit already adopted by the middle-class bourgeoisie of his time (the craftsman, the manufacturer, and the tradesman) and that Weber later treats in his essay.

The "Fate" of Capitalism

Both Hegel and Weber have understood the spirit of modern capitalism as a specific kind of rational life-conduct. The bourgeois ethos of the self-made man contributed to establishing the ethical legitimacy of modern capitalism as an economic system. As such, it differs from the "traditional" way people usually meet their needs and from mere "adventurous," nonsystematic greediness. The ethical legitimacy of modern capitalism is rooted in the very idea of a calling, presented as a systematic way for modern subjects to achieve their "destination." On Weber's thesis, the modern ethic of *Beruf* first appeared within the religious context of "Protestant asceticism" with regard to the "confirmation" the individual believer sought to achieve through hard work and honesty. Hegel's ethic of *Beruf* can be considered as a wholly secularized version of the Protestant ethic of work, wherein "the citizen as bourgeois" acquires social recognition from other members of civil society on the basis of his profession.

Weber was quite pessimistic regarding the shift from the figure of the Puritan to that of the bourgeois entrepreneur. As he famously said when concluding his essay, "[t]he Puritan *wanted* to be a person with a vocational calling (*Berufsmensch*); today we *are forced* to be" (Weber 2002, 123). Due to its secularization the Protestant word ethic has progressively lost any religious foundation, so that the everyday fulfillment of one's profession has become increasingly meaningless for those condemned to live within the "steel-hard casing" of modern capitalism:

Wherever the "conduct of a vocation" cannot be explicitly connected to the highest cultural values of a spiritual nature, or wherever, conversely, individuals are not forced to experience it simply as economic coercion—in both situations persons today usually abandon any attempt to make sense of the notion of a vocational calling altogether. (Weber 2002, 124)

In his later lectures on *Science as a Vocation* (Weber 2004), Weber pleads for a "virile" endorsement of the "fate" of modern capitalism. He attacks the "specialized man" (*Fachmensch*) blindly produced by modern capitalism as well as Romantic attempts to "reenchant" the modern world. In his doctrine of duties, Hegel likewise refers to calling as a "fate" that every individual should freely endorse: "As to what concerns one's specific calling, which appears as *fate* (*Schicksal*), this should not be thought of in the form of an external necessity. It is to be taken up freely, and freely endured and pursued" (Hegel 1986 §44, 44). In order to challenge the "unconscious necessity" (Hegel 2008 §255A, 227) of the capitalist market economy and its "invisible hand," Hegel would have criticized, just like Weber, the narrow-minded specialization that renders individuals unable "to direct their attention to others" (Hegel 2008 §201A, 193) as well as any desperate attempt to rebuild a purely sentimental *Gemeinschaft* within the context of modernity.

Yet Weber and Hegel offer two very distinct ways of tackling the fate of modern capitalism. Nostalgic for the figure of the Puritan, Weber searched for an elite of "entirely new prophets" (Weber 2002, 124).[18] The secularized *Berufmensch* for which, in a rather Nietzschean way, he was hoping was that of "a countersocialized self"[19] whose task was first to rebuild a new range of values and ideals within some small communities before extending them to the entire social world. For Hegel, challenging the "unconscious necessity" produced by modern capitalism meant instead to promote the rational ethic of social cooperation already at work in the professional corporations of his time.[20] The main difference between Weber and Hegel in their responses to the fate of capitalism is likely rooted in their divergent conceptions of modernity. Whereas Weber's *fin de siècle* pessimism saw in modernity a radical "disenchantment" of the world confronting individuals with their existential isolation, Hegel's more optimistic view considered the modern spiritualization of the world as affording them at least the opportunity to collaborate in a truly rational way. If we briefly consider some current debates on the "new" spirit of capitalism, it seems that Weber's diagnosis regarding the increasingly meaningless character of work has largely been proven correct.[21] Yet to articulate an answer to the new fate of capitalism, we might better appeal to the path of a "social" critique inspired by Hegel, whose emphasis on social justice and recognition still appears more promising than a Weberian "artistic" critique, which confronts an alienating capitalism with the values of authenticity and individuality.[22]

Notes

1. To my knowledge, no systematic study on Hegel, Weber, and capitalism has been provided even to this day. On Hegel, Weber and the modern state, see however Colliot-Thélène 1992.

2. Wilhelm Hennis (Hennis 1988) has proposed reinterpreting the whole Weberian enterprise as a historical "science of man."

3. See Weber's "Prefatory Remarks" to his *Collected Essays in the Sociology of Religion*, where he defines modern capitalism through "the rational organization of (legally) *free labor*," "the *separation of the household from the industrial company*," and "the appearance of rational *accounting*" (Weber 2002, 155–156). For a comparison of Marx and Weber, see Karl Löwith's classic essay (Löwith 1993) and more recently Antonio and Glassman 1985.

4. Hegel 2008 §189R. On Hegel and the economic science, see Riedel 2011.

5. Compare Boltanski and Chiapello's recent definition of the spirit of capitalism as "the set of beliefs associated with the capitalist order that helps to justify this order and, by legitimating them, to sustain the forms of action and predispositions compatible with it" (Boltanski and Chiapello 2005, 10).

6. For a similar interpretation of the ambivalent role played by Luther in the economic revolution of the sixteenth century, see Tawney 1972, 99–110.

7. This latter point is more extensively discussed by Weber in his 1920 essay "The Protestant Sects and the Spirit of Capitalism" (Weber 2002, 127–148). See Kim 2004, 57–94, for a discussion of Weber's treatment of sects in this later essay.

8. See, for instance, Weber's reply to one of his Marxist critic Felix Rachfahl: "the emergence of the 'homo oeconomicus' was limited by quite definite *objective* conditions, and it was these conditions—geographical, political, social and other—that limited the culture of the Middle Age, in contrast to antiquity" (Weber 2001, 131).

9. "One of the constitutive components of the modern capitalist spirit and, moreover, generally of modern civilization (*Kultur*), was the rational organization of life on the basis of the *idea of calling*. It was born out of *Christian asceticism*" (Weber 2002, 122).

10. Western rationalism is the main theme of Weber's "Prefatory Remarks" (Weber 2002, 149–164). On Weber and modernity, see Scaff 2000.

11. See Buchwalter 2013.

12. "Amongst the more specific shapes which [the right of subjective freedom] assumes are love, romanticism, the quest for the eternal salvation of the individual, etc.; next come moral convictions and conscience; and, finally, the other forms, some of which come into prominence in what follows as the principle of civil society and as moments in the constitution of the state, while others appear in the

course of history, particularly the history of art, science, and philosophy" (Hegel 2008 §124R, 122).

13. In his *Lectures on the Philosophy of History,* Hegel attributes to the Reformation the idea that "man is not by nature what he ought to be, for he first comes to truth through a process of formation (*Prozess der Umbildung*)" (Hegel 1956, 424).

14. In his early "doctrine of duties," Hegel defines *Gesinnung* as "the subjective side of moral conduct" (Hegel 1986 §34, 37). This seems very close to Weber's own use of the term and its intertwined concepts (such as ethos, *habitus*, and life-conduct).

15. "[R]*ectitude*, the observance of the strict duties toward others, is the first duty and lies at the basis of all others" (Hegel 1986 §60, 48).

16. See also Hegel 2008 §150, 157. For Hegel, a good example of ethical rectitude is the act of returning property (money or goods) loaned by another person for temporary use (Hegel 2008 §135R, 131).

17. See, for instance, how Hegel tackles the problem of Protestant sects (Quakers, Anabaptists) toward which the modern state is to show tolerance (Hegel 2008 §270R, 247).

18. H. S. Goldman 1987, 168: "Weber wants to create an ascetic leadership elite to enter and master the rationalized institutions of society, a band of virtuosos whose quasi-religious devotion to the service of their cause will lead to a form of empowerment similar to Puritan empowerment."

19. Ibid., 170–171: "In Weber's view, the empowered self cannot seek a witness or a companion in others. Indeed, it is formed against others. [. . .] Thus Weber's self is not an interactional or a socialized self, but rather a countersocialized self. One must resist the temptations of others as much as the desires of self." For an opposite interpretation emphasizing the socializing role of sects, see Kim 2004.

20. Hegel seems in this respect much closer to Durkheim's solution. For a comparison of Hegel and Durkheim on modernity, see Honneth 2012 and Carré 2013.

21. "Leaving aside the systemic effects of an unbridled freeing-up of the financial sphere, which is beginning to cause concern even among those in charge of capitalist institutions, it seems to us scarcely open to doubt that at an ideological level [. . .] capitalism will face increasing difficulties, if it does not restore some grounds for hope to those whose engagement is required for the functioning of the system as a whole" (Boltanski and Chiapello 2005, xliii). See also Sennet 1998.

22. The distinction between these two kinds of critique is borrowed from Boltanski and Chiapello 2005, 38–40.

Works Cited

Antonio, R., and Glassman, R., eds. 1985. *A Weber-Marx Dialogue.* Lawrence: University Press of Kansas.

Boltanski, L., and È. Chiapello. 2005. *The New Spirit of Capitalism.* London, New York: Verso.

Buchwalter, A. 2013. "Religion, Civil Society, and the System of an Ethical World: Hegel on the Protestant Ethic and the Spirit of Capitalism." In *Hegel on Religion and Politics*, edited by A. Nuzzo, 213–232. Albany: State University of New York Press.

Carré, L. 2013. "Die Sozialpathologien der Moderne. Hegel und Durkheim im Vergleich." In *Hegel und die Moderne*, edited by A. Arndt, 312–317. Berlin: De Gruyter.

Colliot-Thélène, C. 1992. *Le désenchantement de l'Etat. De Hegel à Weber*. Paris: Minuit.

Goldman, H. S. 1987. "Weber's Ascetic Practices of the Self." In *Weber's Protestant Ethic. Origin, Evidence, Contexts*, edited by H. Lehman and G. Roth, 161–178. Cambridge: Cambridge University Press.

Hegel, G.W.F. 1956. *The Philosophy of History*. Translated by J. Sibree. New York: Dover.

———. 1970. *Vorlesungen über die Geschichte der Philosophie*. Dritter Teil: Neuere Philosophie. Frankfurt am Main: Suhrkamp.

———. 1986. *The Philosophical Propaedeutic*. Translated by A. V. Miller. Oxford: Basil Blackwell.

———. 1990. *Lectures on the History of Philosophy. Medieval and Modern Philosophy*. Translated by R. F. Brown and J. M. Stewart. Berkeley, Los Angeles, Oxford: University of California Press.

———. 2008. *Outlines of the Philosophy of Right*. Translated by T. M. Knox and revised by S. Houlgate. Oxford: Oxford University Press.

Hennis, W. 1988. *Max Weber: Essays in Reconstruction*. Translated by K. Tribe. London: Allen & Unwin.

Honneth, A. 2012. "Labour and Recognition: A Redefinition." In *The I in the We. Studies in the Theory of Recognition*, 56–74. Cambridge: Polity Press.

Kim, S. H. 2004. *Max Weber's Politics of Civil Society*. Cambridge: Cambridge University Press.

Löwith, K. 1993. *Karl Marx and Max Weber*. Translated by H. Fantel. London and New-York: Routledge.

Riedel, M. 2011. "The Influence of Modern Economic Theory." In *Between Tradition and Revolution. The Hegelian Transformation of Political Philosophy*, 107–128. Cambridge: Cambridge University Press.

Scaff, A. 2000. "Weber on the Cultural Situation of the Modern Age." In *The Cambridge Companion to Weber*, edited by S. Turner, 99–116. Cambridge: Cambridge University Press.

Sennet, R. 1998. *The Corrosion of Character. The Personal Consequences of Work in New Capitalism*. New York: Norton.

Tawney, R. H. 1972. *Religion and the Rise of Capitalism*. Harmondsworth: Penguin.

Weber, M. 2001. *The Protestant Ethic Debate. Max Weber's Replies to His Critics*. Translated by A. Harrington and M. Shields. Liverpool: Liverpool University Press.

———. 2002. *The Protestant Ethic and the Spirit of Capitalism*. Translated by S. Kahlberg. Oxford: Blackwell.

———. 2004. *The Vocation Lectures: "Science as a Vocation." "Politics as a Vocation."* Translated by R. Livingstone. Indianapolis, Cambridge: Hackett.

Contributors

ANDREW BUCHWALTER is Presidential Professor at the University of North Florida. He is the author of *Dialectics, Politics, and the Contemporary Value of Hegel's Practical Philosophy* (Routledge 2011) and the edited volumes *Hegel and Global Justice* (Springer 2012) and *Culture and Democracy: Social and Ethical Issues in Public Support for the Arts and Humanities* (Westview 1992). He was Fulbright Research Professor at the Hegel-Archiv Ruhr-Universität Bochum.

LOUIS CARRÉ is postdoctoral researcher of the Fund for Scientific Research—FNRS (Belgium) and works at the Free University of Brussels (ULB). In 2013 he published the book *Axel Honneth: The Right of Recognition*. His research interests include Hegel, contemporary social and political philosophy, and critical theory.

GIORGIO CESARALE is associate professor of political philosophy at Ca' Foscari–University of Venice. He is the author *of La mediazione che sparisce. La società civile in Hegel* (Carocci 2009), *Hegel nella filosofia pratico-politica anglosassone dal secondo dopoguerra ai giorni nostri* (Mimesis 2011), *Filosofia e capitalismo. Hegel, Marx e le teorie contemporanee* (Manifestolibri 2012). He co-edited, with Mario Pianta, a collection of Giovanni Arrighi's essays entitled *Capitalismo e (dis)ordine mondiale* (Manifestolibri 2010).

ARDIS B. COLLINS is professor of philosophy at Loyola University of Chicago. She is the author of *Hegel's Phenomenology: The Dialectical Justification of Philosophy's First Principles* (McGill-Queen's University Press 2013), and the editor of the collection *Hegel on the Modern World* (State University of New York Press 1995). Since 1996, she has served as editor-in-chief of *The Owl of Minerva*, an international journal published by the Hegel Society of America.

LISA HERZOG is postdoctoral researcher at the Institute for Social Research at the University of Frankfurt. During 2014–2015 she was a postdoctoral fellow at the Center for Ethics in Society at Stanford University. Her work lies at the intersection of economics and philosophy, both in the history of ideas and with regard to systematic questions. Her first book, *Inventing the Market: Smith, Hegel, and Political Theory*, was published by Oxford University Press in 2013.

NICHOLAS MOWAD received his PhD from Loyola University Chicago under the direction of Adriaan Peperzak, going on to work at Georgia College and State University and the Community College of Qatar, before accepting a tenure-track position at Chandler-Gilbert Community College. His publications on Hegel's anthropology, political philosophy, and environmental ethics have appeared in *Essays on Hegel's Philosophy of Subjective Spirit*, *Hegel on Religion and Politics* (both State University of New York Press), *Clio*, and *Environmental Philosophy*.

C. J. PEREIRA DI SALVO is a doctoral student in the Department of Philosophy at Northwestern University. His research focuses on social and political philosophy and German philosophy. He is currently working on a dissertation that both offers a contemporary defense of the Kantian cosmopolitan project and seeks to understand the role that social theoretical disagreements have played in its historical development, from Kant down to his contemporary inheritors.

NATHAN ROSS is associate professor of philosophy at Oklahoma City University. His first book is titled *On Mechanism in Hegel's Social and Political Philosophy* (Routledge 2008). He continues to work on Hegel as well as post-Kantian German aesthetics and critical theory.

KOHEI SAITO is a PhD candidate in philosophy at Humboldt University, Berlin. He is also a member of the Japanese MEGA (Marx-Engels-Gesamtausgabe) editorial group. His publications include "The Emergence of Marx's Critique of Modern Agriculture" (*Monthly Review* October 2014).

MICHALIS SKOMVOULIS is postdoctoral researcher at the Aristotle University of Thessaloniki. He earned his PhD in philosophy at the University of Paris 1–Sorbonne with the thesis "Hegel and Political Economy: The Economy of the System and the System of Political Economy." He has published essays in *Theseis* and *Episteme kai Koinwnia* on the epistemology of the political economy of contemporary capitalism. He has also published reviews for the *Bulletin de littérature hégélienne*.

TONY SMITH is professor of philosophy at Iowa State University. His books include *The Logic of Marx's Capital: Replies to Hegelian Criticisms* (1990), *Globalisation* (2005), and *Beyond Liberal Egalitarianism* (forthcoming).

Michael J. Thompson is associate professor of political theory at William Paterson University. His recent books include *The Politics of Inequality* (Columbia), *Georg Lukács Reconsidered* (Continuum), *Constructing Marxist Ethics* (Brill), and the forthcoming *The Republican Reinvention of Radicalism* (Columbia).

Richard Dien Winfield is Distinguished Research Professor of Philosophy at the University of Georgia, where he has taught since 1982. He is the author of *Reason and Justice, The Just Economy, Overcoming Foundations, Freedom and Modernity, Law in Civil Society, Systematic Aesthetics, Stylistics, The Just Family, Autonomy and Normativity, The Just State, From Concept to Objectivity, Modernity, Religion, and the War on Terror, Hegel and Mind, The Living Mind, Hegel's Science of Logic: A Critical Rethinking in Thirty Lectures, Hegel's Phenomenology of Spirit: A Critical Rethinking in Seventeen Lectures,* and *Hegel and the Future of Systematic Philosophy.*

Index